Gothic kinship

MANCHESTER
1824
Manchester University Press

Gothic kinship

Edited by Agnes Andeweg and Sue Zlosnik

Manchester University Press
Manchester and New York
distributed in the United States exclusively by Palgrave Macmillan

Copyright © Manchester University Press 2013

While copyright in the volume as a whole is vested in Manchester University Press, copyright in individual chapters belongs to their respective authors, and no chapter may be reproduced wholly or in part without the express permission in writing of both author and publisher.

Published by Manchester University Press
Oxford Road, Manchester M13 9NR, UK
and Room 400, 175 Fifth Avenue, New York, NY 10010, USA
www.manchesteruniversitypress.co.uk

Distributed in the United States exclusively by
Palgrave Macmillan, 175 Fifth Avenue, New York,
NY 10010, USA

Distributed in Canada exclusively by
UBC Press, University of British Columbia, 2029 West Mall,
Vancouver, BC, Canada V6T 1Z2

British Library Cataloguing-in-Publication Data
A catalogue record for this book is available from the British Library

Library of Congress Cataloging-in-Publication Data applied for

ISBN 978 07190 8860 5 hardback

First published 2013

The publisher has no responsibility for the persistence or accuracy of URLs for any external or third-party internet websites referred to in this book, and does not guarantee that any content on such websites is, or will remain, accurate or appropriate.

Typeset in Sabon by
Servis Filmsetting Ltd, Stockport, Cheshire
Printed in Great Britain by
TJ International Ltd, Padstow

Contents

Acknowledgements		*page* vii
Notes on contributors		viii
	Introduction *Agnes Andeweg and Sue Zlosnik*	1
1	Matriarchal picture identification in first-wave British Gothic fiction *Kamilla Elliott*	12
2	'Those most intimately concerned': the strength of chosen family in Elizabeth Gaskell's Gothic short fiction *Ardel Haefele-Thomas*	30
3	The madwoman in the attic of Labuwangi: Couperus and colonial Gothic *Rosemarie Buikema*	48
4	Seed from the east, seed from the west, which one will turn out best? The demonic adoptee in *The Bad Seed* (1954) *Elisabeth Wesseling*	63
5	'Children misbehaving in the walls!' or, Wes Craven's suburban family values *Bernice M. Murphy*	81
6	Fathers, friends, and families: Gothic kinship in Stephen King's *Pet Sematary* *John Sears*	97
7	Sisterhood is monstrous: Gothic imagery in Dutch feminist fiction *Agnes Andeweg*	115

8 The political uncanny of the family: Patricia Duncker's *The Deadly Space Between* and The Civil Partnership Act *Anne Quéma* 132

9 Violent households: the family destabilized in *The Monk* (1796), *Zofloya, or the Moor* (1818), and *Her Fearful Symmetry* (2009) *Joanne Watkiss* 157

10 'As much a family as anyone could be, anywhere ever': revisioning the family in Poppy Z. Brite's *Lost Souls* *William Hughes* 174

11 Gothic half-bloods: maternal kinship in Rowling's Harry Potter series *Ranita Chatterjee* 196

12 'They fuck you up' – revaluations of the family in contemporary British horror film: Steven Sheil's *Mum & Dad* *Johannes Schlegel* 211

Index 231

Acknowledgements

Gothic Kinship brings together articles commissioned especially for this book and papers presented at two conferences held in 2009: the conference 'Points of Exit: (Un)conventional Representations of Age, Parenting and Sexuality', sponsored and hosted by the Centre for Gender and Diversity at Maastricht University, and the Ninth Biennial Conference of the International Gothic Association held at Lancaster University. We would like to thank our colleagues at Maastricht University and Manchester Metropolitan University for their intellectual and practical support, and two anonymous readers at Manchester University Press for their helpful comments on the original proposal.

Agnes Andeweg and Sue Zlosnik

Notes on contributors

Agnes Andeweg is a lecturer at the Centre for Gender and Diversity of Maastricht University (Netherlands) and a former postdoc at Radboud University Nijmegen. Her dissertation on the Gothic in Dutch contemporary literature was published by Amsterdam University Press in 2011 (*Griezelig gewoon. Gotieke verschijningen in Dutch novels 1980–1995*). She has published numerous articles on gothic, gender and Dutch literature, and contributed to Blackwell's *Encyclopedia of the Gothic*. Her current research focuses on the role of writers and their works in shaping the Dutch national self-image as sexually liberated.

Rosemarie Buikema is professor of Art, Culture and Diversity at Utrecht University. She is the chair of the UU Genderstudies Department and academic director of the Netherlands Research School of Genderstudies. She has widely published on feminist and post-colonial cultural theory and is currently working on the role of the arts in the context of political transitions. Among her recent publications are *Doing Gender in Media, Art and Culture* (Routledge, 2009) and *Theories and Methodologies in Feminist Postgraduate Research* (Routledge, 2011).

Ranita Chatterjee is Associate Professor and Graduate Director of English at California State University, Northridge. She has published numerous articles on queer Gothic, teaching the Gothic, and 1790s British Jacobin writers for journals such as *Gothic Studies* and *European Romantic Review*. Ranita has also contributed entries on feminist and psychoanalytic theorists for Blackwell's

2011 *The Encyclopedia of Literary and Cultural Theory*, and two lengthy entries on William Godwin and Children's Literature for the 2012 *Blackwell Encyclopedia of Romanticism*. She is working on a book on the literary politics of Godwin and radical women writers of the 1790s.

Kamilla Elliott is a senior lecturer in the Department of English and Creative Writing at Lancaster University. She is author of *Rethinking the Novel/Film Debate* (Cambridge University Press, 2003) and *Portraiture and British Gothic Fiction: The Rise of Picture Identification, 1764–1835* (Johns Hopkins University Press, 2012), as well as various articles and essays on literature and visual media.

Ardel Haefele-Thomas was awarded her PhD in Modern Thought and Literature from Stanford University. She is currently the chair of LGBT Studies at City College of San Francisco. Her book *Queer Others in Victorian Gothic: Transgressing Monstrosity* was recently published by the University of Wales Press.

William Hughes is Professor of Gothic Studies at Bath Spa University, and the founder-editor of *Gothic Studies*, the refereed journal of the International Gothic Association. His fifteen published books include scholarly editions of Bram Stoker's *Dracula* (2007) and *The Lady of the Shroud* (2001), and two recent student guides to the criticism and content of *Dracula* (2008, 2009). With Andrew Smith he has coedited *Bram Stoker: History, Psychoanalysis and the Gothic* (1998), *Empire and the Gothic* (2003), *Queering the Gothic* (2009), *The Victorian Gothic: An Edinburgh Companion* (2012) and the forthcoming *EcoGothic*.

Bernice M. Murphy is an Assistant Professor and Lecturer in Popular Literature at the School of English, Trinity College Dublin, Ireland. She has edited the collection *Shirley Jackson: Essays on the Literary Legacy* (McFarland, 2005) coedited *It Came From the 1950s: Popular Culture, Popular Anxieties* (Palgrave Macmillan, 2011,) and written the monograph *The Suburban Gothic in American Popular Culture* (Palgrave Macmillan, 2009). She is co-founder of the online *Irish Journal of Horror and Gothic Studies* and is working on a book about the relationship between horror and the wilderness/rural landscape in American popular culture.

Anne Quéma teaches theories of criticism and modern British fiction and poetry at Acadia University (Wolfville, Nova Scotia). She has published *The Agon of Modernism: Wyndham Lewis's Allegories, Aesthetics, and Politics* as well as articles in *Gothic Studies, Contemporary Issues in Law, English Studies in Canada, Contemporary Literary Criticism, The Canadian Modernists Meet, Philosophy and Literature, West Coast Line, Wider Boundaries of Daring: The Modernist Impulse in Canadian Women's Poetry*, and the *International Journal of Law in Context*. Currently her work focuses on discourses of power in jurisprudence, contemporary Gothic fiction, and family law.

Johannes Schlegel teaches English Literature and Culture at the Georg-August University Göttingen. He is currently completing his PhD thesis on *Anthropology and Mediality of Evil in British Romanticism*. His research interests focus on Romanticism, literary and cultural theory, Gothic and horror studies and contemporary popular culture and its media.

John Sears is a Reader in Contemporary Literature at Manchester Metropolitan University, and author of *Stephen King's Gothic* (2011) and *Reading George Szirtes* (2008).

Joanne Watkiss is a lecturer in English Literature at Leeds Metropolitan University. Her research focuses on the interplay between contemporary gothic texts and literary theory, in particular the later works of Jacques Derrida. In 2012 her monograph *Gothic Contemporaries: The Haunted Text* was published by the University of Wales Press as part of the Gothic Literary Studies series.

Elisabeth Wesseling is the director of the Centre for Gender and Diversity, a research centre of the Faculty of Arts and Social Sciences of Maastricht University, the Netherlands. She publishes on the cultural construction of childhood in fiction (film, (children's) literature, photography) and science (developmental psychology, anthropology). More specifically, she works on the cultural construction of the adoptable child in transnational adoption from a comparative perspective, studying narrative strategies for the 'kinning' of foreigners in the United States, France and the Netherlands. Her work has been published in journals such as *Arcadia, Science in Context*, and *Children's Literature in*

Education. She co-authored a monograph with Rosemarie Buikema on Dutch Gothic fiction by Amsterdam University Press.

Sue Zlosnik is Professor of Gothic Literature at the Manchester Metropolitan University, UK. With Avril Horner, she has published five books, including *Daphne du Maurier: Writing, Identity and the Gothic Imagination* (1998), *Gothic and the Comic Turn* (2005), the edited collection *Le Gothic: Influences and Appropriations in Europe and America* (2008) (all Palgrave Macmillan) and an edition of Eaton Stannard Barrett's *The Heroine* (Valancourt, 2011). Alone, she has published essays on Meredith, Stevenson, Tolkien and Palahniuk. Her most recent book is *Patrick McGrath* (University of Wales Press, 2011). She has contributed an essay to the forthcoming collection *Global Gothic* edited by Glennis Byron (Manchester University Press). She is currently working on invited contributions to the new *Cambridge Companion to Modern Gothic* and the *Palgrave History of British Women's Fiction*.

Introduction

Agnes Andeweg and Sue Zlosnik

Gothic is always in some way a family matter. Indeed, as Anne Williams has pointed out, the critical history of Gothic itself, its 'organizing myth', is often couched in terms of the patriarchal family: it is the 'black sheep' of the literary dynasty; it descends from a founding father in the figure of Horace Walpole, to give just two examples of familial metaphor at work in many accounts. For Williams, this alerts us to pervasiveness of the metaphorical use of family relationships as we attempt to structure the world.[1] She also draws attention to the ambiguity of the word 'house' in the context of Gothic fiction: it is both 'structure' and 'family line'.[2] Thus the importance of the Gothic edifice noted by so many critics from Maurice Lévy and Eve Kosofsky Sedgwick onwards, whether it be castle or suburban villa, is intrinsically related to the kinship ties within it, ties that both bind and oppress. From *The Castle of Otranto*, through 'The Fall of the House of Usher' to the parodic *The Addams Family*, families loom large in Gothic. It is perhaps no coincidence either that Gothic's historical trajectory coincides with the emergence of the modern nuclear family. In Gothic fiction, the family is not the safe refuge of the ideological construct of the private sphere but the site of threat, particularly, as many critics have noted, for its female members.[3] As James Twitchell suggests, 'if the Gothic tells us anything it is what "too close for comfort" really means'.[4] It is nothing new to state that Gothic fiction revels in family secrets, incestuous bonds and bastard children. As Jerrold E. Hogle notes: 'in some way the Gothic is usually about some "son" both wanting to kill and striving to be the "father" and thus feeling fearful and guilty about what he most desires, all of which applies as well to Gothic heroines who seek both to appease and to free themselves from the excesses of male and patriarchal dominance'.[5]

The burgeoning of Gothic studies over the last thirty years has been characterized by both the psychoanalytically informed mode of interpretation exemplified by Hogle's observation and detailed historical research into Gothic's engagement with social, political and economic developments from the late eighteenth century onwards. Both modes of interpretation have identified Gothic's tendency, in its preoccupation with transgression, to call into question those boundaries that appear to underpin social relationships. Thus Gothic, while often seeming conservative in its plot closures, also opens up a radically transformative space in which alternative relationships may be configured. Both contesting and reinforcing notions of the nuclear family, Gothic fiction may offer figurations of alternative kinship ties. As early as 1818, the biological basis of kinship ties were radically challenged by Mary Shelley in the form of Victor Frankenstein's relationship with his monster, who exclaims that they are 'bound by ties only dissoluble by the annihilation of one of us'.[6]

Starting from the assumption that Gothic fiction is a key site where sociocultural figurations of the family are negotiated, this volume aims to analyse how Gothic figurations of kinship both contest and reinforce orthodox notions of the nuclear family. The chapters address such questions as: how does Gothic fiction mediate the ways in which the family is understood, both as a shifting constellation of social and personal ties and as a powerful regulatory ideal; how does Gothic fiction configure, refigure or disfigure conceptualizations and representations of kinship; when do cultural figurations of kinship become Gothic? Alternative relationship structures, not based upon genitally determined reproduction or legalistic dynasties, are characteristic of much modern Gothic. An example of such an alternative family setting is Anne Rice's vampire family arrangement, consisting of two male vampires and the vampiric child who is doomed to be a little girl until her final destruction. By choosing the term 'Gothic kinship' as the title for this volume, we are acknowledging the way in which Gothic often draws attention to alternative quasi-familial relationships.

Surprisingly, perhaps, Gothic kinship has hardly been studied in its own right so far, and in that sense, *Gothic kinship* aims to fill a gap. There are a few notable exceptions; disparate in the period and the regions they cover. Tony Williams analysed the subversion of the modern family ideal in twentieth-century American horror films in *Hearths of Darkness* (1996), and showed the ambivalence residing in the bosom of the American family. Margot Gayle Backus's *The Gothic Family Romance* (1999) argued that Anglo-Irish Gothic fiction shows the devastating impact of imperialism especially for children. Biological reproduction, according to Backus, served a colonial order whose violent origins were expressed through Gothic elements like child sacrifice. Nancy Armstrong, in her analysis of the novel's role in shaping the modern individual, *How Novels Think* (2005), reserved a special place for Gothic fiction. Gothic, according to Armstrong, provides a possible alternative to the reproductive system of the nuclear family.

The notion of what entails a family has changed considerably in the past two hundred years; who may be recognized as a relative, both by other family members, outsiders and the state, have all been the subject of study. Kinship and the family are studied by a variety of disciplines, most notably anthropology. Anthropologists have traditionally located kinship as the basis of culture. Kinship relations were conceived of as a given set of normative categories, as natural (as defined by blood ties) and unchangeable. With the arrival of new reproduction technologies, queer families and surrogate mothers, questions about what constitutes kinship have become all the more pressing. This has resulted in anthropologists becoming increasingly interested in the social and cultural dimensions of kinship and in the ways the separation between 'natural' and 'cultural' definitions of kinship has become untenable.[7] Janet Carsten conceptualizes kinship therefore as a process rather than as a given – in Carsten's view, kinship is negotiated, experienced and shaped in cultural exchange – within and without the home.[8] Carsten's interest in houses as the places where kinship is experienced and shaped provides an easy link to the Gothic.[9] This new approach in kinship studies also foregrounds how 'being related' does not refer just to the ties between people, but also to the ways in which these ties are related or, in other words, narrated. The various chapters in this volume look at how kinship is enacted in narrative, through the prism of the Gothic.

Analysis of kinship structures is inevitably bound up with issues of normality and deviance. What constitutes a family – socially, politically and legally? Who is included, and who is excluded? As such, kinship theory has become a matter of interest for queer theorists as well, notably Judith Butler and Elizabeth Freeman.[10] Whereas Butler discusses the desirability of state-ratified arrangements of kinship (gay marriage), for Freeman the importance of the notion of kinship also lies in the envisioning of new forms of belonging 'whether they are addressed by state policy or not'.[11] If Gothic moments, or events, mark a digression from normality, the question is always 'which norm is being violated'? As several contributors to this volume demonstrate, the Gothic can fruitfully be read as a critical dismantling of the ideal of the nuclear family, both in the eighteenth century and more recently. Gothic fiction presents us with the queerness of families and with families of queers, as Ardel Haefele-Thomas in Chapter 2, William Hughes in Chapter 10 and Anne Quéma in Chapter 8, in particular, demonstrate.

Within cultural studies, the analysis of representations of the family has accelerated in the past fifteen years. Studies like *Family Fictions* (Harwood, 1997), *Representing the Family* (Chambers, 2001), *Shooting the Family* (Pisters and Staat, 2005), and *Mediating the Family* (Tincknell, 2005), which all focus on visual representations of the family in television dramas, films and news media, signify the increasing interest in how our understanding of familial relationships is mediated through narrative and image. These works tend to overlook the Gothic as a crucial site of mediations of the family, or only mention it in passing. However, it could well be argued that Gothic fiction is one of the privileged discourses on kinship that displays a profound cultural ambivalence toward families. One of the most detailed accounts about transformations in literary representations of kinship to date is Ruth Perry's *Novel Relations* (2004). While demonstrating a tendency to regard Gothic only as a nostalgic yearning, she offers insights into the ways in which literature engaged with the 'seismic shift in the eighteenth century, from the consanguineal to the conjugal' as the basis of the family. Perry argues that the definition of what constituted the primary kin group was transformed: 'the biologically given family into which one was born was gradually becoming secondary to the chosen family constructed by marriage'.[12] For Perry, incest is 'the hallmark of the Gothic genre'; Gothic heroines are usually terrorized by those who are supposed to be their protectors.[13] For David Richter, however, early Gothic presents its readers with a wide variety of family styles: 'from feudal (Falkland in *Caleb Williams*) to patriarchal (the Frankensteins) to matriarchal (the Vivaldis in Radcliffe's *The Italian* or the Moncadas in *Melmoth*)'.[14] Perry's rendering of the Gothic family may therefore be considered too one-sided. As the chapters that follow will show, both early and contemporary Gothic display very diverse kinship ties, ranging from metaphorical to triangular, from queer to nuclear-patriarchal.

This volume aims at thinking about kinship through Gothic, and thinking about Gothic through kinship. What is it that makes certain forms of relatedness Gothic? In what sense may kinship be regarded as monstrous, or evil, or haunting? *Gothic kinship* brings together case studies of Gothic kinship ties in film and literature and makes a first attempt at synthesizing and theorizing the different appearances of the Gothic family. The various contributions show that Gothic, as a mode of cultural representation that stages ambivalences at times of change, proves to be a rich source of expressing both subversive and conservative notions of the family.

Kamilla Elliott in Chapter 1 shows the importance of maternal miniature identification for first-wave Gothic heroines. Elliott focuses on how first-wave Gothic fiction pits matriarchal against patriarchal pictorial identifications to reinforce the bourgeois attack on aristocratic patriarchy with gendered as well as class-based narratives of kinship. While *The Castle of Otranto* uses picture identification to shore up aristocratic patriarchy, subsequent Gothic fiction sets interpenetrating resemblances among mothers, sons, daughters and portraits against the patriarchal *imago dei*. Gothic texts such as *Evelina*, *The Confessional of Valombre* and others demonstrate that, against an overt play of binary oppositions, and against the prevailing emphasis on difference in contemporary literary studies, the greatest power of matriarchal picture identification lies in its ability to produce and project devastating *resemblances*.

Ardel Haefele-Thomas in Chapter 2 analyses Elizabeth Gaskell's pioneering of alternative family ties in her short Gothic fictional texts. Gaskell utilizes the Gothic genre to explore and provide points of escape for women confined within abusive, heteronormative situations. From her understanding of the ways that gender, class and subversions of 'normative' heterosexual family structures can function together to create transgressive critiques and narratives, Gaskell finds a place to carry out queer family re-structurings within her Gothic short fiction. Haefele-Thomas explores contemporary queer theory focusing specifically on ideas of transgender and genderqueer positionality as well as historic references to famous nineteenth-century cross-dressing cases that may have influenced Elizabeth Gaskell's thinking about the topic.

In her Chapter 3 analysis of the Dutch colonial novel *De stille kracht* (*The Hidden Force*) (1900), by Louis Couperus, Rosemarie Buikema evaluates the plethora of Gothic machinations in the novel not only against the background of the changing Dutch colonial policy of around 1900 but also in relation to the corresponding specific kinship relations as they were engrained in notions of masculinity, femininity and European identity at the time. The downfall of both colonial European power and the colonial patriarchal family in the novel pivots upon the position of the colonial woman who with her arrival drove the indigenous wife off the colonial stage.

Elisabeth Wesseling's Chapter 4 traces the genealogy of evil children, by analysing the success of William March's portrayal of the demonic adoptee in *The Bad Seed* (1954) and its remediations. The success of this unprecedented work becomes all the more remarkable when we take its cultural context into account. *The Bad Seed*, Wesseling argues, takes issue with the two dominant US discourses on adoption at the time. It subverts the adoption professionals' paradigm of similarity, by suggesting that even when parents and children are perfectly matched, conforming as closely to the ideal of the white middle-class family as one could wish for, a bad seed could nevertheless still assert itself and wreak havoc. It is also at odds with the 'love-and-faith-will-conquer-all' optimism of inter-country-adoption-enthusiasts, suggesting that the normative nuclear family may not be such a great model for world politics after all.

The cult of the happy home as personified by the American suburban nuclear family is scrutinized in Chapter 5 by Bernice Murphy on Wes Craven's horror films. The American horror film since 1960 has frequently used suburbia as a setting for narratives in which the concepts which allegedly lie at the very heart of the national psyche – the privacy and safety of the home, the sanctity and inherent moral worth of the nuclear family, and the superiority of the capitalist, consumption-driven way of life – are systematically and, at times, gleefully deconstructed. Fictional suburbanites are seldom menaced by a terrible 'other' of alien origin: instead, they tend to be violently despatched by one of their own, usually a murderous family member. Murphy analyses how, from the very beginning of his career, Craven's horror films have depicted brutality and horror at the heart of the modern suburban family.

John Sears in Chapter 6 is also concerned with the American nuclear family in his discussion of *Pet Sematary*, Stephen King's most complex and pessimistic analysis of the American family. This Gothic novel presents the family from the outset as an effect of significations produced and read in faces. Faces demarcate structures of communication, exchange and power that regulate and organize the family and its relations to friends, neighbours and others – and, eventually, to Otherness itself. Sears argues that King deploys facial codes to figure this displacement and fracturing. Defaced elements of the family return as murderously persistent trace-effects of patriarchal desire. *Pet Sematary* deploys these faces and facelessnesses to envisage a critique of fatherhood itself as a dangerous surplus to its own structures, deluded, irrational, driven by the very forces it seeks to repress. Sears reads the facial troping of King's novel as a definitive intervention in contemporary Gothic's rethinking of the family.

In her Chapter 7 contribution, Agnes Andeweg focuses on the Gothic dimensions of sisterhood in Dutch feminist fiction. Renate Dorrestein's (1954) fictional autobiography *Het perpetuum mobile van de liefde* (*The Perpetual Motion Machine of Love*, 1988) offers a case of Gothic monstrosity perceived from a feminist perspective. Whereas the feminine monster has usually been read as indicator of the register of difference, in Dorrestein's work the monster is monstrous because of an uncanny resemblance between Self and Other. Dorrestein investigates the feminist notion of sisterhood through the autobiographical narrative about her sister's suicide and fictional monsters. By making the political personal again, Dorrestein finds modes to express the unspeakable rivalry and competition between sisters – and that includes feminists.

Moving into the twenty-first century, Anne Quéma analyses in Chapter 8 uncanny kinship narratives in Patricia Duncker's *The Deadly Space Between* (2002) and the British Civil Partnership Act (CPA) (2004). Quéma argues that the uncanny can be interpreted as the manifestation of the effects of normative power as we adhere to dominant norms such as family norms. In Duncker's novel, cultural performatives of kinship, sexuality and gender identification relentlessly haunt the protagonist. The CPA betrays a fundamental contradiction: while legitimizing the deletion of binary gender differences by same-sex union, it applies an interdict that reinstates the Oedipal logic of binary relations and undoes the acknowledgment of same-sex union. This constitutes the political uncanny at the heart of English family law. If the uncanny characterizes both the legal discourse and the novel, it is not so much because they operate under sexual and cultural repression; rather, the uncanny effect derives from the ways in which these two texts remain trapped in and haunted by ancestral patterns of gender and sexual identification that posture as universal, natural and commonsensical ways of doing things.

Joanne Watkiss in Chapter 9 aligns anxieties regarding family lineage in Audrey Niffenegger's *Her Fearful Symmetry* (2009) with similar anxieties in classic Gothic texts such as *The Monk* and *Zofloya, or the Moor*. Watkiss shows how the familiar, the linear and the domestic are revealed to be fragile constructions. Events do not proceed as they should; these are families that are 'out of joint', redundant in their ability to sustain themselves and future generations. In addition, qualities aligned with the institution of the family such as the familiar, the domestic and the homely are exposed as unstable foundations. Unlike early Gothic texts such as *The Monk* and *Zofloya, or the Moor*, whose Gothic families are denied lineage, *Her Fearful Symmetry* allows the Gothic family to continue through the non-linear; a perverse rendering of familial relations that accumulates three generations into one body.

In Chapter 10, William Hughes considers the representation of an alternative grouping – not based upon genitally determined reproduction or legalistic dynasties, simultaneously vampiric and homosexual – in Poppy Z. Brite's *Lost Souls* (1992). *Lost Souls* generally, and this vampiric alternative to mortal reproductive culture in particular, critiques two outwardly conventional and yet utterly deviant types of the American family – the incestuous, Christian one-parent family of the vampire-obsessed teenager; and the bourgeois, liberal, new-age-inflected two-parent adoptive family. The alternative to these families is the vampire family. In a sense, the novel embodies familial models which seemingly emblematize social structures that reflect a repressive past, a liberal present and a speculative and truly liberated future. The twenty-first-century significance of this novel is, arguably, its revision of both the failed heterosexual families and the faulted homosexual families of the twentieth century.

Ranita Chatterjee explores in Chapter 11 the Gothic kinship ties between hero Harry Potter and villain Lord Voldemort in J.K. Rowling's famous novel series. Their physically intertwined existence – Harry is Voldemort's monstrous soul progeny – gives occasion to analyse blood ties beyond the nuclear family. Chatterjee argues that that the Potter series, with its prominence of literal and figurative blood ties, reconfigures the act of sacrifice as not only feminine and maternal, but also problematically generative insofar as Harry's mother's blood both protects the hero and empowers the villain.

Johannes Schlegel in Chapter 12 examines evaluations of the nuclear family in a contextual analysis of the recent Gothic film *Mum & Dad* (2008, dir. Steven Sheil). This film, as medium of a discursive transformation of familial semantics, reflects and negotiates a paradoxical notion of order and cultural discontent in a way that can no longer be described adequately with the Gothic *topoi* of transgression and the monstrous. According to Schlegel, Steven Sheil's film aims at a radical revaluation of familial values, which results in a notion of the family as an entity that is intrinsically perverted, yet the ineluctable condition of being and of subjectivity. *Mum & Dad* circumvents the inherent dialectics of transgression, by shifting towards something rather 'ceremonial', reflecting and negotiating a paradoxical notion of order and uneasiness in contemporary culture.

In summary, the contributions to this volume explore the many ways in which Gothic fiction, be it textual or visual, questions the often seemingly natural legitimacy of kinship ties. The Gothic may show how 'natural' family relations have to be established or supported by identification techniques (Elliott, Sears, Chatterjee); how the use of family metaphors to create bonds between people are to be distrusted – either in world politics (Wesseling) or in the women's movement (Andeweg); how shaky the nuclear family ideal is (Murphy, Schlegel); or how blood ties wreak havoc rather than creating a family (Buikema, Watkiss). This volume develops fresh insights about these issues by analysing new case studies from Europe and North America, as well as texts that may be more familiar to a Gothic-studies audience – although in the light of these discussions, 'familiar' may be a rather suspect term.

Notes

1. Anne Williams, *Art of Darkness*, p. 11.
2. Ibid., p. 45.
3. See for example Joanna Russ, 'Somebody's trying to kill me'; Kate Ferguson Ellis, *The Contested Castle*; and Julie Shaffer, 'Familial love'.
4. James B. Twitchell, *Forbidden Partners: The Incest Taboo in Modern Culture*, p. 152.
5. Jerrold E. Hogle, *The Cambridge Companion to Gothic Fiction*, p. 5.
6. Mary Shelley, *Frankenstein: or The Modern Prometheus*, p. 102.
7. Good examples of this new approach in anthropology are Sarah Franklin and Susan McKinnon (eds), *Relative Values*; Janet Carsten (ed.), *Cultures of Relatedness*; and Janet Carsten, *After Kinship*.
8. Carsten, *After Kinship*, pp. 6–9.
9. Ibid., Ch. 2, 'Houses of Memory and Kinship', pp. 31–57.
10. Judith Butler, 'Is kinship always already heterosexual?'; Elizabeth Freeman, 'Queer belongings'.
11. Elizabeth Freeman, 'Queer belongings', p. 295.
12. Ruth Perry, *Novel Relations*, p. 2.
13. Ibid., p. 103.
14. David Richter, 'Review', p. 201.

References

Armstrong, Nancy, *How Novels Think: The Limits of Individualism from 1719–1900* (New York: Columbia University Press, 2005).

Backus, Margot Gayle, *The Gothic Family Romance: Heterosexuality, Child Sacrifice, and the Anglo-Irish Colonial Order* (Durham, NC and London: Duke University Press, 1999).

Butler, Judith, 'Is kinship always already heterosexual?' *Differences*, 13:1 (2002), 14–44.

Carsten, Janet, *After Kinship* (Cambridge: Cambridge University Press, 2004).

Chambers, Deborah, *Representing the Family* (London: Sage, 2001).

Ellis, Kate Ferguson, *The Contested Castle: Gothic Novels and the Subversion of Domestic Ideology* (Urbana: University of Illinois Press, 1989).

Franklin, Sarah, and Susan McKinnon (eds), *Relative Values. Reconfiguring Kinship Studies* (Durham, NC and London: Duke University Press, 2001).

Freeman, Elizabeth, 'Queer belongings: kinship theory and queer theory',

in George Haggerty and Molly McGarry (eds), *A Companion to Lesbian, Gay, Bisexual, and Transgender Studies* (Malden, MA: Blackwell Publishing, 2007), pp. 295–314.
Harwood, Sarah, *Family Fictions: Representations of the Family in 1980s Hollywood Cinema* (London: Macmillan, 1997).
Hogle, Jerrold E. (ed.), *The Cambridge Companion to Gothic Fiction* (Cambridge: Cambridge University Press, 2002).
Perry, Ruth, *Novel Relations: The Transformation of Kinship in English Literature and Culture, 1748–1818* (Cambridge: Cambridge University Press, 2004).
Pisters, Patricia and Wim Staat, *Shooting the Family. Transnational Media and Intercultural Values* (Amsterdam: Amsterdam University Press, 2005).
Richter, David, Review of *The Contested Castle: Gothic Novels and the Subversion of Domestic Ideology* by Kate Ferguson Ellis; *Dead Secrets: Wilkie Collins and the Female Gothic* by Tamar Heller; *In the Name of Love: Women, Masochism, and the Gothic* by Michelle A. Massé, *Modern Language Review*, 89:1 (Jan 1994), 200–3.
Russ, Joanna, 'Somebody's trying to kill me and I think it's my husband: the modern Gothic', *Journal of Popular Culture* 6:4 (1973), 666–91.
Shaffer, Julie, 'Familial love, incest, and female desire in late eighteenth and early nineteenth-century British women's novels', *Criticism* (Winter 1999), 67–99.
Shelley, Mary, *Frankenstein: or The Modern Prometheus*, ed. Maurice Hindle (1818; London: Penguin, 2003).
Tincknell, Estella, *Mediating the Family: Gender, Culture and Representation* (London: Hodder Arnold, 2005).
Twitchell, James B., *Forbidden Partners: The Incest Taboo in Modern Culture* (New York: Columbia University Press, 1987).
Williams, Anne, *Art of Darkness: a Poetics of Gothic* (Chicago: University of Chicago Press, 1996).
Williams, Tony, *Hearths of Darkness. The Family in the American Horror Film* (London: Associated University Press, 1996).

1
Matriarchal picture identification in first-wave British Gothic fiction[1]

Kamilla Elliott

This chapter examines various ways in which first-wave British Gothic fiction ties matriarchal picture identification to bourgeois ideology to delimit, undermine and reform aristocratic ideology. Addressing numerous Gothic texts, it attends particularly to Eleanor Sleath's *The Orphan of the Rhine* (1796), and Louisa Sidney Stanhope's *The Confessional of Valombre* (1812).

For Michael McKeon, '"Aristocratic ideology" names the impulse, operative in a wide diversity of cultures, to conceal the perennial alteration in ruling elites by naturalising those elites as a unity of status and virtue, the ongoing "rule of the best"'.[2] Aristocratic ideology maintains 'a unity of status and virtue' in part through ideologies, practices and narratives of picture identification. Picture identification grows out of *imago dei* (man made in the image of God): both portraits and sons are made in the images of fathers, forging parallel chains of hierarchical, patriarchal imaged identities. Ancestral portrait galleries tie aesthetically created imaged identities to humanly procreated imaged identities. Portraiture 'articulated the patriarchal principle of genealogy upon which aristocratic ideology was built. The authorising relationship between the living model and its imaged likeness was analogous to that between father and son.' Through imaging, 'the subject was situated within chains or hierarchies of resemblance leading to the origin of Nature herself: God'.[3]

Against cycles of aristocratic despotism and underclass revolution, Anne K. Mellor suggests that 'women writers of the Romantic era offered an alternative programme grounded on the trope of the family-politic, on the idea of a nation-state that evolves gradually and rationally under the mutual care and guidance of both mother and father', with 'domestic affections as the model for all political action', producing an 'equality of the sexes' and an 'egalitarian rather than patriarchal family'.[4] Nancy Armstrong argues similarly that nineteenth-century fiction sets domesticity against genealogy, attaching 'psychological motives to what had been the openly political behavior of contending groups' in order 'to evaluate these according to a set of moral norms that exalt[s] the domestic woman over and above her aristocratic counterpart'.[5] My argument builds on and departs from these and similar critical connections made between class and gender. In contrast to Mellor's account, it locates points at which matriarchal picture identification is militant and destructive; in contrast to Armstrong's focus on 'a form of power that works through language – and particularly the printed word – to constitute subjectivity',[6] it demonstrates how the verbal-visual intersemiotics of picture identification construct social rather than solely subjective identity. A focus on picture identification furthermore situates matriarchal dynamics between Romantic studies of absent mothers[7] and psychoanalytic accounts of maternal bodies.[8]

Before we turn to examine Gothic matriarchal picture identification, the aristocratic patriarchal portrait identification that such representations undermine must be established. Gothic fiction's founding father provides one.

Patriarchal picture identification in *The Castle of Otranto*

Although there are no maternal or matriarchal portraits in Horace Walpole's *The Castle of Otranto*, the novel contains the seeds that would produce them in subsequent Gothic fiction and manifests the vulnerabilities in patriarchal chains of imaged identity that later fiction would exploit. In Walpole's novel, divine right has gone wrong: sequences of lineal and portrait imaging have been broken; the grandson of a usurping steward sits on the throne; the usurper's portrait hangs in the ancestral gallery. The legitimate heir is missing; the 'sickly, puny'[9] heir of the illegitimate line indicates the failure of usurpers to procreate with potency.

By contrast, ancestral portraits are present and active. When the helmet of the usurped Prince Alfonso's funerary statue, supersized and animated, kills the sickly heir, a legitimate afterlife destroys an illegitimate one; a portrait wreaks revenge on progeny, setting two forms of imaged afterlives in violent conflict, against aristocratic traditions in which they were to shore each other up. Portraits from both legitimate and usurping lines work against the continuation of the illegitimate one. When Manfred, his wife infertile, tries to force his dead son's fiancée to produce another heir with him, the portrait of his *own* grandfather, the original usurper, prevents him (19). As Manfred is 'unable to keep his eyes from the picture, which began to move', the princess escapes. The portrait subsequently 'quit[s] its panel, and descend[s] on the floor with a grave and melancholy air' (20), a tacit admission that it does not belong in the ancestral gallery. Beckoning Manfred to follow, the portrait prefigures his descendant's subsequent abdication.

By contrast, the legitimate heir, an apparent peasant, is identified and entitled by resemblance to the portrait of his grandfather: 'is not that youth the exact resemblance of Alfonso's picture in the gallery?' (78). Identified by resemblance to 'Alfonso the good' (92), when Theodore becomes Prince of Otranto, he represents a new kind of patriarch, blending aristocratic and non-aristocratic values. The modern bourgeois values that Theodore incorporates into his medieval aristocratic identity derive implicitly from his matriarchal line of descent. As much as Theodore resembles his grandfather, his descent from Alfonso is matrilineal rather than patrilineal; his mother was Alfonso's only daughter.

Mothers and sons: rebirthing and re-identifying patriarchy

'[I]f the physiognomonical germ exist in the father, how can it sometimes resemble the mother?' – Johann Caspar Lavater[10]

'People are as often like their mothers as their fathers.' – Theresa Lewis[11]

Just as Roman Catholicism had historically checked unbridled regal and aristocratic power, subsequent Gothic fiction draws on Roman Catholic theology and iconology to empower matriarchal and bourgeois identities against patriarchal and aristocratic ones, even though most Gothic authors officially disavow Roman Catholicism. As Roman Catholic icons disperse power from God the Father to other identities, matriarchal portraits in Gothic fiction disperse symbolic and social power among non-patriarchal identities.

Pseudo-religious secular iconographies representing dead mothers as saints and angels further position them with heavenly authority over earthly fathers, inspiring worship, empowering progeny and terrorizing guilty patriarchs. That such representations border on idolatry and blasphemy only intensifies the power of such representations for Protestant readers.

Crucially, Mariology offers a symbolic means of bypassing and erasing the earthly father in procreation and the formation of social identity. Gothic fiction secularizes Mariology to symbolically erase aristocratic patriarchal genealogies and rebirth sons in the images of mothers aligned with bourgeois ideologies. Sons may take the patriarchal name but, as the 'the exact resemblance' or 'the very picture' of mothers, they inhabit a matriarchal *imago dei*.

While *The Castle of Otranto*'s Theodore is identified by a patriarchal portrait, nearly half a century later *The Confessional of Valombre*'s Theodore is identified by a matriarchal one:

> One form, one countenance the most attracted his attention; it was the beauteous semblance of a matron, on whose white bosom a sleeping boy reclined. The smile of maternal exultation glowed upon the canvas, as her snowy hand seemed in the act of parting the golden ringlets on the forehead of the child.
>
> 'Ah!' exclaimed Theodore, as he gazed upon the picture, 'how nature speaks in every perfect feature! ... blessed cherub! rich in a mother's love.'[12]

The painting represents the infant Theodore with his mother, omitting his father, after traditions of Madonna and child portraiture. The narrator's picture identification apotheosizes 'maternal exultation' over paternal blood; the child is 'rich in mother's love' rather than a father's property. The maternal *imago dei* manifested in progeny and portrait is produced by Mother Nature rather than Father God: 'Nature stamped the smile of matchless sweetness, marking the calm of virtue and the soul of honour' (Vol. 3, 44–5).

Cloistered since infancy, Theodore nevertheless has an enraptured bourgeois vision of a new kind of patriarchy:

> I become a husband! – I become a father! God of nature! ... I alleviate, soften, soothe the cares of affection! I catch the lisping accents of tender infancy! I breathe the proud, the grateful prayer of praise for growing virtues, for budding promises, for parental transports! I, when the winter of age steals o'er my being, freezing my youthful

ardour, I retrace that ardour, re-acted, re-existing in [my children!]. (55–6)

Theodore's vision, which invokes the 'God of nature' rather than the God of the Church, does not simply or even primarily express sexual desire: its desire is political, setting a romanticized, sentimental, middle-class paternalism against both aristocratic and ecclesiastical patriarchies. Theodore's paternal pride lies in the virtues, not the lineage, of his children; he dreams of infusing them with his sentiments rather than his blood.

When Theodore's position as the infant in the Madonna-child portrait subsequently identifies his aristocratic birth, that matriarchal picture identification rebirths him symbolically as a new kind of patriarch identified with feminine, bourgeois concepts of virtue. Rejecting the usual Gothic endings ('Thinking it immaterial to state the tedious process of judicatory proceedings, the evidence of Du Plessis, the penitent Lambelle, &c. &c. ... the confessions of Montauban, and the wretched Ermissende'), the novel focuses instead on Theodore's 'visit to the unconsecrated grave of a murdered mother, embalmed in the tears of filial tenderness' (Vol. 4, 247; 251). Spilled tears are set against aristocratic blood and bloodshed, embalming the bourgeois sentiment they express as well as the maternal grave.

Yet for all their sentimentality and innocence, maternal picture identification and Mother Nature are formidable social forces. Armstrong has demonstrated the role of romantic desire in reorganizing social relations, arguing that 'narratives which seemed to be concerned solely with matters of courtship and marriage ... contest the reigning notion of kinship relations that attached most power and privilege to certain family lines' (p. 5). *Valombre* touts 'love' as 'the boasted prerogative of nature', 'the master-passion, which subdues man's lordly mind' (Vol. 4, 247; 251). Here Mother Nature asserts herself in a masculine, aristocratic rhetoric of prerogative, mastery, and subjugation against the pragmatism of aristocratic marriages and 'lordly' masculine reason. Taking on traditionally masculine functions, simultaneously rebelling against authority and declaring her omnipotence, Nature is positively autocratic: 'Nature, spurning the innovation of authority, proclaims the omnipotence of passion and stamps her laws irreversible!' (Vol. 3, 137). Her 'irreversible laws' are joined by principles impervious to social forces:

'I have seen the world in its busy maze ... but it cannot destroy the principles of nature' (Vol. 2, 165).

Concomitantly, Nature reconstructs an aristocratic patriarch made in 'the image of his Creator' as 'a slave', overriding the *imago dei* held to lie at the core of aristocratic identities:

> Nature, perhaps in sport, sometimes violates her own stamp of perfection by affixing to man, the image of his Creator, the blackening dye of a corrupt heart. She had neither gifted [the usurping duke] with external charms or internal qualification, for his features, the direct index to his mind, bespoke him proud, morose, unbending, a slave to his passions. (Vol. 2, 52–3)

Paradoxically, although Nature makes him, 'Nature was dead within him, for no relenting softness pleaded a brother's cause; he pined to possess the title, the dignity of his ancestors' (Vol. 4, 146). Here *desiring* the aspects of aristocratic identity inaccessible to the middle ranks – the title of duke and aristocratic lineage – renders the Duke 'a slave'. At the end of the novel, bourgeois class values displace erotic desire. For all the rhetoric lauding romantic love, at the culmination of their courtship, Theodore and Juliette pontificate rather than procreate, reproducing bourgeois values before progeny: 'of what avail had been the boasted pride of birth ... the lasting stamp of eternal devotion, virtue, generosity, is the true essence of greatness – is the noblest distinction of man. Honours are hereditary, but honour, free, unconfined, harbours in obscurity and stamps a peasant oft superior to a prince' (Vol. 4, 260). And yet birth, rank, and wealth do matter: this peasant turns out to be an aristocrat by birth; he marries a marquis's daughter and inherits aristocratic property, which he 'soften[s] into order' by the 'chisel of improvement' (Vol. 4, 258). Drawing on a Romanticized Nature and a pseudo-religious, feminine iconography, matriarchal picture identification has likewise softened, ordered, and improved patriarchy in this novel; more militantly, it has pseudo-usurped aristocratic titles, property, power, and prestige and bestowed them on pseudo-middle-class identities.

Mothers, daughters, and miniatures: resisting and reforming patriarchy

'Remember, he is thy father still!'

'But you are my mother too,' said Matilda fervently, 'and you are virtuous, you are guiltless! – Oh! must not I, must not I complain?' – Horace Walpole, *The Castle of Otranto*. (150–1)

More often than Gothic sons and much earlier in the Gothic tradition than they, Gothic daughters are identified with and by matriarchal portraits. As sons and portraits serve as parallel, imaged afterlives of patriarchs, daughters and portraits serve as parallel, imaged afterlives of matriarchs, reinforcing matriarchal identities and their alignment with bourgeois agenda. As interpenetrating resemblances among fathers, sons and portraits shore up aristocratic patriarchy in *Otranto*, interpenetrating resemblances among daughters, mothers and portraits undermine it in other Gothic texts. As sons and portraits share terminology, so do daughters and portraits. As Theodore is the 'exact resemblance' of his grandfather in *The Castle of Otranto* (78), a daughter in Francis Lathom's *The Castle of Ollada* (1795) is 'the exact resemblance of her deceased mother', 'the very picture of poor Rosala'.[13] Even in *Otranto*, although Manfred has Hippolita's greater love (he 'is dearer to me even than my children', 15), her core identification is with her daughter: 'Life of my soul,' she cries, 'I lived but in her and will expire with her' (191).

Gothic fiction is particularly vested in exploring imaged identities among mothers, daughters and miniature portraits. Gesturing doubly to the diminutive size of newborns and of portraits, infant daughters are frequently figured as 'miniatures' of their mothers. In Catherine Smith's *Barozzi* (1815), a mother brings 'into the world a sweet girl, a miniature resemblance of herself',[14] as does a mother in Marianne Breton's *The Wife of Fitzalice* (1817): 'she expired in giving birth to a female infant, the miniature resemblance of herself'.[15] In Catherine Cuthbertson's *Santo Sebastiano* (1806) the clause, 'She left him this sweet miniature of herself to twine her memory more closely round his neck' refers to the woman's daughter, not her own portrait.[16]

Marcia Pointon argues that 'miniatures are historically, quintessentially, about the oscillation between self and other'.[17] For Gothic heroines, however, miniatures are more often about the oscillation between self and *m*other. When Gothic heroines wear portraits of the mothers they resemble, such portraits serve as outward-facing mirrors of inherently imaged matriarchal identities. The maternal image unfolds from mothers to both daughters and miniature portraits, creating interpenetrating resemblances that shore up female power in social contexts that disempower them. A daughter described as her mother's 'sweet semblance' receives her mother's portrait: '"Look," [he said], extending a miniature towards her, "is not this your own image?" She started – the picture trembled in her hand; – it was indeed her own image.'[18] 'Her own image' resonates multiply: her mother's image is her own; the portrait's image is her own; she owns the image by resembling it, by recognizing it and by possessing it as property. Such multifaceted ownership undermines patriarchal imaged identities, hierarchies, sequencing, property and lineages.

In Sophia Lee's *The Recess* (1783–85), the first Gothic novel to picture-identify women, matriarchal lineages displace patriarchal ones, as queens rather than kings or princes vie for power. In contrast to the supernatural, militant authority of patriarchal picture identification in *Otranto*, *The Recess* authorizes matriarchal picture identification through an aesthetics that unites nature, art, memory and mirror. Their foster mother informs twin princesses: 'I would describe the Queen of Scots to you, my dear children, had not nature drawn a truer picture of her than I can give. Look in the glass, Matilda, and you will see her perfect image'.[19] Nature rather than God or a father has made this daughter in the image of her mother.

Hitherto Matilda has seen only self-sameness in the mirror; after her matriarchal picture identification in, with and through it, the mirror henceforth functions as a reflection of self and of (m)other. Although it is conventional to read such dynamics in Lacanian terms, this is not so much an unconscious projective identification as a consciously perceived, socializing one. The process is not one of image prior to words or against words, but of image joining forces with words to produce social identification. The picture identification produces a re-cognition, which the daughter experiences simultaneously as return to origin and coming of age. Produced by an adoptive mother rather than by a patriarch, the mirror shatters the daughter's identification with that maternal foster mother, reconstructing it with a matriarchal birth mother. It is this picture identification, not the Name of the Father, which ushers the daughter into the social order. Following her picture identification by both mothers, Matilda moves from the womb-like space of the recess into the political and social domain.

Matilda has previously looked in the mirror to understand how others perceive her and to differentiate herself from her twin sister (who intriguingly resembles their father). Prior to her matriarchal re-identification, she has located her power to forge potential social alliances in her beauty: 'When I looked in the glass, I did not think I should be neglected' (Vol. 1, 20). Now she sees that her power to form social alliances lies in resemblance to her royal mother, which testifies to kinship. Turning to the bonds of kinship rather than courtship, she uses picture identification to fix, proclaim and circulate her matriarchal resemblance. Writing to request 'alliance' and 'protection' from her mother's former allies, she 'enclosed my picture in little, not doubting but that would identify my birth' (Vol. 2, 50). Here and elsewhere, in contrast to psychoanalytic emphases on unconscious, projective negotiations between self and (m)other, picture identification's vacillation between self-sameness and sameness with (m)other produces conscious processes of representation and social negotiation.

Since their British origins in the court of Henry VIII, miniature pictures had been exchanged among royals and courtiers to forge secret political and sexual alliances against official ones. *The Recess* fictionalizes such exchanges. Bourgeois Gothic fiction co-opts such uses of miniatures to set private, middle-class identities against official, ruling identities and to valorize bourgeois over aristocratic modes of affiliation. Miniatures exchanged secretly support the formation of marriage bonds that oppose aristocratic family values and diminish aristocratic power.

The heyday of miniature portraits in England, 1760–1840, coincides almost exactly with the first wave of Gothic fiction; miniatures appear in it more often than any other kind of portrait. They do so because they are ideal forms for promoting middle-class identities, ideologies and iconographies and opposing aristocratic ones. Miniature portraits stand in diametric contrast to the gigantic funerary portrait of *Otranto*, which Clara Reeve deems more laughable than formidable in her preface to *The Old English Baron*,[20] and which seems to protest a threatened aristocracy too much.

Eleanor Sleath's *The Orphan of the Rhine* (1798) inscribes a continuum between Roman Catholic icons of female saints and miniatures of dead mothers, granting them power to instill and preserve virtue (synonymous with social value in this period) in daughters.

What begins as a prayer to an icon of Saint Rosalie ends as a prayer to a heroine's mother, 'the companion of angels':

> 'Forgive me, holy Saint,' resumed she, falling meekly upon her knees before a small image of Saint Rosalie, 'forgive me if I have dared to murmur ... endeavor to fortify my mind with those invaluable principles of religion which were instilled into my heart from the earliest period of my existence by my first and dearest friend ... if she is already released from the shackles of mortality and is become the companion of angels, may she look down with compassion upon her adopted child, strengthen her weak resolves, and lead her, by secret inspiration, to that excelling and unassuming piety which dignified her character!'[21]

The Orphan of the Rhine (1796) spiritualizes the *resemblances* among mothers, daughters, and miniature portraits. When 'the person of [a daughter], recall[s] the image of her beloved mother' for a monk, he sacramentalizes the resemblance by giving the girl an outward sign of his inward recognition: 'Take this, it is the portrait of thy mother; wear it as an invaluable gift' (423; 189). The artefactual resemblance carries the maternal *imago dei* from embodied and subjective domains (like memory) into the domain of sacred objects. The resemblance is, moreover, a reciprocal rather than hierarchical or linear one; when 'she pressed ... to her lips ... the picture ... whose saint-like countenance so finely imaged her own' (323), her mother's portrait images *her*. The miniature redoubles the resemblance; the daughter's 'person' is the image of her mother; she now wears an image of her mother on her person.

Daughters manipulate maternal portraits to exert power over patriarchs. As Mary and the angels are positioned above mortals in Roman Catholicism, so too sainted, angel, spirit and ghostly mothers are positioned above mortal patriarchs in Gothic fiction. The pseudo-supernatural associations of maternal portraits, conjoined with the sentimentality accorded portraits of dead mothers, lead patriarchs to submit themselves to matriarchal iconography and to teach progeny to do likewise. In Cuthbertson's *Santo Sebastiano*, a father instructs and joins his daughter in worship of a maternal portrait:

> clasping me with the convulsive grasp of anguish to his throbbing heart, and taking from his bosom the miniature of [my mother], [he] press[ed] it with agonised tenderness to his lips: – again, and still, still, again; then he would hold it for me kiss to give it and bid me

'look with high reverence upon it and love it beyond all things at all, except my Creator'. (Vol. 1, 180)

Even as 'my Creator' raises the spectre of the patriarchal *imago dei*, the father subjugates himself to the maternal icon.

Most dead Gothic mothers remain buried on earth or up in heaven; some, however manifest as ghosts. In addition to progeny and portraits, these ghosts constitute a third form of imaged afterlife for mothers that strengthens matriarchal power. Ghosts too are made in the images of bodies – ambivalently so as 'a substance yet a shadow, in thy living likeness'.[22] As Alfonso's ghost resembles and seems to emanate from and return to his portraits in *The Castle of Otranto*, so too does the ghost of a murdered matriarch in Matthew Lewis's *The Castle Spectre* (1797):

> ANGELA. *(Kneeling before Evelina's portrait.)* Mother! Blessed Mother! If indeed thy spirit still lingers amidst these scenes of sorrow, look on my despair with pity! fly to my aid! ...
>
> *(A plaintive voice sings within, accompanied by a guitar.)*
>
> 'Lullaby! – Lullaby! – Hush thee, my dear,
> Thy father is coming and soon will be here!' ...
>
> *(The folding-doors unclose, and the Oratory is seen illuminated. In its centre stands a tall female figure, her white and flowing garments spotted with blood; her veil is thrown back and discovers a pale and melancholy countenance; her eyes are lifted upwards, her arms extended towards heaven, and a large wound appears upon her bosom ... She then turns, approaches Angela, seems to invoke a blessing upon her, points to the picture, and retires to the Oratory. The music ceases. Angela rises with a wild look and follows the Vision, extending her arms towards it.)*
>
> ANGELA. Stay, lovely spirit! – Oh! stay yet one moment!
>
> *(The Spectre waves her hand, as bidding her farewell. Instantly the organ's swell is heard; a full chorus of female voices chant 'Jubilate!' A blaze of light flashes through the Oratory, and the folding doors close with a loud noise.)*[23]

The matriarchal spectre enters to the sound of a lullaby rather than to the thunder and earthquake accompanying Alfonso's ghost (194); she exits to Christian choral music. Even bleeding, she is a 'lovely spirit' rather than an object of terror or horror.[24] Like the

Virgin Mary, the maternal 'vision' reaches 'towards heaven' and blesses her daughter. By contrast, when Manfred's servants see the gigantic replica of Alfonso's funerary statue, they nominate it 'Satan himself' and beg Manfred to 'have the castle exorcised' (37; 40). From Alfonso on, Gothic patriarchal ghosts are generally associated with violence and revenge. While both are deemed necessary to the destruction and unseating of 'bad' aristocrats, maternal ghosts work to *sanctify* changes in power.

Maternal ghosts and portraits possess ideological, psychological and supernatural power *because* the mothers they represent, powerless against patriarchs in the social sphere, are dead and removed from that sphere. On the one hand, ghosts and portraits empower mothers by removing them from the power of the social sphere over them, positioning them over and above it; on the other, they situate mothers as insubstantial spectres and inanimate objects in the social realm. Interpenetrating resemblances among mothers, daughters and portraits, however, shore up matriarchal power, as one imaged identity compensates for what the others lack. Where ghosts are unstable and daughters changing, portraits fix the maternal *imago dei*. Where mothers are dead, portraits grant them an imaged afterlife; ghosts give mothers a supernatural afterlife, while daughters offer them an embodied and social afterlife. As incarnate resemblances of mothers, daughters restore the social and physical power evacuated by ghosts and portraits. Concomitantly, where daughters lack symbolic power, their resemblance to mothers bestows it on them, giving them authority in the social domain. While mothers cannot be literal virgins and virgin daughters cannot be literal mothers, resemblance allows each to image both, an exchange exemplified when *The Orphan of the Rhine*'s second-generation heroine resembles both her mother and one of Raphael's *Madonnas* (245).

Their possession of maternal resemblance joins their possession of maternal portraits to grant daughters power over patriarchs. In Charlotte Smith's *Montalbert* (1795), resemblance renders the daughter a 'representative' of her mother, reversing conventions in which fathers acknowledge daughters: 'dear representative of the most beloved and most injured of women – Speak to me – Speak to and acknowledge your unhappy father!'[25] In Frances Burney's *Evelina* (1779), which some critics consider to be a Gothic novel, a daughter's resemblance to a deceased mother – 'thou image of my long-lost Caroline'[26] – forces an aristocratic father to acknowledge paternity. Maternal resemblance is her sole source of authority. Evelina, legally a bastard raised by a clergyman, lacks social, physical, economic and legal power. Her performativity – her behaviour and speech toward him – remains entirely submissive and self-abasing. Yet Evelina's passive *resemblance* to her mother becomes a violent, avenging, rapacious force: 'thy countenance is a dagger to my heart! – just so thy mother looked' (Vol. 2, 180). But since resemblance is never identical identity, it equally empowers Evelina by rendering her *un*like her victimized mother, who died from her husband's refusal to recognize her as wife. Evelina's non-resembling resemblance to her mother allows her to emerge as embodied, social victor in contrast to her mother, who is dead, angel victim. The resemblance vindicates the mother posthumously; mother and daughter conjoin to punish and reform the patriarch: the mother constructs him as tyrannical villain; the daughter, as humble penitent. Such dynamics do not represent the power of 'women' over 'men' so much as the power of matriarchal *resemblance* over patriarchy.

In *Evelina*, memory produces matriarchal resemblance; other Gothic novels artefactualize it in portraits. A father in *The Orphan of the Rhine* wears the miniature portrait of his dead wife, turning to it as confessional and icon: '"Have I not been an unnatural parent, a cruel husband? Yes,' resumed he, fixing his hollow eyes upon a small picture, which was fastened round his neck with a black ribbon, 'my Helena! My much injured Helena! I was thy murderer!"' (18).

Even where guilty patriarchs are impenitent, they are disempowered by resemblances among mothers, daughters and portraits. Miniature portraits of mothers save heroines on the brink of forced marriages to the uncles who murdered their parents in both *The Orphan of the Rhine* and *The Confessional of Valombre*. In the former, 'astonishment and terror' are 'delineated on [the Marchese's] countenance on the discovery of the picture' (307); the latter expands the miniature's patriarchal disempowerment:

> My mother's cherished image, torn from my neck, still trembled in [the Duke's] hand, whose every feature wore the stamp of horror and amazement. 'Quick, name the original of this accursed picture!' he demanded, in loud appalling accents. But when my trembling lips pronounced, 'Mother,' the picture dropped from his grasp; breath-

less, he clung to the arm of his servant and was supported from the chapel. (Vol. 3, 50–1)

Between 1796 and 1812, 'astonishment' becomes 'amazement' and 'terror' metamorphoses into 'horror'. The Duke, deprived of breath, speech and mobility, becomes dependent on a servant. The common noun *mother* overpowers the titled man; he is unable to maintain his grasp upon her image.

The earlier novel, however, is more radical in other regards, declaring the ability of maternal miniatures to reveal the hidden face of patriarchy:

> The language of nature is indelibly engraven on the human countenance and, however the slave of vice and insincerity may hope to seclude it from the eagle eye of Truth, there are moments when the mask of dissimulation will drop ... The Marchese ... betrayed a secret which the wealth of the world could not have wrested from him. (313)

The mother's sainted picture identification produces the Marchese's criminalizing identification.

Aristocratic patriarchal titles and social status are more permanently and tangibly overthrown when matriarchal picture identification establishes both heroines as entitled to them. While patriarchal picture identification is entirely absent in *The Confessional of Valombre*, in *The Orphan of the Rhine* it is present, but ineffectual. One woman gives birth to a son 'who bore the name as well as the resemblance of his father, but of whom death early deprived me' (226); another loses her father's miniature; found by her enemies, it is read as a sign that she is plotting against the novel's archpatriarch (142; 170). By contrast, the matriarchal miniature given to an orphan lacking a patriarchal name: ('She was called Laurette, but no other name was added', 187) is worn 'continually in her bosom, carefully conceal[ed] from observation ... secretly cherish[ed] ... as an invaluable relic' (231). Here, as in *Evelina*, when women lose their patriarchal names, matriarchal resemblances restore them. Resemblances among mother, daughter and portrait, as well as between two maternal portraits, affirm the heroine's right to possess the patriarch's property: 'That it was really the portrait of her mother was beyond a doubt. The resemblance that it bore to herself she was perfectly aware of'; indeed, it was 'too striking to escape the penetration of the most transient observer' (275).

This Gothic tale dramatizes what happens to matriarchal names under patriarchy in society: patriarchal names swallow them up in marriage. Facial resemblances, however, bear witness to the matriarchal affiliations that patriarchal names have overwritten. Facial resemblances mark the return of the matriarchy that patriarchy has repressed. Bearing the names of mothers as maternal portraits do, daughters become picture identifications of mothers and are in turn picture-identified by maternal portraits.

In *The Orphan of the Rhine*, Laurette produces her *own* picture identification, joining passive physical resemblance to her mother's portraits to active mental constructions of resemblances between the miniature and a full-length portrait of her mother:

> As she examined the features of the portrait, rendered infinitely more touching by the sweet pensive cast of the countenance, she thought she had somewhat seen a painting that strongly characterised it and, as the castle contained all that had ever fallen under her observation, she was resolved to regard them more attentively and, if possible, to trace the resemblance. (190)

Turning empiricist and detective, Laurette relocates the full-length portrait in the castle gallery that 'strikingly resembled the miniature that she wore in her bosom' (423). Tracing their resemblances, she produces picture identification in the same way that art historians do – by matching picture to picture. The portable property of the miniature matched to the large portrait in the castle allows her to lay claim to real property. When Laurette subsequently produces another picture identification in the same way that artists do – 'she had been attempting to sketch his likeness. Memory had been too faithful to its task not to portray his exact resemblance' (355) – both modes extend the power of resemblance from her passive, unconscious possession of it to her active construction and production of it. At the end of the novel, Laurette displays the hitherto secreted miniature of her mother and tells her previously untold story. In so doing she moves from a picture identification in which a given name is matched to an inherited face, producing her own more expansive picture identification in the form of an illustrated personal narrative (421).

Matriarchal picture identification in Gothic fiction, then, draws on the dead and the living, the animate and the inanimate, the religious and the secular, the natural and the artefactual, interiority and exteriority, aesthetics and science, the supernatural and the empirical, as well as on ruptures and contradictions in all of these binarisms. Indeed, in spite of their oppositions and contradictions, they ally in matriarchal and maternal picture identifications to attack aristocratic patriarchy on all fronts. Against the overt play of binary oppositions (matriarchy vs patriarchy, middle vs aristocratic classes, etc.) *and their deconstructions*, the most formidable power of matriarchal picture identification lies in its ability to project and produce *resemblances* that destabilize, undermine and overthrow the capacity of patriarchy to establish and maintain hierarchical difference and authority through its modes and ideologies of imaging.

Notes

1. This chapter is taken in part from Kamilla Elliott, *British Gothic Fiction and the Rise of Picture Identification*.
2. Michael McKeon, *The Origins of the English Novel, 1600–1740*, p. 169.
3. Joanna Woodall, 'Introduction', in Joanna Woodall (ed.), *Portraiture*, p. 3.
4. Anne K. Mellor, *Romanticism and Gender*, pp. 65–7.
5. Nancy Armstrong, *Desire and Domestic Fiction*, p. 18; p. 5.
6. Ibid., p. 25.
7. See for example Elizabeth A. Fay, 'Women and the Gothic: literature as home politics', in *A Feminist Introduction to Romanticism*, pp. 107–48.
8. See for example Julie Kipp, *Romanticism, Maternity, and the Body Politic*.
9. Horace Walpole, *The Castle of Otranto*, p. 16. Subsequent page numbers are cited parenthetically in the text.
10. Johann Caspar Lavater, *Physiognomy*, p. 151.
11. Lady Theresa Lewis, *Dacre: A Novel*, 3 vols, ed. by the Countess of Morley, Vol. 2, p. 68.
12. Louisa Sidney Stanhope, *The Confessional of Valombre*, Vol. 2, pp. 250–1. Subsequent page numbers are cited parenthetically in the text.
13. Francis Lathom, *The Castle of Ollada*, pp. 89–90.
14. Catherine Smith, *Barozzi: or, The Venetian Sorceress*, p. 77.
15. Marianne Breton, *The Wife of Fitzalice, and the Caledonian Siren*, Vol. 1, p. 82.
16. Catherine Cuthbertson, *Santo Sebastiano*, Vol. 3, p. 246. Subsequent page numbers are cited parenthetically in the text.
17. Marcia Pointon, '"Surrounded with brilliants"', p. 63.

18 Louisa Sidney Stanhope, *Striking Likenesses*, Vol. 3, p. 8; Vol. 2, p. 71.
19 Sophia Lee, *The Recess*, Vol. 1, p. 55. Subsequent page numbers are cited parenthetically in the text.
20 Clara Reeve, *The Old English Baron*, p. v.
21 Eleanor Sleath, *The Orphan of the Rhine*, pp. 315–16. Subsequent page numbers are cited parenthetically in the text.
22 William Harrison Ainsworth, *Rookwood*, Vol. 2, p. 202.
23 Matthew G. Lewis, *The Castle Spectre, a Drama*, Vol. 4, pp. 50–1.
24 Icons often represent the Virgin Mary with a sword through her heart; there are numerous accounts of her icons bleeding. See Maria Vassilaki, 'Bleeding icons', in Antony Eastmond and Liz James (eds), *Icon and Word*, pp. 121–34.
25 Charlotte Turner Smith, *Montalbert*, Vol. 3, p. 243.
26 Frances Burney, *Evelina*, Vol. 2, p. 166. Subsequent page numbers are cited parenthetically in the text.

References

Ainsworth, William Harrison, *Rookwood: A Romance*, 2 vols (Philadelphia: Carey, Lea & Blanchard, from the 2nd London edn, 1834).

Armstrong, Nancy, *Desire and Domestic Fiction: A Political History of the Novel* (Oxford: Oxford University Press, 1990).

Breton, Marianne, *The Wife of Fitzalice, and the Caledonian Siren: A Romance*, 5 vols (London: Minerva Press, 1817).

Burney, Frances, *Evelina: or, The History of a Young Lady's Entrance into the World*, 3 vols (London: T. Lowndes, 4th edn, 1779 [1778]).

Cuthbertson, Catherine, *Santo Sebastiano: or, The Young Protector*, 5 vols (London: Longman, Hurst & Co., 1820 [1806]).

Fay, Elizabeth A., 'Women and the Gothic: literature as home politics', in *A Feminist Introduction to Romanticism* (London: Blackwell, 1998), pp. 107–48.

Kamilla Elliott, *British Gothic Fiction and the Rise of Picture Identification, 1764–1835* (Baltimore: Johns Hopkins University Press, 2012).

Kipp, Julie, *Romanticism, Maternity, and the Body Politic* (Cambridge: Cambridge University Press, 2003).

Lathom, Francis, *Human Beings*, 3 vols (London: B. Crosby & Co., 1807).

——, *The Castle of Ollada* (Kansas City, MO: Valancourt, 2005 [1795]).

Lavater, Johann Caspar, *Physiognomy: or, Corresponding Analogy between the Conformation of the Features and the Ruling Passions of the Mind* (London: Cowie, Low, & Co., 1826).

Lee, Sophia, *The Recess: or, A Tale of Other Times*, 3 vols (London: A.K. Newman & Co., 1821 [1783–5]).

Lewis, Lady Theresa, *Dacre: A Novel*, 3 vols, ed. the Countess of Morley (London: Longman, Orme, Brown, Green, & Longman, 1834).

Lewis, Matthew G., *The Castle Spectre, a Drama*, in William Oxberry (ed.), *The New English Drama*, Vol. 4 (London: W. Simpkin & R. Marshall, 1818 [1797]).

McKeon, Michael, *The Origins of the English Novel, 1600–1740* (Baltimore: Johns Hopkins University Press, 2002).

Mellor, Anne K., *Romanticism and Gender* (London: Routledge, 1993).

Pointon, Marcia, '"Surrounded with brilliants": miniature portraits in eighteenth-century England', *The Art Bulletin*, 83.1 (March 2001), 48–71.

Reeve, Clara, *The Old English Baron: A Gothic Story* (London: Longman, Hurst, Rees, Orme & Brown, 9th edn, 1811 [1777]).

Selden, Catharine, *The Count de Santerre: A Romance*, 2 vols (Bath: R. Cruttwell, 1797).

Sleath, Eleanor, *The Orphan of the Rhine* (Gloucester: Dodo Press, 2009 [1798]).

Smith, Catherine, *Barozzi: or, The Venetian Sorceress* (Kansas City, MO: Valancourt Books, 2006 [1815]).

Smith, Charlotte Turner, *Montalbert: A Novel*, 3 vols (London: B. Booker, 1795).

Stanhope, Louisa Sidney, *Striking Likenesses: or, The Votaries of Fashion: A Novel*, 4 vols (London: J.F. Hughes, 1808).

——, *The Confessional of Valombre: A Romance*, 4 vols (London: Minerva Press, 1812).

Vassilaki, Maria, 'Bleeding icons', in Antony Eastmond and Liz James (eds), *Icon and Word: The Power of Images in Byzantium* (Aldershot: Ashgate, 2003), pp. 121–34.

Walpole, Horace, *The Castle of Otranto: A Gothic Story* (London: William Bathoe, 3rd edn, 1766 [1764]).

Woodall, Joanna (ed.), *Portraiture: Facing the Subject* (Manchester: Manchester University Press, 1997).

2

'Those most intimately concerned': the strength of chosen family in Elizabeth Gaskell's Gothic short fiction

Ardel Haefele-Thomas

Introduction

Unitarian biographers Maryell Cleary and Peter Hughes posit that Elizabeth Gaskell, 'believed and acted on a religion of works, "the real earnest Christianity which seeks to do as much and as extensive good as it can." Local action for change by those most intimately concerned, not government legislation, was her solution to social problems.'[1] Elizabeth Gaskell tightly wove her expansive brand of Christianity into her Gothic short fiction, creating a sense of Gothic kinships that often become more divine and pure than recognized legal relations mandated by patriarchal authority, the Church, or the bonds of blood. Through her exploration of these kinships, Elizabeth Gaskell examines biological familial relations and often finds them, especially for the girls or young women involved, lacking at best, if not downright dangerous in comparison to the safety of *chosen* 'kinships'. Two of her works that clearly exemplify the detrimental nature of blood relations are 'Clopton House' (1840) and *Lois the Witch* (1859). Almost in answer to the problems these two stories illuminate, Gaskell's curious tales, 'The Old Nurse's Story' (1852) and 'The Grey Woman' (1861) employ the Gothic as a means to make some subversive arguments about family and what constitutes 'true' familial relations in the face of growing mid-Victorian ideologies – embodied both in novels and in legislation – bent on moving societal norms (for the middle class in particular) towards a more restricted, heteronormative, class-bound, blood-bound and private nuclear configuration.

'Clopton House'

In one of her earliest known tales, 'Clopton House' which first appeared in 1840 as part of William Howitt's book, *Visits to Remarkable Places*, Gaskell describes Clopton Hall, a dilapidated family estate located a mile from Stratford-on-Avon:

> We passed through desolate, half-cultivated fields, till we came within sight of the house ... In front was a large formal court, with the massy pillars surmounted with two grim monsters; but the walls of the court were broken down, and the grass grew as rank and wild within the enclosure as in the raised avenue walk down which we had come. The flowers were tangled with nettles. ...[2]

The overgrown and untended estate becomes metaphoric for the family's inability to care for their house, *as well as* the inhabitants therein. In particular, this neglect costs their daughter Charlotte her life.

The narrator of the tale wends her way through the 'rank and wild' lawn, and then enters the house and stops in 'one of the bed-rooms (said to be haunted ... with its close, pent-up atmosphere')' (58). Here, the narrator encounters the haunting portrait of a 'sweet-looking girl' whose eyes '"looked like violets filled with dew" – for there was the glittering of unshed tears before their deep dark blue' (58). This melancholy painting of the Cloptons' daughter Charlotte underscores and foreshadows the family tragedy when she becomes the victim of an epidemic. Presuming their daughter dead, the family buries her 'with fearful haste in the vaults of Clopton chapel' (58). Rushing the contagion-riddled body out of the house, however, does not prevent another Clopton, this time an unnamed male, from succumbing. Upon entering the vault with the second body, the family discovers, to their horror, that Charlotte had actually been buried alive:

> As they descended the gloomy stairs, they saw, by torchlight, Charlotte Clopton in her grave-clothes leaning against the wall; and when they looked nearer, she was indeed dead, but not before, in the agonies of despair and hunger she had bitten a piece from her white round shoulder! Of course she had *walked* ever since. (59)

The family's inability to read the signs of illness and properly take care of their sick daughter, coupled with their fear of spreading the disease to other people in the household causes them to commit a horrible (albeit accidental) act when they bury her alive. It takes little imagination to visualize the horrors the sick child must have gone through entombed in the airless and dark family vault literally suffocating amidst the bones of her ancestors. Charlotte Clopton's living relatives have sent her to die among her dead ones.

Lois the Witch

Just as Gaskell's 'Clopton House' explores a family tragedy in which biological relatives mistakenly send their kin off to die a hideous and claustrophobic death, *Lois the Witch* (1859) also begins with a family mistake which will, ultimately, cost yet another daughter her life. Set in New England in 1691, Gaskell's novella focuses on the newly orphaned eighteen-year-old Lois Barclay from Barford, England. As the story opens, Lois sits on Boston pier in her new homeland and reflects upon her mother's dying wish – that she contact her maternal uncle Ralph, a schismatic ex-patriot in Salem, Massachusetts. In a fevered state in which she anxiously awaits death so that she can rejoin her husband, Lois's mother tells her, 'he will take thee in, and love thee as a child, and place thee among his children. Blood is thicker than water.'[3] Gaskell places a cliché on the lips of the dying mother, perhaps to signal to her readers that we need to be wary of the simplistic assumption that a genetic connection equates love. Gaskell pushes her point further when the narrator reproaches the dying mother for her joy at the coming reunification: 'Such was the selfishness of conjugal love; she thought little of Lois's desolation in comparison with her rejoicing over her speedy reunion with her dead husband!' (90).

When Lois finally arrives at Ralph and Grace Hickson's home in Salem, her Puritan aunt coldly views her as one of the sinful English relations who had remained faithful to Charles Stuart (104).[4] Lois's elderly, dying uncle greets Lois with kindness, but it is clear that Grace Hickson rules this household. Grudgingly, Grace assents to Lois's becoming part of the family. Manasseh, the Hicksons' only son and eldest child, implores his mother to accept Lois; however, his motives are not pure since he has set his sights on marrying his pretty English cousin. In the following scene, Manasseh takes advantage of Lois's pity for him, having just lost his father, but also of Lois's grief over the only member of the Hickson household to show her any true kindness, since neither his mother nor his two sisters Faith and Prudence have accepted her:

> 'My father was very kind to thee, Lois; I do not wonder that thou grievest after him ... This is not the time to talk of marriage and giving in marriage. But after we have buried our dead, I wish to speak to thee.'
>
> Lois did not cry now, but she shrank with affright ... She avoided him carefully – as carefully as she could, without seeming to dread him ... Sometimes she thought it must have been a bad dream, for if there had been no English lover in the case, no other man in the whole world, she could never have thought of Manasseh as her husband. (120)

In fact, Manasseh becomes more and more forceful as he stalks Lois throughout the story. In a fraught scene, Manasseh claims that religious visions have told him they must get married: 'Thou canst not escape what is foredoomed' (123). The fear of being raped by her cousin, however, turns out to be the least of Lois's worries.

Grace, Faith and Prudence Hickson hold Lois's fate in their hands when they not only refuse to defend, but actually contribute to her persecution as a witch. Elizabeth Gaskell utilizes Grace Hickson to critique a type of Christianity that was not 'the real earnest Christianity which seeks to do as much and as extensive good as it can'.[5] It would seem that part of an 'extensive good' would be to open one's home to an orphaned and impoverished relative. Interestingly, the social code to help those most in need is broken in Gaskell's novella in much the same ways that it was ignored during the actual historic events – the witch hunts – that took place in Salem in 1691 and 1692.

In their Introduction to *The Salem Witchcraft Papers*, Paul Boyer and Stephen Nissenbaum examine the witch-hunts in terms of a changing socio-economic landscape:

> [A] good candidate for an accusation of witchcraft was some impoverished person who had appealed to the traditional code of communal responsibility by requesting a favour – characteristically *food or lodging* [emphasis mine] – of a relatively more prosperous individual. In this model, the *accuser* was an individual who had denied the beggar's request, thus failing to conform to the traditional code of behaviour ... This accusation itself took the form of a claim that it was really the beggar (now the alleged witch) who was morally culpable in the incident.[6]

Grace Hickson's hateful attitude towards her niece underscores this sense that she views Lois as 'morally culpable'. In Gaskell's story (and in the historical register) we know that some of the first victims to be hanged as witches were people seen as outsiders who existed on the fringes of society and were thus suspect – the poor, the orphaned, the disabled and the elderly.

Interestingly, it is not Grace Hickson whose actions damn Lois to the gallows, but rather those of her youngest cousin, Prudence. As the witch frenzy heats up in Salem, Prudence attempts to sneak out of the house to witness the public hanging of the first victim, Hota, who is modelled after the actual first victim, Tituba (whom we now know was beaten until she 'confessed' to being a witch). In an attempt to shield her little cousin from witnessing a brutal hanging, Lois refuses to allow her out of the house. In retaliation, Prudence begins the rumour that her English cousin is a witch. Rather than protecting her niece, Grace Hickson allows the tragic events to unfold.

Lois's life ends on an agonizing note as she cries out, 'Mother!' just before she swings from the noose. With this exclamation Gaskell clearly reminds the reader that Lois's mother (albeit unknowingly like the case of the Cloptons) has actually turned out to be responsible for sending her daughter to her death. Gaskell's critique of blood relations does not end with Lois's pathetic cry, for while we might forgive a dying mother who knew not what she was doing, the reader is still acutely aware that Aunt Grace and cousins Faith and Prudence have, in essence and without hesitation, committed murder.

'The Old Nurse's Story'

Feminist author and biographer Patsy Stoneman writes that 'the care of children is Elizabeth Gaskell's crucial test of moral values; seen as a communal duty (though undertaken by individuals), it takes precedence over all other responsibilities and is never restricted to biological mothers or conventional households.'[7] Clearly, the biological families in both 'Clopton House' and *Lois the Witch* have failed Gaskell's moral litmus test. In her classic ghost tale, 'The Old Nurse's Story' (1852) and her curiously queer 'The Grey Woman' (1861), however, Gaskell not only utilizes a Gothic framework to explore the ways that biological family can be detrimental to the well-being of 'the daughter'; she also goes a step further by including a subversive twist via two revolutionary servant-class women who are not afraid to defy patriarchal laws of heredity and marriage in order to choose to create safe and *unconventional* households. 'The Old Nurse's Story' and 'The Grey Woman' exemplify Gaskell's Gothic kinships, those bonds forged outside the biological tie, at their strongest.

Charles Dickens asked Elizabeth Gaskell to write a ghost story for his 1852 Christmas issue of *Household Words*; 'The Old Nurse's Story' became, as Glennis Stephenson has suggested, 'one of the most powerful ghost stories of the century'.[8] In this tale, Gaskell takes on the trope of 'sins of the father being visited upon by the children' and reworks it in a radical vein; the ghost story provides a perfect platform for her. In her essay, 'Uncanny Stories: The Ghost as Female Gothic', Diana Wallace claims that 'the ghost story as a form has allowed women writers special kinds of freedom, not merely to include the fantastic and supernatural, but also to offer critiques of male power and sexuality which are often more radical than those in more realist genres'.[9] What haunts the text of this ghost story is, yet again, a tale of a biological family that has failed to protect the daughters. Patriarchal power, in the name of what is 'proper' has, in fact, done nothing but cause the death of a daughter and her helpless child (the granddaughter) and the emotional destruction of the remaining spinster sister. It takes the love of a nursemaid, Hester, for her young charge, Rosamond, as well as her refusal to cooperate with societal norms to save the little girl from the same fate other female members in this family have suffered.

'The Old Nurse's Story' begins with an elderly Hester who tells her grandchildren (they are not related to her by blood, yet she clearly sees them as her grandchildren), 'You know ... that your mother was an orphan and an only child ...'[10] When Hester herself was merely a teenager, Miss Rosamond's mother (the wife of a vicar) selected her to be the baby's nursemaid because she was 'a steady, honest girl, and one whose parents were very respectable, though they might be poor' (1). Hester proves to be an excellent nursemaid who fits perfectly into the vicar's immediate family. Suddenly, when Miss Rosamond is only four or five, both of her parents die within a fortnight of one another. Knowing how close the bond between Rosamond and Hester is, Rosamond's mother, on her deathbed, asks Hester to stay with her daughter. Hester states that, 'but if she had never spoken a word, I would have gone with the little child to the end of the world' (2). Here, a mother takes her last responsibility seriously by not begging to find long lost blood relations, but rather by relying on someone whom she knows to be good and true to the little girl; the biological mother *chooses* the adoptive one. Hester, too, understands that, had the dying woman not had the capacity to ask, Hester already knew that this child was going to be hers, and at this point, Hester makes it clear that she wishes she could take Rosamond to her own family's dwelling where they would both be welcomed. However, Hester also knows that she needs to adhere to the societal rules *at this point*.

The little girl and the nursemaid barely have time to mourn before they are whisked off to Miss Rosamond's distant relatives' isolated estate on the edge of the Fells:

> Then we saw a great and stately house, with many trees close around it, so close that in some places their branches dragged against the wall when the wind blew, and some hung broken down; for no one seemed to take much charge of the place; – to lop the wood, or to keep the moss-covered carriage-way in order. (4)

Like the decrepit and untended yard at Clopton Hall, the neglect at Furnivall Manor symbolizes the haunted and dangerous situation for the little girl. Hester comments that 'Poor little Miss Rosamond held very tight to me, as if she were scared and lost in that great place; and as for myself, I was not much better (5). Other occupants of the house include servants and an aunt, Miss Furnivall, and her elderly nurse Mrs. Stark who spend their days weaving a tapestry, though they do take time out to enjoy the company of the precocious Miss Rosamond.

As the days grow shorter and autumn gives way to winter, everyone in the mansion is held hostage by the haunting music from a decrepit organ emanating from the forbidden east wing of the house. As Hester investigates the mystery of the music, she slowly comes to realize that the organ is being played by the angry ghost of Miss Furnivall's father, and as the howling winter weather encompasses the house, his playing grows louder and lasts longer. On a frigid November Sunday, Hester decides that the bitter wind will be too much for Miss Rosamond, but the nursemaid still wants to walk to the nearest village to attend church. Reluctantly, she leaves her charge with the family, who prove to be unable to protect her.

As if one ghost were not enough to set the house upon its ear, this is the evening that Miss Rosamond is lured into the frigid night air and up onto the Fells by the spectre of a little girl her own age who, as we come to learn, is the granddaughter of the mournful organ player. Hester rescues her young charge and brings the half-frozen Rosamond back to life, the entire time castigating herself for leaving the child with people who cannot sufficiently care for her – i.e., the biological family.

The moment that particularly stands out in this story, though, the moment that actually defines 'The Old Nurse's Story' as subversive, is when Hester, after rescuing Miss Rosamond, declares that she will take *her* little girl and move out of the horrid mansion and away from danger – away from Rosamond's blood relations:

> I would carry my darling back to my father's house in Applethwaite; where if we lived humbly, we lived at peace. I said I had been frightened enough with the old lord's organ-playing; but now that I had seen for myself this little moaning child, all decked out as no child in the neighbourhood could be, beating and battering to get in … with the dark wounds on its right shoulder; and that Miss Rosamond had known it again for the phantom that had nearly lured her to her death …; *I would stand it no longer* [emphasis mine]. (17)

Hester's focus is her chosen child's safety even if the actions she takes are not supported by Victorian laws or mores. This scene in 'The Old Nurse's Story' also serves to remind the reader about the horrific family crypt scenario in 'Clopton House' as though in this later story, Gaskell is trying to exemplify how we can 'get it right' where the care of children is concerned. Surely, Gaskell's readership would have connected this little girl with the shoulder wound to poor Charlotte Clopton who had chewed her own shoulder in hungry desperation before she died only to return as the village ghost. Hester cannot save the child who wanders the Fells; however, she can save her little girl by ignoring society's rules and absconding with her to Applethwaite.

Dorothy, one of the other servants and *not* one of the aristocratic authority figures, reminds Hester that Miss Rosamond is legally the ward of the absent lord of the manor, even though he has nothing to do with the child. So, within this legally binding patriarchal frame, Hester chooses to stay and mother Miss Rosamond: 'I would not leave her, and I dared not take her away. But, oh, how I watched her, and guarded her!'(21). We know that eventually, Hester and Miss Rosamond find their way out of the Gothic mansion together because the story ends with Hester telling Miss Rosamond's children (her grandchildren) the strange tale.

While there may not be anything inherently radical about a nursemaid putting her own life on the line out on a bitter winter's night in order to save her young charge, there are many points to Gaskell's famous ghost story that do defy social norms. Most notably, Hester does not care who has legal claims over Miss Rosamond; Miss Rosamond is her daughter. Hester is a truly loving parent in that she defies the laws of state which dictate how and by whom Miss Rosamond should be raised; a loving working-class home for a girl born a young lady is far better, in Gaskell's eyes, than the aristocratic, disturbed, Gothic family mansion with its decrepit inhabitants, regardless of their biological connection to the little girl. Through Hester, Gaskell rejects societal 'norms' that point to patriarchal laws and nuclear blood relations as those best suited to raise a child. She also rejects the notion that a working-class woman cannot successfully raise a young lady. In this story, the nursemaid *needs* to remain with Rosamond in order to protect her *from* her blood relations. Gaskell cleverly employs the ghost story frame to carry out her critique of Victorian family laws.

'The Grey Woman'[11]

'The Old Nurse's Story' exemplifies the notion that class boundaries can be traversed successfully when the best interests of the child are concerned; however, the crossings are still limited in that Hester chooses to remain in the decayed aristocratic mansion in order to mother Rosamond. It is a price she must pay to maintain the Gothic kinship, that which challenges the primacy of biological ties. Nine years after the publication of her classic ghost story, Gaskell returned to the theme of boundary transgressions as she took up her pen to again critique the plethora of restrictions placed upon women in the patriarchal, heteronormative, gender normative and class-bound Victorian societal structure.

'The Grey Woman' was printed in three parts in Dickens's *All The Year Round* on 5, 12, and 19 January 1861; with each section, Gaskell carefully sculpts multilayered and complex Gothic kinships that ultimately show the monstrosity of societal 'norms' and weaves sympathy for the transgressors. As in 'The Old Nurse's Story', Elizabeth Gaskell introduces us to a young woman, Anna Scherer, who is forced to leave her comfortable family home in Germany by the Neckar River, and is relocated to a treacherous and isolated Gothic setting, this time in France – *Les Rochers*. Unlike Rosamond from Gaskell's earlier work, however, Anna Scherer is not a helpless child who becomes orphaned by the ravages of an epidemic. Rather, at the age of eighteen, Anna's father, a prosperous miller, shames her into marrying an odd French aristocrat, Monsieur de la Tourelle:

> One day I said to my father that I did not want to be married, that I would rather go back to the dear old mill; but he seemed to feel this speech of mine as a dereliction of duty as great as if I had committed perjury; as if after the ceremony of betrothal, no one had any right *over me* except for *my future husband* [emphasis mine].[12]

Perhaps Anna's father insists because he holds a grudge against her for not originally accepting his apprentice's marriage proposal. Gaskell hints that the dowry might have seduced the miller: 'all the money arrangements were liberal in the extreme, and more than satisfied, almost surprised, my father. Even Fritz [Anna's brother] lifted up his eyebrows and whistled' (260). Monsieur de la Tourelle's money becomes more important to Anna's biological family than her happiness. This is underscored when her father points out that the French fiancé has not been abusive and, therefore, she must marry him. The message is clear: marriage – *almost any* marriage – is preferable to becoming an 'old maid'.

Anna's first reaction to her new home in the isolated Les Rochers is one of despair:

> I thought that perhaps it was because I was so unhappy that the place looked so dreary. On one side, the chateau looked like a new building, hastily run up for some immediate purpose, without any growth of trees or underwood near it, only the remains of the stone used for building ... on the other, were the great rocks from which the place took its name, and rising close against them, as if almost a natural formation, was the old castle, whose building dated many centuries back. (261–2)

Not only is the castle itself isolated but, furthermore, Anna is confined to her bedroom and sitting room within the walls of the Gothic abode. La Tourelle, seemingly in a moment of pity for his homesick wife, builds a small garden to which she has access outside one of her windows, but her other windows open onto a chasm of several hundred feet. On both a literal and a metaphoric level, Gaskell signals to the reader that Anna must very carefully 'watch her step' because one wrong move could plunge her to her death.

Aside from the garden, the one indulgence that M. de la Tourelle concedes to Anna is hiring a 'maid of middle age, experienced in the toilette, and with so much refinement that she might on occasion serve as a companion' (264). The second instalment begins with the arrival of this refined servant-class woman, Amante (which translates as 'lover'), who was 'tall and handsome' and as Anna remarks, 'by birth we were not very far apart in rank' (265). Anna reminds the reader of their class status initially in defence of herself as a 'a great lady ... of a castle' who spends too much time with her 'Norman waiting-maid' (265). As the story progresses, however, Gaskell will count on her readers remembering this comment when both Anna and Amante cross several boundaries including socio-economic and gender.

Anna and Amante's relationship begins to take on a mother-daughter tone, possibly heightened by the fact that Anna has grown up without her biological mother. Within the confines of this menacing Gothic castle, Amante's protection of Anna on a daily basis signals what the reader could call a mother's instinct about Anna's well-being:

> And with all her shrewdness to others, she had quite tender ways with me; all the more so at this time because she knew, what I had not yet ventured to tell Monsieur de la Tourelle, that by-and-by I might become a mother – that wonderful object of mysterious interest to single women, who no longer hope to enjoy the blessedness themselves. (266)

While a companion's knowledge of her charge's pregnancy might not be at all unusual, in 'The Grey Woman' la Tourelle *never* learns of his wife's condition because he commits a horrendous crime which causes Anna to run in fear for her life before she has a chance to tell him that he will become a father. This is a critical point in the story because by the tale's end, the first *father* that Anna's baby, Ursula, will know is Amante. It is at this moment that Gaskell begins to create a very subversive Gothic kinship.

During a late October evening, Anna finds out that her husband has been hiding her father's letters from Germany. Amante attempts to steal them for Anna, but is stopped by another servant. Finally, the two women decide that after everyone has gone to bed (Monsieur de la Tourelle is away on one of his secret trips for a few days) they will sneak into his study to get the mail. In a highly suspenseful scene, the two women attempt to creep into the office (in the part of the castle where Anna is not allowed) when the candle Amante is holding goes out. She leaves Anna in the dark office to go and retrieve another light.

In Amante's absence, the doors to an outside terrace open, Anna dives under a table covered with a large cloth, and listens as her husband and a small group of men bring in the dead body of a neighbour whom they have killed. They drop the corpse down by the table, and at one point, Anna's hand reaches out and touches the cold flesh. In her fear of fainting, Anna bites out a piece of her own hand so that she will not give herself away.[13] After a prolonged discussion about Anna (we find out that la Tourelle's first wife had been murdered for knowing too much) and whether or not she suspects that her husband is actually one of the leaders of an infamous murderous gang called *Les Chauffeurs*, the men all leave the room – without Anna having been discovered. In this situation, it is not the biological family (although Anna's father certainly pressured her into the union) but the family created legally through the institution of marriage that could likely kill the wife. This is also the moment when chosen family literally steps in and saves the day.

Amante has, through a psychic bond or a Gothic familial instinct, during this entire time of the dumping of the corpse and the discussion about Anna's fate, found a way to go unnoticed and to be at the ready when the men quit the castle:

> The sound of her voice gave me strength; I walked straight towards it, as one benighted on a dreary moor, suddenly perceiving the small steady light which tells of human dwellings, takes heart, and steers straight onward. Where I was, where that voice was, I knew not; but go to it I must, or die ... She took me up in her vigorous arms and laid me on my bed ... I let her put her arm under my head and raise me, and pour something down my throat. All the time she kept talking in a quiet, measured voice, *unlike her own* [emphasis mine]. (278–9)

Amante's actions in this scene are stereotypically maternal as she places the terrified young woman on the bed and then coaxes her to drink some calming elixir. The comment that Amante's voice was not her own also signals that she has suddenly, amidst the terror of the evening's events, taken on more responsibility beyond her prescribed job description and has assumed the role of a protector. Amante's quick decision to then remove the pregnant woman from her husband's house and steal away into the wilderness becomes subversive; she is relocating M. de la Tourelle's 'property' in the form of his wife and unborn child. Gaskell's radical transgression does not stop with the Norman maid becoming Anna's mother, but rather with Amante transforming herself to masquerade as Anna's husband. Amante's actions move them both outside the heterosexual paradigm, but it is in order to save the pregnant woman. And in this way, Elizabeth Gaskell's categories of mother and husband elide within the structure of Anna and Amante's Gothic kinship.

The transformations for the pair become more complex when Anna has to cross-dress in Amante's servant's clothes (and thus another layering of Anna as Amante) so that anyone they encounter on the road that autumnal night will think that he or she has seen two maids. It is also during this initial fraught departure from Les Rochers that a more intimate tone creeps in between the two women, 'We had not spoken a word; we did not speak now. Touch was safer and as expressive' (280). When Anna and Amante finally make their way to a miller's house, the old woman there initially refuses them entry because she believes that, with her masculine voice, Amante is a man (282). Once the old woman 'satisfied herself [that they were women], and unbarred the heavy door' (282), she asks them to climb a ladder and sleep in the loft so that her master will not beat her if he comes home to find out she has let strangers into the house. In a plot twist, the elderly woman removes the ladder, leaving Anna and Amante trapped in a confined space yet again – this time in the miller's loft. During the night, the old woman dies – without giving up her refugees – and Anna and Amante are left to eavesdrop on the miller who tells one of his mates the story of an evil and unfaithful wife (Anna) who is being hunted down by Monsieur de la Tourelle and a band of men. It occurs to Amante and Anna that, although they may pass well enough as two maids in the middle of the night, they must further transform themselves in order to survive.

In *Transgender Warriors*, Leslie Feinberg argues that 'Passing means having to hide your identity in fear, in order to live … It is *passing* that is a product of oppression.'[14] Amante and Anna are forced to go into transition and to 'pass' or they will not make it out of the village alive. As part of this transition, Amante cuts off Anna's flaxen hair and then dyes it with walnuts that have been stored in the loft: 'I let her blacken my teeth, and even voluntarily broke a front tooth to better effect my disguise.' (286). As the relationship between the two women changes and as they move further into the margins and away from expected societal roles, Anna comes out of her state of shock and finds a reason to live: 'I absolutely recollect once the feeling of a smile coming over my stiff face as some new exercise of her cleverness proved a success' (286). In the early part of the process, Anna refers to their actions as a disguise. As the action of this final instalment moves forward, though, Gaskell makes a subtle shift in Anna's narration; she and Amante move from 'disguise' into the reality of their lives as a rough and ready tailor and his wife. (Amante has managed to find a man's suit of clothes stored in the loft.)

Marjorie Garber's groundbreaking text *Vested Interests* explores various modes of cross-dressing throughout history. In her investigation of the nineteenth century, Garber is correct to point out that the term 'third sex' was used to indicate both homosexuality and cross-dressing: 'the "third" is that which questions binary thinking and introduces crisis – a crisis which is symptomatized by *both* the overestimation *and* the underestimation of cross-dressing ... The "third" is a mode of articulation, a way of describing a space of possibility'.[15] For Gaskell's two characters, this 'space of possibility' is enriched by their having chosen to trust one another – first as mother and daughter and then when that would no longer keep them safe, again as a working-class husband and wife. The Gothic kinship between Anna and Amante is so strong that the boundaries and definitions of their relationship remain fluid and flexible, which enables them to survive because they constantly evade la Tourelle and his henchmen. Are Amante and Anna mother and daughter? Are they Sapphic lovers? Are they a tailor and his pregnant wife? Part of the queer space that Gaskell has created for them in her Gothic framework allows the two women to simultaneously embody *all* of these positions. In a mid-1980s essay, Maureen T. Reddy writes that 'in a way, Amante really *is* Anna's husband ... I do not mean to suggest that the two women have a sexual encounter, but simply that there is a sexual spark between them'.[16] Clearly, Reddy is wrestling with the confounding position of Amante as Anna's *male* husband as well as the lesbian possibility between them. Given these categorical confusions, a genderqueer or transgender lens makes clearer the complexity found within Anna and Amante's relationship.[17]

Throughout the third instalment, Gaskell utilizes phrases like 'she entered the house, and boldly announced herself as a traveling tailor, ready to do any odd jobs of work that might be required, for a night's lodging and food for *herself and wife* [emphasis mine]' (288). Or 'I close behind her, sewing at another part of the same garment, and from time to time well scolded by my … husband (288) and 'she [Amante] brought him to see me, her sick wife'(299). Through the use of 'her wife' and the constant switching between 'her' and 'husband' Gaskell creates a space where gender categories elide creating neither a specifically heterosexual nor a specifically homosexual marriage. Gaskell gracefully utilizes this genderqueer space in her Gothic narrative to carry out her critique of women's roles as wives in Victorian culture. To drive her point home, Gaskell actually leaves Anna and Amante in drag as the working-class tailor and his wife long after they need to be. Upon the birth of their daughter, Anna writes about Amante's 'delight and glory in the babe [which] almost exceeded mine; in outward show it certainly did' (298). Now, this chosen family has become more complicated in that Amante serves as both baby Ursula's first father as well as a grandmother figure given the earlier nuances of her relationship with Anna.

In the last three pages of 'The Grey Woman', the reader is informed that Amante has been hunted down and killed by la Tourelle's men while on her way to work. When Amante is found maimed in the street, her biological sex is not revealed until the doctor removes her clothing. Interestingly, the juxtaposition of Amante's biological sex and her gender identity is *not* treated as part of the Gothic horror of the situation. Many nineteenth-century authors would have made this revelation the climax of the Gothic story. Instead, Gaskell writes the scene poignantly, leaving the reader in mourning along with Anna as she grieves for her dead husband. 'Mrs Gaskell' writes with a deep sense of respect and dignity for these two boundary transgressors.

Conclusion

In 'Clopton House' and *Lois the Witch*, Elizabeth Gaskell uses a Gothic framework to explore the ludicrousness of a patriarchal heteronormative culture that assumes blood relatives are inherently superior when it comes to the rearing and well-being of children. Neither Charlotte Clopton nor Lois Barclay is allowed to escape her fate – they are both the victims of biological family structures that utterly fail to care for the children. Whereas, in 'The Old Nurse's Story' and 'The Grey Woman', Gaskell takes her critique a step further when she not only exposes the weakness of biological family bonds, but through her Gothic kinships, looks to the strength and the tenacity of chosen families that are forged through adversity. Through those who are truly 'most intimately concerned' – the plucky Hester and the daring Amante – Gaskell exemplifies the ways that emotional ties rather than legal or familial ones can act as revolutionary examples of the ways that 'family' can be defined. These two tales illustrate the ways that gender, class and subversions of 'normative' heterosexual family structures could function together to create transgressive critiques and narratives.

These 'devious' families actually prove to be much more loyal and loving than the ones society then (and now, for that matter) would deem 'normal' and 'good'. For Gaskell, love makes a family. And while this may sound trite, even now in the early twenty-first century, we are facing numerous cultural and social wars as 'non-traditional', single-parent, and non-heteronormative families fight for the right to raise our children in a society that certainly harkens back to the same push for 'normativity' that Elizabeth Gaskell interrogated within her Gothic short fiction.

Notes

1 Maryall Cleary and Peter Hughes, 'From the biography of Elizabeth Gaskell'.
2 Elizabeth Gaskell, 'Clopton House', in William Howitt, *Visits to Remarkable Places*, pp. 57–60. Subsequent page numbers are cited parenthetically in the text.
3 Elizabeth Gaskell, *Lois the Witch*, in Jenny Uglow (ed.), *Curious, If True*. Subsequent page numbers are cited parenthetically in the text.
4 This refers to the time of the English Civil War, when Henrietta's

father had remained loyal to the king rather than espousing the Puritan cause.
5 Note that this quote comes from the Cleary and Hughes resource; however, this was taken from Gaskell's own writings.
6 Paul Boyer and Stephen Nissenbaum (eds), *The Salem Witchcraft Papers*, p. 12.
7 Patsy Stoneman, *Elizabeth Gaskell*, p. 49.
8 Glennis Stephenson, 'Bibliographical Note', in Glennis Stephenson (ed.), *Nineteenth-Century Stories by Women*, pp. 307–9, pp. 307–8.
9 Diana Wallace, 'Uncanny Stories', p. 57.
10 Elizabeth Gaskell, 'The Old Nurse's Story', in Jenny Uglow (ed.), *Curious, If True*, pp. 1–25, p. 1. All references will be made to this edition of the story. Subsequent page numbers are cited parenthetically in the text.
11 The framing device Gaskell uses for 'The Grey Woman' is one of the story within the story. At the outset, it is narrated by an Englishwoman (possibly Gaskell herself recounting a trip to Heidelberg and the surrounding area) although the narrator most present in the text is a dead woman via an epistolary narrative she has left for her daughter. What is interesting to note is that the Englishwoman's attention is caught by a haunting portrait on the wall of a pretty girl whose complexion has gone completely grey through fright. This scene harkens back to the narrator's viewing the portrait in 'Clopton House'.
12 Elizabeth Gaskell, 'The Grey Woman', in *A Dark Night's Work and Other Stories*, pp. 249–303, p. 260. All references will be made to this edition of the story. Subsequent page numbers are cited parenthetically in the text.
13 Readers will be reminded of Charlotte Clopton's attempt to survive in the airless family crypt by eating her own flesh. Here, Anna has to literally bite a piece of flesh out of her hand to keep from fainting or screaming out in horror, either of which would have caused her to be discovered and murdered.
14 Leslie Feinberg, *Transgender Warriors*, p. 89.
15 Marjorie Garber, *Vested Interests*, p. 11.
16 M.T. Reddy, 'Gaskell's "The Grey Woman": a feminist palimpsest', p. 190.
17 'Transgender' often denotes people who do not identify with the sex and subsequent gender assigned to their body at birth. As a term, 'transgender' carries with it a set of complexities rooted in Western medicine, even while many transgender activists and theorists have attempted to move away from this medical model. 'Genderqueer' has only recently come fully into use as a term that goes beyond the gender binary. Some theorists and activists have suggested it as an alternative

to 'transgender', which still implies a crossing from one fixed gender position to the opposite pole of the binary. 'Genderqueer' and 'queer' are useful terms for looking at the nineteenth century because they are flexible terms that can hold multiple gender identities and sexual behaviours of a Victorian culture that was beginning to consolidate rigid definitions of the connection between identity and behaviour.

References

Boyer, Paul, and Stephen Nissenbaum (eds), *The Salem Witchcraft Papers: Verbatim Transcripts of the Legal Documents of the Salem Witchcraft Outbreak of 1692* (New York: Da Capo, 1977).

Cleary, Maryell and Peter Hughes, 'From the biography of Elizabeth Gaskell', in *The Dictionary of Unitarian and Universality Biography, an on-line resource of the Unitarian Universalist History & Heritage Society.* http://www25.uua.org/uuhs/duub/articles/elizabethgaskell.html, (Accessed 7 March 2012).

Feinberg, Leslie, *Transgender Warriors: Making History from Joan of Arc to Dennis Rodman* (Boston, MA: Beacon Press, 1996).

Garber, Marjorie, *Vested Interests: Cross-Dressing and Cultural Anxiety* (New York: HarperCollins, 1993).

Gaskell, Elizabeth, 'Clopton House', in William Howitt *Visits to Remarkable Places* (London: Longmans, Green, and Co, 1890), pp. 57–60. On-line e-book digitized by Google, http://books.google.com/books?id=B6e7ypxTzywC&printsec=frontcover&source=gbs_ge_summary_r&cad=0#v=onepage&q&f=false (Accessed 8 March 2012).

——, 'The Grey Woman', in Suzanne Lewis (ed.), *A Dark Night's Work and Other Stories* (Oxford: Oxford University Press, 1992), pp. 249–303.

——, *Lois the Witch*, in Jenny Uglow (ed.), *Curious, If True: Strange Tales by Mrs Gaskell* (London: Virago Press, 1995), pp. 88–186.

——, 'The Old Nurse's Story', in *Curious, If True: Strange Tales by Mrs Gaskell*, ed. Jenny Uglow (London: Virago Press, 1995), pp. 1–25.

Reddy, M.T., 'Gaskell's "The Grey Woman": a feminist palimpsest', *Journal of Narrative Technique*, 15:2 (1985), 183–93.

Stephenson, Glennis, 'Biographical note', in G. Stephenson (ed.), *Nineteenth-Century Stories by Women: An Anthology* (Peterborough, ON: Broadview Press, 1993).

Stoneman, Patsy. *Elizabeth Gaskell* (Bloomington, IN: Indiana University Press, 1987).

Wallace, Diana, 'Uncanny stories: the ghost story as female Gothic', *Gothic Studies*, 6:1 (2004), 57–68.

3

The madwoman in the attic of Labuwangi: Couperus and colonial Gothic

Rosemarie Buikema

Haunting always implies a debt.

Jodey Castricano (2001)

If there is anything Gothic literature causes us to experience, then it is that life is a matter of dealing with the dead. We might as well get used to the idea, so the adage of many a Gothic tale runs, that people generally at some point in their personal or political history will encounter ghosts and spirits. The things animate and/ or the living dead of Gothic narratives often embody, as it were, a symbolic debt that has not been settled and that goes beyond the physical presence of debtors. Injustice does not fade with the passage of time. The Gothic tale, in other words, has a long tradition of plot structures in which the sins of the fathers are visited upon the children. Inexorably each Gothic text forces the progressive insight upon the reader that the denial of one's indebtedness to the past will defy the realm of ghosts, and that the dead could be mightier than the living, the oppressed more powerful than the oppressors.[1]

Usually in Gothic tales the living and the dead, the past and the present, are interconnected in a very specific mediated manner. In all cases, the embodiment of that relationship is situated in an intermediate area, a space turned Gothic, where one's reliance on the ability to perceive proves problematic. Did or didn't one hear the cries of souls, was it a ghost or just a patch of fog one just saw, is that writing materializing on the wall or does it just look like that? Not infrequently, access into the Gothic space is gained in the narrative by a piece of text looming up, a found manuscript or an enigmatic letter. The texts emerging from the depths of the Gothic story are, however, difficult to interpret because they are difficult to read, either literally or metaphorically speaking. The texts are already intermediate in themselves. In the literal case the writing may be difficult to read because the paper has partly decayed or the ink has faded, or because one text was written over the other and we are dealing with a palimpsest. In the metaphorical case, the text may be difficult to read because its content, for example, breaks a taboo and its meaning must not or cannot become manifest. Above all, from the nature of things these manuscripts are always dissociated from the sender. The text stays on, the sender disappears. The author is present only in spirit, otherwise absent. Writings, in other words, function independently from either sender or receiver and as such exist autonomously in the Gothic tale.

The search for the role and meaning of a text hard to read and/or for the identity of the sender often forms the core of the genre of Gothic narrative and the driving force behind many a Gothic plot.[2] The Gothic context then determines that deciphering such an encrypted text inevitably involves a meeting with the proverbial madwoman in the attic as the embodiment of the spirits of a neglected past: a meeting eventually affecting the perception of the narrative present. The Gothic ghosts and spirits populating the narrative present do not, therefore, solely refer to the legacy of the past but also hold promises for a possible future.

The structure of obscure texts functioning as an index for unsettled debt also drives the plot of *The Hidden Force* (*De Stille Kracht*, 1900), the popular colonial novel by the Dutch author Louis Couperus (1863–1923). The novel was adapted for Dutch television in 1974. Couperus, indisputably a primary representative of the Dutch literary canon, is the Netherlands' major nineteenth century author. He is known for his psychological 'The Hague novels' (The Hague being the town where many so-called expatriates from the former Dutch East Indies settled after returning from the colony), as well as for historical novels and colonial novels including *The Hidden Force*. Couperus grew up in the East Indies in the city of Batavia on the island of Java, where his family owned a coffee plantation. In 1878 the family returned to The Hague. Later, in his adult life, the author on two occasions visited relatives in Java. Early twentieth-century critical reception designated his work as decadent, immoral and perverse, but he was widely read nonetheless. Up to today Couperus has remained a very popular author in Dutch literature.

Evaluating the complex load of Gothic machinations in *The Hidden Force* therefore means that Couperus's great East Indies novel should not only be read against the background of the changing Dutch colonial policy of around 1900: in particular, it should also be related to the corresponding specific kinship relations such as they were engrained in notions of masculinity, femininity and European identity. As for the former: the Dutch East Indies colonial policy was characterized by a structure of so-called indirect rule. This meant that the various regions of the archipelago were governed by indigenous regents appointed by order of the colonial administration. These regents, local aristocrats from the archipelago's various regions, were presided over by a Dutch so-called 'resident'. The resident was initially supposed to grant regents an ample right of self-government, but growing economic and political interests would cause a change in colonial relations. Around 1900, it was considered necessary to impose a more efficient administration, to the effect that indigenous leaders were increasingly reduced to mere executors of colonial rule. Their power thus became largely ceremonial.[3]

Against this background it will probably come as no surprise to the post-colonial reader that the central conflict of *The Hidden Force* involves a confrontation between Resident Otto Van Oudijck and Regent Sunario Adingrat. This conflict is fascinating and also literarily interesting, not so much because of its historical and post-colonial relevance as regards relations between ruler and ruled, but rather for the way it is mixed up with the theme of incest that arises from the resident's private sphere. This well-meaning but complacent executor of colonial rule is blind in all respects to the hidden force, that is, to the specific spirituality of Asian culture and the coded response of the subaltern voice. This blindness to the perspective of the colonized Other turns out to be fatal in a parallel process of decay both in his professional life and in his private sphere. The colonial and industrial divide between private and public, rationality and irrationality, the visible and the invisible, the living and the dead, the knowable and the unknowable, cannot withstand the machinations of the hidden force. In Couperus's best-selling novel, colonial European power as well as the colonial patriarchal family suffer defeat. In this sense, this Gothic tale has turned out to be a visionary document.

Right from the first page *The Hidden Force* falls into the Gothic mode to make clear that something ominous is about to happen. Night is falling, with the blood pink full moon shining low behind the tamarind trees. Except for some melancholy *gamelan* sounds in the distance, it is quiet. Here and there some lights are lit. Light and dark, reason and the irrational, the visible and the invisible – the thematics of the Gothic tale are apparent right away in *The Hidden Force*. Resident Van Oudijck leaves his lit house and enters the dark, responding to the mystique of the East Indian night with an evening stroll towards the ocean. Hindering him is a sense of the uncanny that at first he blames on the fact that his wife has of late been away from home quite frequently. Consequently, his family is somewhat orphaned, but he instantly represses his unease – exacerbated by twilight melancholy – through breathing the fresh sea air. The fresh air connects him to European colonialist reason. His response to what becomes felt but as yet is not immediately comprehensible typifies his personality: 'He denied mystery. It was not there: there was only the sea and the cool wind'.[4] The unknown is not explored, but instantly reduced to the familiar and therefore temporarily covered up and sidelined. All in the name of Western reason characterized by a tradition of transformation or control of natural forces.[5] So the seemingly innocent but ideologically loaded appropriation of the sea air turns Van Oudijck's exchange with the sea on the novel's very first pages into a symbol of the gulf stretching between the colonial authorities' sphere of life on the one hand and that of the indigenous population on the other. The colonizer believes he can rule and maintain control, whereas the native sees a world full of uncontrollable phenomena one must simply endure. The indigenous servant accompanying Van Oudijck therefore observes his boss's evening reverie with disquiet. In his view it is a very bad idea to provoke the spirits of the sea at nightfall. Caimans dwell in the water, and every caiman is a spirit ... 'How strange, those Hollanders, how strange! ...' (48). The natives have just brought offerings to the spirits; banana and rice are still floating on the waves on tiny bamboo rafts; and the resident should really leave the sea spirits in peace now. The tone of the novel is definitively set: there is a yawning chasm between the soul of the native and that of the colonizer. It is immediately evident that the impending calamity announced on almost every following page has to do with that unbridgeable gap between the worldview of colonial rulers and that of the natives. In the course of the novel it becomes apparent that the political and ethical conflict is inextricably intertwined with Van Oudijck losing patriarchal control in the private sphere.

One day after this exchange with the sea, the resident's wife Leonie returns from her mundane outings and Van Oudijck together with his son goes and picks her up from the railway station. The narrator lets no opportunity pass to slowly build the tension which, mediated by anonymous letters and other writings, will come to an outburst by the end of the novel. Initially Van Oudijck persists in feeling secured by the context of family and colony, despite the vague unease concerning his family and a simmering conflict with Sunario, the Javanese regent. Complacently he rattles off in his carriage, horses trampling as he drives through the velvet silence of fictional Labuwangi on the island of Java. He does not note how his town has fallen into decay. He does not see that the legacy of colonial villas, once testifying to planters' prosperity, is one of abandonment and neglect. Certain districts in the town of Labuwangi he governs are in the same state of disarray as the colonial family that is falling apart right before his eyes even though Van Oudijck does not yet acknowledge this. The tension between what the reader sees on the one hand and what protagonists see on the other is one component of the growing tension in the novel, producing the typically Gothic effect of the double perspective in which the two sides of same coin are active at the same time.

The family founded by Van Oudijck is a true reflection of the route taken by Dutch colonial rule in the nineteenth century. His marriage to the blonde Leonie was preceded by a so-called pre-marriage with an indigenous woman. She runs a gambling den and lives somewhere deep in the *kampong*, as we learn in passing much later in the story. The two almost adult children Theo and Doddy incorporated in the present family are therefore of mixed racial descent. This ethnic marker appears at the very first introduction of these characters, because their language bears characteristics of the Indo-Dutch syntax familiar to the Dutch reader. Later in the novel the description of the two pre-marriage children continuously plays on the clichés of an identity formed in the tropics, such as precocious sexuality (Doddy being described as a hurried rose blossoming too soon, [50]), a slow rhythm of moving (there's nothing brisk in Doddy's and Theo's stroll), no excess of vigour and/or intelligence (Theo failing in many jobs). Often we read about such external features as full lips, olive skin and so on. As for Leonie, she is white, but on the grounds that she was born in the Dutch Indies she has, according to the prevailing views at the time, in a sense become Creole. She is a pretty phlegmatic blonde woman who spends the time purchasing luxuries and conducting extramarital affairs, which partly explains her being outside the home so often. Outside the narrative her being away from the family initially takes shape in the form of visits to Batavia, but in the course of the story these outward trips gradually take place at closer range. Her transgressive and semi-incestuous relationship with her stepson Theo also turns her own home into an uncanny place.

Apart from the adulterous nature of Leonie which I will presently explore extensively, the ethnically mixed family situation of the Van Oudijcks is quite typical for the composition of the Indo-European community around 1900. In the last decades of the nineteenth century, the colony was not deemed a safe destination for European women. At the end of the nineteenth century a change in this situation was brought about by the increasing institutionalization of colonial rule, improved hygiene, the invention of the steamship, the opening of the Suez Canal, and the development of the railway system. The distance between the Dutch Indies and Europe had become more manageable. Where at first the journey from the Netherlands to Java was a matter of months, it only took a few weeks around 1900. European men were from the turn of the century encouraged to take along a wife from Europe or to make one join him later. European women were then supposed to reinstall and fortify European culture within the European community. The single European colonizers had in the preceding period massively resorted to indigenous housekeepers, *nyais*, who looked after them in all respects. They were therefore not only increasingly going native (the Dutch term being '*verindischt*', become Indian), but also caused a whole new population group to emerge: Eurasians, or 'Indos' as the Dutch said. Indos are the children born of the union between colonial men and indigenous women. Some of these children were legitimized and incorporated in the European father's new European family, as was the case with Theo and Doddy Van Oudijck. Many of these children, however, were not acknowledged and were in danger of not being accommodated by society. A contemporary from the Indies characterized their state as follows: that they float between indigenous and European society, scraping a living and constituting an unhappy, dissatisfied, and damaging part of the population.[6] They were too Indian to be European and too European to be incorporated in the indigenous village community. Eventually they often lived in miserable conditions. They were there and they were not there. Thus around 1900 a Eurasian proletariat began to take shape which constituted a threat to the colonial values of economic prosperity and racial purity.[7] This is the proletariat that in the end becomes a disturbing force in *The Hidden Force*.

While Van Oudijck tries to solve his conflict with a dissolute and drunken regent, using the familiar colonial rhetoric of the benevolent patriarch who acts in the best interests of his children, Leonie Van Oudijck abandons herself into an affair with her stepson. The family rhetoric of the colonizer towards the native implies, as the authoritative post-colonial critic Anne McClintock conclusively analyses, that hierarchical relations within the colony are not constructed in history and geopolitics, but are a natural given fact, just like relations between family members. Just as it is the father who bears responsibility for his children, so the colonial ruler is the one who knows best how the natives under his administration may come to fulfilment.[8] It also follows therefore that if the colonizer is no sensitive father, he fails in his role as governor and guardian of the law. In *The Hidden Force* the rhetoric of failing fatherhood becomes the theme of the novel in the simultaneous development of the two storylines relating to Van Oudijck as resident and as head of the family. Van Oudijck is so convinced of his role as protector of the natives and so uncomplicated in his adoration for his wife, that he barely heeds the anonymous letters reaching him with great regularity. These letters inform him about the turmoil in the kampong as well as the adulterous behaviour of his wife. Van Oudijck does not want to know or see anything. Right under his nose his son Theo and his wife Leonie are having an affair, but 'his eyes blinked, as though tired from working' (178). When at long last Van Oudijck becomes aware of Leonie's semi-incestuous relationship and, above all, when this affair has been threatened too often by a series of incidents – apart from the anonymous letters, a hidden force unaccountably causes the casting of stones during her secret meetings with Theo; white *hajis* appear; the trees are filled with the wailing voices of children's souls; and then the incomprehensible low point: when taking a bath Leonie is spattered with blood-red betel juice

– Leonie shifts to an affair with Addy, her daughter Doddy's lover and another Indo. Her role as femme fatale has reached completion: 'it made her husband jealous – perhaps for the first time, for she had always been very careful – and made Theo and Doddy jealous. She aroused the jealousy of every young married woman and of every girl, and since she, as the resident's wife, stood above them all, she had an ascendancy over all of them' (195). Leonie is the woman who is conscious of her colonial power not only over colonized women but also over colonized men. Even though her erotic power is compounded by her social standing, she leaves the actual execution of the function of resident's wife and guardian of European culture to another woman altogether: Eva Eldersma, the gentle wife of Onno Eldersma, secretary of the resident. Eva is the only protagonist Van Oudijck actually relates to. Oriented on Europe, she is the one to hold, as a European woman is expected to do, the European community together, performing charitable works and organizing receptions at the residency where Leonie behaves as the indifferent, languid guest. Above all, Eva is a monogamous wife and a loving mother to her son. Potential lovers are amiably converted to platonic friends. Eva's only weakness is that she is too vulnerable to the hidden force and cannot resist the menace emanating from a hostile landscape and a climate alien to her. Her creativity, her artistic home as well as her exquisite wardrobe become mouldy in the course of the story and are corroded by moisture and termites.

Although, as already noted, there are quite a few Gothic signs of domestic and colonial decay in the story, as well as numerous indications of a simultaneous process of increasing tension between the different communities, culminating in the conflict between the regent and the resident, it seems that the real cause of the collapse of Van Oudijck's universe lies in the fact that his wife Leonie in all respects withdraws from her role as his wife. Not only does she neglect her duty to keep the European community European, she is above all explicitly sexually active. One could also say: because she is sexually active – and on top of that with members of the Indo community (Addy is the son of the prominent Indo family De Luce) – she neglects her duty to keep the European community together, that is, racially pure and distinct from the other ethnic communities. Her body is a guilty body.[9] Instead of bearing European children, taking care of her husband's pre-marriage children and doing her duty as the resident's wife, she violates the laws that gender, race and class impose upon her by being actively promiscuous. The red betel spit inexplicably descending on her body while she is taking a bath suggests that incest, the violation of patriarchal and colonial laws, are the cause of the decline steadily setting in after the bathing scene: the decay of the houses in Labuwangi, the collapse of the colonial community, the disintegration of the Van Oudijck family. But there is more.

Few critics have so far ventured an interpretation of the novel's crucial bathing scene. The novel has become known for it, but the secret has not been fully disclosed in interpretations, as befits a good Gothic plot. In his preface to the English translation of the novel, E.M. Beekman indicates that the hidden force refers to the overwhelming power of 'the other' which is destructive of the European subject.[10] The 'other' then is the flip side of the whole package of values representing Cartesian thinking; it represents the insignificance of man against the backdrop of Nature in Asia, the non-linear relation between cause and effect, the unity of body and mind. But Beekman also takes care to point out that the perception figuring so prominently in *The Hidden Force* of falling stones, the moaning *pontianaks* (tree-dwelling souls), and the appearance of *hajis* and other phenomena are not only widely reported in colonial writings and thus rely on historical sources, but that these supernatural phenomena still form part of Indonesian consciousness today. In support, he cites president Sukarno's 1958 injunction which proclaimed that spiritual and mystical practices should not slip into black magic.[11] It is therefore important to see these phenomena not as symbols alone, but also as the essential elements of a culture. Just like the Gothic tale, in other words, non-Western culture features the intertwining of the perceptible and the imperceptible, the living and the dead, those present and those absent. Nevertheless, with the dramatic betel spit incident a text is written on Leonie's body by an unknown hand, causing to appear more specifically, to those knowledgeable in the post-colonial, the intersection of three invisible pillars of colonial policy: gender, class and race. The text on the body of Leonie is the ultimate and equivocal Gothic script figuring a constellation of returning instances of the repressed in such a way that relations in the narrative present are irrevocably changed. So the question is: how should we read the script on Leonie's body? What kind of text is it, who wrote it? Whose ghost is stirring in Van Oudijck's house and why?

The madwoman: Couperus and colonial Gothic

To begin with, the dramatic incident is the only moment in the story where Leonie's cool, indifferent sensuality overtly loses out to her wild panic. Often when she and Theo met there had been bats, white *hajis*, falling stones and the cries of souls, *pontianaks*. On the evening prior to the bathing scene the wailing souls are stirring again and Leonie confesses to Theo that she is beginning to feel afraid and that their incestuous affair might have defied the spirits. Then when during her evening bath 'slimy spittle' (184) inexplicably descends on her body, on 'her eyes, her breasts, her lower belly … and the red dripped from her buttocks', she flees naked and screaming for help into the nocturnal garden. The only one she allows to approach her is her servant Oerip: 'In her utter madness, with her eyes staring wildly, she felt ashamed not of her nudity but of her defilement' (184). In order to understand what is actually happening here in this crucial scene, it is important to highlight a third storyline here. The affair of Leonie and Theo leads, at a relatively late point in the narrative, to Si-Oudijck, Van Oudijck's forgotten bastard son who lives on the *kampong*. As I mentioned above, Leonie's flirtation with Addy, the potential son-in-law, arouses at some point the jealousy of stepson Theo. He decides to go to search for Addy to settle the matter. But Addy is Leonie's male counterpart: sensual, beautiful, feminine, made to love and be loved. Addy remains completely indifferent to Theo's wrath and manages to win Theo over in a fraternal way. The two young men exchange confidences and Addy informs Theo about the existence of a half-brother, Si-Oudijck, on the *kampong*. (The prefix 'si' indicates son, the Dutch Indies version of the suffix 'son' as in Stevenson for example). This unknown son of his father was conceived in a relationship with a now deceased housekeeper that preceded the one with Theo's biological mother. When the two lovers of Leonie, stepson and son-in-law, look up the third Indo deep in the *kampong* where he lives in a ramshackle hut amid soured opium fumes, Theo experiences an identity constitutive kinship with this illiterate half-brother who lives in such miserable conditions. They are both sons of an indigenous mother. Both were sired by a European father who actually looks down on them. Van Oudijck, that is, shares with his contemporaries an increasingly less veiled dislike of the Indo. He does not want Doddy to marry the Indo young man Addy, preferring instead a thoroughbred European as son-in-law (197). And he considers his son Theo as lazy and unintelligent, refusing to help him climb the social ladder. The manifest hatred of the abandoned illegitimate son with respect to the father now suddenly mobilizes the latent hatred Theo, equally quite unsuccessful socially, feels for a father who is perfect in all respects. The encounter between the two brothers therefore epitomizes the fates of both the impoverished-class and middle-class Indo communities.

Based on contemporary reports on poor relief, Meijer argues that the position of Indo children was marginal and without perspective.[12] They were at the fringe of Dutch Indies society. Because of their poor education and fluency in Dutch, Indo children barely qualified for a job with a Dutch company. Around 1900 their chances even diminished because of the sugar crisis, which caused a dramatic growth in unemployment rates among the Indo population, compounded by the arrival of Dutch young men who often had left their homeland not for the best of reasons, seeking refuge in the Indies. Indos came to be mocked for their 'funny talk' and saw how these newcomers appeared to land all the jobs. It is plausible therefore that the anonymous letters Van Oudijck receives are sent by this forgotten son on the *kampong*. The dark hut is strewn with papers and there is a man with the boy who is writing for him.

Of course this son might be after his father's downfall for the obvious Oedipal reasons, but it is more likely that this socially underprivileged son is after his father's money and a better life. When Van Oudijck has to face up to the existence of this son, he does indeed hand him that money later in the story without, however, acknowledging that he actually is his son. More disruptive for familial relations within the Van Oudijck family is the effect on Theo of this encounter with Van Oudijck's interracial sexual history. This interracial son who fails to achieve social standing now for the first time experiences the Oedipal triumph of possessing his father's wife: 'And Theo hid his secret, hid his weapon deep down within himself' (121). Having access to Leonie assures Theo that he is superior to both his father and his half-brother, although he has little use for this knowledge apart from cultivating the seeds of hatred to further fruition, causing in the end the implosion of the Van Oudijck family. Van Oudijck ends up a lifeless man, without office, sickly and abandoned by his wife and children. The position of the sexually active resident's wife therefore plays a crucial part in the complex constellation of father and sons, colonizer and colonized. As Pamela Pattynama concludes in her lucid post-colonial and feminist inspired analysis of the novel, the fact that Leonie neglects her role as guardian of the patriarchal and colonial family announces the demise of both organizational structures and reveals the intrinsic and geopolitically specific enmeshment of private and public, the personal and the political.[13]

Yet this all still does not quite explain why in a visionary novel like *The Hidden Force*, which treats the consciousness of the indigenous population with such respect and empathy, Leonie's body should be defiled with betel spit. She undermines colonial and patriarchal authority, and in this sense her body symbolizes guilt and decay, but that as such should not cause the *pontianaks* to be disturbed. According to popular belief, a *pontianak* is a demon alluding to women who died in childbirth. The term is a contraction of *perempuan beranak mati*, the woman who died in childbirth. This spirit is often disguised as a beautiful woman and announces its presence through the cries of children's souls.[14] If we associate this particular meaning of the wailing souls with beautiful Leonie, it suddenly becomes clear which repressed is manifested here, whose ghost is seeking revenge among the living.

In the analysis of Anne McClintock as well as that of Ann Stoler, Western imperialism is based on three principles: the transmission of white, male power through control of colonized women; the emergence of a new global order of cultural knowledge; and the imperial command of commodity capital.[15] Part of this contract is the complex position of the colonial woman who is, as McClintock puts it, no hapless onlooker of empire, but ambiguously complicit both as colonizer and colonized, privileged and restricted, acted upon and acting.[16] It is clear that Leonie has tried to manoeuvre away from that ambivalent position. It is also clear that she has used her colonial power to wrest herself from patriarchal laws by her consummation of sexual freedom. The *pontianak* unmistakably recalls the way in which colonial women have benefited from the oppression of indigenous women. The only voice systematically remaining unvoiced in the novel and unaddressed in its reception is that of the mothers of Indo sons. That is the voice which writes itself in and on Leonie's body.

In this perspective Leonie embodies the position of the colonial woman who, with her arrival, drove the indigenous wife off the colonial stage. If up to 1900 it was common practice for white men to live with an indigenous woman, after the turn of the century this practice was exchanged for one of regulated ethnic segregation. The aversion against interethnic relations gained ground rapidly and the *nyai* disappeared from the colonial picture.[17] Often they could only survive through prostitution (cf. Theo's mother leading a gambling den), or they just died an early death (as Si-Oudijck's mother). It is the *nyai*, the indigenous woman who was used colonially but who now has become disposable, who writes back in *The Hidden Force*. The *nyai* is the madwoman in the attic of Labuwangi. While the resident is embattled with the regent and slowly loses his grip on both colonial relations and his family, the *nyai* reminds white Leonie's body of an unpaid debt.

Leonie's emancipatory behaviour, her liberal morality and her subversion of colonial and patriarchal laws are achieved at the cost of silencing her indigenous sisters, just as in *Jane Eyre*, as Gayatri Spivak has shown us, the heroine emancipates herself at the expense of Bertha Mason.[18] Unlike that novel, the title of *The Hidden Force* alludes to the non-Western underpinnings of Western culture. As with Spivak's inescapable vision of Bertha Mason's role in the *Bildung* of Jane Eyre, however, a post-colonial and complex feminist perspective is needed for a reading of the Gothic manuscript in *The Hidden Force*, in order to allow for colonial, Western and patriarchal taboos being challenged by a Gothic plot.

Notes

1 See Jodey Castricano, *Cryptomimesis* and David Punter, *The Literature of Terror*.
2 See Rosemarie Buikema and Elisabeth Wesseling, 'Contesting consensus culture: the case of Dutch Gothic'; and Anne Williams, *Art of Darkness*.
3 J.S. Furnivall, *Netherlands India*, p. 299; Hans Meijer, *In Indië geworteld*, p. 29. See also Gert Oostindie, *Postkoloniaal Nederland*.
4 Louis Couperus, *The Hidden Force*, p. 47. Subsequent page numbers are cited parenthetically in the text.
5 Genevieve Lloyd, *The Man of Reason*, p. 3.
6 See Victor Ido, *De Paupers*.
7 For the persistent stereotype of the Indo, see also Meijer, *In Indië geworteld*, p. 36.
8 See Anne McClintock, *Imperial Leather. Race, Gender and Sexuality*.

9 See Elisabeth Bronfen, *Over her Dead Body* for a detailed analysis of this trope.
10 E.M. Beekman, Introduction to *The Hidden Force*, p. 31.
11 Ibid., p. 22.
12 See Meijer, *In Indië geworteld*.
13 Pamela Pattynama, 'Secrets and danger: interracial sexuality in Louis Couperus's *The Hidden Force* and Dutch colonial culture around 1900'.
14 For a discussion of the *pontianak*, see Marion Valent, 'Over De Stille Kracht van Louis Couperus'.
15 See McClintock, *Imperial Leather*; and Ann Laura Stoler, *Race and the Education of Desire*.
16 McClintock, *Imperial Leather*, p. 7.
17 See Pollmann, 'Bruidstraantjes: de koloniale roman'; and Locher-Scholten, 'Monogamous marriage and female citizenship'.
18 See Gayatri Spivak, 'Three women's texts and a critique of imperialism'.

References

Beekman, E.M., 'Introduction', in *The Hidden Force* (London: Quartet Books, 1992).
Bronfen, Elizabeth, *Over her Dead Body: Death, Femininity and the Aesthetic* (Manchester: Manchester University Press, 1992).
Buikema, Rosemarie and Elizabeth Wesseling, 'Contesting consensus culture: the case of Dutch Gothic', *Journal of European Studies*, 41:2 (2011), 123–43.
Castricano, Jodey, *Cryptomimesis: The Gothic and Jacques Derrida's Ghost Writing* (Montreal/Kingston: McGill/Queen's University Press, 2001).
Couperus, Louis, *The Hidden Force* (London: Quartet Books, 1992).
Furnivall, J.S., *Netherlands India: A Study of Plural Economy* (Cambridge: Cambridge University Press, 1939).
Gouda, Frances, *Dutch Culture Overseas: Colonial Practice in the Netherlands Indies, 1900–1942* (Amsterdam: Amsterdam University Press, 1995).
Ido, Victor, *De Paupers: Roman uit de Indo-Europeesche Samenleving* (Amersfoort: Valkhoff & Co., 1915).
Lloyd, Genevieve, *The Man of Reason: Male and Female in Western Philosophy* (Minnesota: Minnesota University Press, 1993).
Locher-Scholten, Elsbeth, 'Monogamous marriage and female citizenship in the Dutch East Indies 1898–1938', in M. Grever and F. Dieteren (eds), *Een vaderland voor vrouwen. A Fatherland for Women: The*

1898 'Nationale tentoonstelling van Vrouwenarbeid' in Retrospect (Amsterdam: IISG/VVG, 2000).

McClintock, Anne, *Imperial Leather. Race, Gender and Sexuality in the Colonial Contest* (New York and London: Routledge, 1995).

Meijer, Hans, *In Indië geworteld. De 20ste Eeuw* (Amsterdam: Uitgave Bert Bakker, 2004).

Oostindie, Gert, *Postkoloniaal Nederland* (Amsterdam: Uitgeverij Prometheus, 2010).

Pattynama, Pamela, 'Secrets and danger: interracial sexuality in Louis Couperus's *The Hidden Force* and Dutch colonial culture around 1900', in Julia Clancy-Smith and Frances Gouda (eds), *Domesticating the Empire: Race, Gender, and Family Life in French and Dutch Colonialism* (Charlottesville, VA and London: University Press of Virginia, 1998).

Pollmann, Tessel, 'Bruidstraantjes: de koloniale roman, de njai en de apartheid', in Jeske Reijs et al. (eds), *Vrouwen in de Nederlandse Kolonien, Jaarboek voor Vrouwengeschiedenis*, 1986), pp. 98–126.

Punter, David, *The Literature of Terror*, Vol. II: *The Modern Gothic* (Harlow: Pearson ELT, 1996).

Smith, Andrew and William Hughes (eds), *Empire and the Gothic: The Politics of Genre* (Basingstoke: Palgrave McMillan, 2003).

Spivak, Gayatri, 'Three women's texts and a critique of imperialism', *Critical Inquiry*, 12:1 (1985), 243–62.

Stoler, Ann Laura, *Race and the Education of Desire: Foucault's History of Sexuality and the Colonial Order of Things* (Durham, NC: Duke University Press, 1995).

Valent, Marion, 'Over de stille kracht van Louis Couperus', *Literatuur*, 1 (1984), 203–9.

Williams, Anne, *Art of Darkness* (Chicago: Chicago University Press, 1995).

4

Seed from the east, seed from the west, which one will turn out best? The demonic adoptee in *The Bad Seed* (1954)

Elisabeth Wesseling

Adoption is a means of forging kinship with great Gothic potential. An innocent-looking little stranger from unknown background is received within the bosom of a well-meaning family, and then what? Clearly, anything may and does happen in Gothic fiction, although it took a while before things became really nasty. To be precise, it took until 1954, when the Southern American novelist William March published *The Bad Seed*, a seminal adoption horror story about an eight-year-old all-American girl, Rhoda Penmark, who turns out to be a serial killer. It was March's last novel, published posthumously one month after he had died of a heart attack. As Elaine Showalter points out in her introduction to the 1999 edition, he thought rather poorly of the work himself,[1] and would have been very surprised had he lived to see it become his biggest literary success by far. Immediately after publication, it turned into one of those rare literary phenomena that fared well with both the critics and the public at large. It did not take long before *The Bad Seed* was adapted for the stage as a Broadway play in 1955, which was the basis for a Hollywood movie in 1956, great critical and commercial successes both of them. From this point onwards, the demonic adoptee became a dominant phenomenon in Gothic narrative, with Rhoda as the founding mother of an extensive genealogy of evil children who have either been adopted or sired by some alien force, beginning with John Wyndham's *Midwich Cuckoos* (1957) and provisionally ending with Jaume Collet-Serra's horror movie *The Orphan* (2009), which may be regarded as a remake of *The Bad Seed*.

The spectacular success of *The Bad Seed* in all of its (re-)mediations gives us ample cause for amazement, not only because the phenomenon of a downright evil child was largely unprecedented[2] in the history of English literature and film, but also because it departed from all culturally dominant and scientifically authoritative perspectives on procreation and adoption in the 1950s. This novel was at odds with both the literary and the cultural context of 1950s America. Nevertheless, it became popular with a very large audience indeed[3] and so it must have touched a sensitive chord somehow. But which one? Addressing this question will illuminate the highly complex ways in which this novel renegotiates the family values of the baby-boom era in the USA. This chapter will explicate the dissident nature of *The Bad Seed* before venturing an explanation for its mysterious success.

Literary genre

At first sight, Rhoda Penmark comes across as the perfectly accomplished daughter of a devoted mother, Christine, and a doting father, Kenneth, who are still very much in love with each other. In short, the Penmarks seem to embody the ideal all-American family. In the course of the story, however, it turns out that neither Rhoda nor Christine is what she appears to be. Christine gradually discovers that she is not the biological, but the adopted daughter of the criminologist Richard Bravo, a brave man indeed, who was killed in action during the Second World War. Although Christine is very sweet-natured and even-tempered, it turns out that she is the daughter of an infamous serial killer, Bessie Denker, who did not even shirk from butchering her own children.[4] Christine accidentally escaped this fate while she was hidden away in a shed, and at the age of two she was subsequently adopted by Bravo. The plot of *The Bad Seed* is based on (pseudo-)scientific hereditary determinism, suggesting that Christine unwittingly passed on a criminal gene to her one and only daughter. Obviously, it bore fruit in Rhoda, as evidenced by the fact that at the tender age of eight she manages to kill three people. This murderous gene is not so much described as an active force that makes you commit crimes, but rather as the inherited lack or absence of an inhibitory power such as conscience or empathy. Rhoda kills without hesitation or remorse, simply removing anyone out of the way who steps between her and the objects of her desire, for she is extraordinarily acquisitive. She first kicks down the stairs an old lady who possesses a trinket she covets. Then she drowns her class-mate Claude Daigle, who has been rewarded with a medal that Rhoda felt she had deserved. Finally, she sets the janitor of her family's apartment building ablaze, calmly licking a popsicle while she watches him burn to death. In between the lines, we are also given to understand that Rhoda has defenestrated a puppy she had received as a birthday present when she had become tired of it.

The uncanny thing about Rhoda is that she is a perfectly obedient, well-disciplined child, who does everything adults want children to do to perfection. She is a talented and diligent pupil at school, she is perfectly neat, never dirtying or tearing her outfit, she is extremely well behaved and polite, and she accepts authority without any questioning. It is 'just' that she kills. When Christine has finally uncovered the full truth about her family origins, she realizes that she is to some extent culpable, as the bad seed has been passed on from grandmother to granddaughter through her. Accordingly, she assumes full responsibility for Rhoda by taking matters into her own hands. She realizes that Rhoda can only go from bad to worse, given her awful genetic inheritance. So to prevent this from happening, Christine administers a lethal dose of sleeping pills to Rhoda and subsequently shoots herself through the head. Ironically, Rhoda survives her ordeal through the intervention of the upstairs neighbor Monica Breedlove, while Christine dies on the spot. Breedlove tries to comfort the bereaved husband with the following misguided words in the wryly ironic, final scene of the novel: 'You must not despair, Mr. Penmark, and become bitter. We cannot always understand God's wisdom, but we must accept it. At least Rhoda was spared. You still have Rhoda to be thankful for' (227). End of story.

In generic terms, *The Bad Seed* may be defined as a crossbreed between the Naturalist novel, Southern Gothic and the thriller. It shares the Naturalist obsession with issues of heredity, as well as its amoral, scientific stance and anti-religious determinism. The story is divulged to us by an external, omniscient narrator in a cold, detached, almost clinical tone. This scientific stance is enhanced by the various real-life case histories of famous criminals that punctuate the fictional plot, all perfectly in keeping with the literary conventions of Naturalism. It is not insignificant that the novel is set in the American South and that March was a Southerner himself. Its affinity with Southern Gothic becomes manifest in its obsession with perversion and degeneration. Most characters in this novel are perverted in some way or other (according to 1950s standards, that is). Even those characters who seem to be the very epitome of normality at first, i.e. Rhoda and her mother, turn out to have serious flaws. More specifically, the novel could be subsumed under the denominator of what Fred Botting calls 'homely Gothic'[5] in that it brings horror home, situating it within the bosom of the nuclear family. In this case, it is even situated within the very core of the maternal body, the womb. Finally, this novel is also obsessed with race, albeit in a highly roundabout way. It certainly does not deal in any sort of way with the mixing of whites and blacks, an issue that belongs to the staple of Southern Gothic, as March's characters are all white, up to and including the janitor, which should surprise us, given the fact that this novel is set in the American South, where menial jobs such as Leroy's were mostly performed by blacks. Clearly, whatever forms of degeneration or perversion his characters are prone to, March does not want us to blame their defects on the admixture of 'alien' blood. In his all-white, all-too-white universe his characters carry the seeds of their own destruction within themselves. Rounding off the generic classification of *The Bad Seed*, it should be added that it is also a suspense story or thriller, whose plot revolves around Christine Penmark's gradual, excruciatingly painful discovery that she is in fact the offspring of the cold-hearted butcher Bessie Denker. Glimmerings of early childhood memories ('recovered' memories one would say nowadays) intimate the truth to Christine. She follows up on these leads through solid research in the municipal library, where she retrieves the history of her notorious mother step by step.

For several reasons, these generic labels only augment the mystery of the landslide victory of *The Bad Seed*. For one thing, this Naturalist novel conquered the literary scene in an era in which literary Naturalism had decidedly fallen into disrepute as an overly determinist, atheist, socialist, in short, un-American, literary style.[6] This is corroborated by the fact that several literary critics found fault with the biological determinism of this work, discarding it as implausible or scientifically unsound. Even practising scientists felt compelled to criticize March's suggestion that flawed genes could skip a generation, which accidentally also underscored the novel's strong cultural impact.[7]

Furthermore, although *The Bad Seed* fits the category of 'homely Gothic' perfectly, there are only very few Gothic or horror stories antecedent to *The Bad Seed* that feature an adoptee as patently demonic as Rhoda. Certainly, there is the girl-vampire Carmilla in Sheridan Le Fanu's novella *Carmilla* (1872). However, it turns out that Carmilla is not really a girl, but an age-old Austrian countess. There are also Miles and Flora in Henry James's much-discussed *The Turn of the Screw* (1898), but in their case we can never really know for sure whether they are complicitous with sexual depravity or not. One should also mention 12-year-old Josephine in Agatha Christie's *Crooked House* (1949) here, who is as whimsical and carefree a murderess as Rhoda, but there is no history of orphanhood or adoption in her family. The only Gothic orphan to come close to Rhoda is Emily Brontë's Heathcliff. Like so many other evil orphans after him, Heathcliff is branded as a 'cuckoo' by the housekeeper Nelly Dean in the frame story of *Wuthering Heights*. As cuckoos are wont to do, Heathcliff throws all his 'siblings' out of their parental nest, completely disinheriting the rightful heirs of the powerful land-owning families he had become linked with through the benevolence of his adoptive father. Like Rhoda, Heathcliff seems to be utterly devoid of tender sentiments after the loss of his beloved Cathy, engaging in wilful acts of cruelty such as hanging the lapdog of Isabella Linton for no good reason at all, which seems to be a foreboding of Rhoda's cold-hearted defenestration of her puppy. Like Rhoda, Heathcliff is ruthless, and stops at nothing. He also seems to share her acquisitiveness, as he carries out his master-plan of usurping the lands and homes of both the Linton and the Earnshaw families, who had owned these properties for centuries. But here the resemblances end. Heathcliff, for one, is capable of love, considering his lifelong devotion to Catherine Earnshaw, while Rhoda does not seem to know this sentiment, nor for that matter any other feeling but greed. Furthermore, Heathcliff is not really greedy at all, for he obviously does not care for the goods he has amassed, living in highly austere living conditions at Wuthering Heights, in spite of his fabulous wealth. All Heathcliff cares about is revenge. He is indeed extremely vindictive, but for a reason, and therefore he only derails after childhood, while Rhoda is innately heartless and cruel, already manifesting her evil nature as a girl. In other words, Heathcliff is both tyrant and victim, while Rhoda falls only in the first category. Lastly, the framing of

Catherine's and Heathcliff's derailment is metaphysical, rather than scientific in nature. Their cardinal sin is that they seek eternal bliss in each other, rather than in the deity. Accordingly, they prefer each other's company to anything and everything, even if this would imply eternal damnation. Heathcliff is indeed, as Irving H. Buchen suggests, the Doctor Faustus of love, who is willing to sell his soul to the devil in order to gain eternal possession of the woman he so ardently desires.[8] The framing of Rhoda's depravity, on the contrary, is (pseudo-)scientific in nature. Her destiny is in her biology. Thus, we have to conclude that Rhoda the Ruthless is something of a *novum* in the history of fiction, which makes the instant success of *The Bad Seed* all the more surprising.

The unconventional nature of *The Bad Seed* becomes even more glaring when we confront the story with the wider cultural context of the shared pro-natalist and pro-adoption family values of 1950s America. The novel drives the message home that procreation and adoption are dangerous affairs. The theatre and movie versions spell out this fear quite explicitly. At the hospital where Rhoda is treated after her mother's attempt to kill both of them, a doctor tells Richard Bravo (who is still alive in the remediated versions of *The Bad Seed*) to put the idea out of his head that Bessie Denker was the cause of Rhoda's derailment, suggesting that if that were true, then nobody would adopt a child or even have children of their own. But of course, it is 'true' within the context of this story, which therefore does not exactly encourage family-making of whatever variety. This did not only undercut the mounting pressure on American women to produce children, but it also conflicted with ruling perspectives on adoption, as I will point out below.

Adoption paradigms

In 1950s America, adoption practices were shaped by two rival paradigms. The first has been aptly called 'kinship by design' by the adoption historian Ellen Herman. This paradigm was inspired by the genetic determinism of Arnold Gesell and his pupils. It governed adoption from the 1920s up to the 1960s. Up to the 1950s, adoption was an exclusively domestic affair, in that prospective parents were only allowed to adopt children from American orphanages and children's homes. The norm that kinship by design aspired to was that of the biological family, meaning that adoptive parents and adoptees ideally resembled each other as closely as possible in terms of physical features, intelligence, religion and class background. This paradigm was developed in response to the turn-of-the-century eugenics movement, which was outspokenly anti-adoption. From a eugenic point of view, it was irresponsibly risky to import children from largely unknown family backgrounds into successful, healthy middle-class families, where they could become a liability as soon as they would start sowing their 'bad seeds'. Advocates of kinship by design claimed that these risks could be reduced through a rigorously scientific approach to the whole process. Science was to ensure a perfect match by controlling and monitoring the adoption process from the starting point of the selection of suitable adoptive parents and their matching with adoptees, through post-adoption counselling and supervision services to studies that attempted to assess the final outcome of the adoption process.[9]

From the post-war period onwards, the 'kinship-by-design' paradigm was challenged head-on by an alternative that may be called 'kinship by humanitarian vocation'. This social practice took its lead from the plight of war orphans in Europe and Asia, especially from the large-scale discrimination and abandonment of Korean GI-babies in the wake of the Korean War – i.e., children of American fathers and Korean mothers. The internationalization of adoption was inspired by religion rather than science, more specifically by Christian Americanism, a culture religion that fused a selection of vaguely outlined Christian principles with specifically American values, most notably a paternal sense of responsibility for the rest of the world and a strong emphasis on the importance of family. The religious motives behind this new adoption paradigm become evident from the autobiographies of transnational adoption pioneers such as Bertha Holt's[10] *The Seed from the East* (1956) and *Bring my Sons from Afar* (1986). Both titles derive from a biblical scripture, as Bertha Holt has emphasized on several occasions, namely a passage from the Old Testament book of Isaiah:

> I will bring thy seed from the east, and gather thee from the west; I will say to the north, Give up; and to the south, Keep not back: bring my sons from afar, and my daughters from the ends of the earth; Even every one that is called by my name: for I have created him for my glory, I have formed him; yea, I have made him. (Isaiah 43: 5, 6, 7)

The Holts applied this passage to their own adoption work, which construed the United States as a transracial haven that was destined to receive and unite the children of different peoples of the world. The paternal sense of global responsibility was premised on the cliché of the United States as a morally superior nation, a shining beacon on a hill or symbol of hope that had a missionary duty to Christianize and Americanize less privileged peoples abroad, redeeming their plight by welcoming them inside the borders of God's own country if necessary. Considering the importance of family relationships, what better way could there be for bringing the poor and wretched into the American fold than by turning them into family members? Thus, Christian Americanists took on transnational adoption as a new kind of missionary work, quickly shifting from fostering Korean orphans in their birth country to importing them into their very homes.[11]

Kinship-by-humanitarian-vocation downplayed the significance of ethnic differences. Physical and cultural similarities between adoptive parents and adoptees were considered to be utterly unimportant, as all children were God's children and equal members of The Family of Man. Christian Americanists such as Helen and Carl Doss,[12] Pearl Buck[13] and Bertha and Harry Holt were outspokenly anti-racist, chiming in with the overall tendency within post-war culture to discard racial differences as only skin deep and therefore unimportant. Christian Americanism tied in with a larger cultural imaginary that Christina Klein has dubbed 'Cold War Orientalism'.[14] Contrary to old-school European Orientalism, this body of images and ideas about ethnic difference emphasized the possibilities of bridging otherness by de-essentializing and de-biologizing race. Certainly, we tend to associate the Cold War period with the policy of containment that was to put a *cordon sanitaire* around the Communist states. However, American politicians realized quite clearly that in order to bring newly decolonized countries within the orbit of the USA as satellite states, it was not going to be enough to merely be against something. Containment could only become a success if one would also give citizens at home and abroad something positive to identity with. One also had to be in favour of certain things in order to effectively combat communism. The affirmative side of containment policy assumed the shape of Cold War Orientalism, that was effectively propagated by post-war popular culture, as becomes evident from a whole spate of novels, musicals and movies about Americans in Asia, such as the Asian trilogy[15] by Richard Rodgers and Oscar Hammerstein that featured memorable songs such as 'Getting to Know You' (*The King and I*) or 'You've Got to Be Carefully Taught' (*South Pacific*). These songs expressed the idea that human beings are essentially the same everywhere and that racism is therefore a misconception that does not come naturally to human beings, and would not exist at all if citizens were not indoctrinated by racism from early childhood onwards. The musicals by Rodgers and Hammerstein, the travel writing of James Michener and the widely read autobiographies of the Dosses and Holts all demonstrated to the public at large how family ties could be forged across the divides of ethnicity and nationality. Global relationships were represented as family relationships and vice versa or, in Klein's words, the forging of family ties became a 'political obligation',[16] with the United States donning the guise of a caring, global parent. Such an image suited this upcoming imperial power that aspired to bring the newly decolonized nations into its orbit by positively distinguishing itself from its European predecessors.

Returning to William March's novel, one has to conclude that he parts ways with both paradigms that divided the adoption field among themselves during the 1950s. Christine and Rhoda Penmark defy the kinship-by-design paradigm by meeting its selection criteria all too perfectly, wreaking havoc nonetheless. Christine, Rhoda and her infamous grandmother are all strikingly good-looking. Bessie Denker is credited with a deceptively sweet and charming outward appearance that fooled three consecutive juries into believing her incapable of murder. Christine is also portrayed as a highly charming and attractive woman, while Rhoda is exceptionally intelligent and competent to boot.

It is striking that March went out of his way to dispel any possible taint of ethnic otherness from his leading characters. Bessie Denker, the source of all evil, has a Dutch- or German-sounding name, Christine Penmark is cast as a blonde in the novel, and Rhoda as a brunette. The Broadway and Hollywood adaptations reverse this, turning Christine into a brunette, and Rhoda into a platinum blonde, who sports two thick braids that give her a German, if not to say 'Aryan' look. This is indeed extraordinary from both a literary and a cultural point of view. Returning to Heathcliff once more, we have to observe upon the fact that his ethnic otherness is emphasized all throughout the novel. Heathcliff has black hair while the colour of his skin is dark, we are told time and again. Indeed, the characterization of his outward appearance is in keeping with Victorian modes of simianizing and orientalizing the Irish. Clearly, his wild and violent nature is to be somehow attributed to his 'impure' blood.[17] Rhoda, on the other hand, is not just white, she is ultra-white. From the look of it, the genetic material of the Penmarks is of an outstanding quality if we abide by the standards of the kinship-by-design advocates. So, if adoption even misfires in their case, what could adoption professionals possibly have to go by?

Meanwhile, *The Bad Seed* is also out of tune with the adoption-by-humanitarian-vocation paradigm. Advocates of transnational adoption believed that love will conquer all barriers and disadvantages. Any child will turn out all right, if it enjoys the privilege of growing up in a warm and loving family. Indeed, the autobiographies of Bertha Holt and Helen Doss are full of miraculous anecdotes about magical transformations. Children enter into their households with all sorts of physical, psychological and mental defects and disabilities. They tend to be cured of their disorders within a month, as a tribute to the transformative power of parental love.[18] The advocates of transnational adoption were environmentalists, in short. Environmentalism, however, is obviously the target of March's sinister story, and even more so of the play and the movie that departed from the novel by adding to their cast Richard Bravo, who was killed in action during the Second World War in March's story, dying before he could witness his adoptive daughter's tragedy. The idealist, high-flown Bravo is ideally suited for personifying the humanitarian and environmentalist viewpoint in the movie and play. Notwithstanding his likeability and integrity, he is proven utterly wrong. Although Bravo is a loving and protective father to Christine, and in spite of the fact that Christine is totally devoted to Rhoda, parental love is obviously incapable of overruling a flawed genetic heritage in this story. Moreover, as a staunch atheist, March did not have any affinity with the religious underpinnings of the kinship-by-humanitarian-vocation paradigm, which comes out quite clearly in the stab at religion in the concluding paragraph.

If March can be fitted into any adoption paradigm at all, his sympathy seems to lie with the outdated, turn-of-the-century eugenics movement, as he shared its genetic determinism, its atheism, its scientism and its radical anti-adoption stance, in spite of the fact that the eugenics movement lost all its authority after Nazism. This returns us to our starting point, the puzzling nature of March's success, for aligning yourself with an outmoded, disreputable socio-political movement hardly seems to be the ticket to high sales numbers. As Joyce Carol Oates put it in a review that appeared on the occasion of *The Bad Seed*'s reprint in 1997:

> Why, when a taboo is repudiated, is there such a rush of communal relief and excitement? Do we secretly yearn to hate that which we have been obliged to love? Is there a perverse thrill in believing the very worst about what had seemed to us only yesterday the very best? ... and what is the curious consolation of 'bad seed' politics – the belief that genetic inheritance determines entire lives? Does it comfort us to be told that our efforts at social amelioration are worthless?[19]

To me, these are real, rather than rhetorical, questions. In conclusion, I will now try to answer them.

Gender and ethnicity

If *The Bad Seed* is so out of tune with the literary and cultural values of its own day and time, then how did it gain access to such a wide audience? The answer is to be sought in the 1950s trade-off between racism and sexism. Several historians have pointed out that the persistent de-essentializing and de-biologizing of 'race' in 1950s America went hand in hand with the surreptitious essentializing and biologizing of 'sex'.[20] In other words, biological determinism was deflected from ethnicity onto gender. This trade-off became manifest in the continual attacks on 'momism'[21] and 'she-tyranny' that were fuelled by deep-seated worries about female sexuality as being essentially volatile and uncontrollable, although women were continually called upon to procreate. According to the literary historian Perin Gurel, fear and loathing of female sexuality 'lurked dangerously close to the surface of the pronatalist zeitgeist of the baby boom years'.[22] In other words, sexism was the dark flipside of the enlightened, anti-racist humanitarianism of cold war Orientalism. I would like to devote the final section of this chapter to the further substantiation of Gurel's thesis by forwarding additional evidence from the text of the novel.

The social universe of *The Bad Seed* is not just all-white, but it is also strongly dominated by women. Men are either absent or inadequate in this novel. Christine's husband is conveniently moved out of the way at the opening of the story and only returns to the scene after events have run their course, while her father, Richard Bravo, has died before the onset of the story. These two are the only respectable men in *The Bad Seed*, and they are both of them absent. All the other males can hardly be taken seriously, judging from a 1950s perspective. The upstairs neighbour Monica Breedlove lives together with her brother Emory, who is categorized in Monica's pseudo-psycho-analytical jargon as a 'larvated homosexual' (40). There is a hint of incest as well to their relationship. Claude Daigle, Rhoda's classmate and second victim, displays all the features of a sissy. He is very small, highly sensitive, artistically gifted and overly fond of his mother. Claude Daigle's father also comes across as a wimp, incapable of controlling his hysterical wife, who turns into a drunkard after the loss of her boy. Then there is the mystery writer Reginald Tasker, who does not seem to have much of a real job, spending most of his time drinking tea with the ladies. Tasker knows all there is to know about serial killers, but only in an armchair sort of way, for he fails to recognize one when he sees one – i.e., Rhoda. Last but not least, there is the janitor, Leroy, 'white trash' obviously, and a sexual pervert to boot, lusting after both Christine and her daughter.

In this world in which men are either absent or inadequate, women rule. Rhoda is raised by her mother only, as Kenneth is on the road most of the time for professional reasons. Christine, in her turn, lost her father prematurely. Rhoda's school is run by three spinster sisters, and the apartment building where the Penmarks live is presided over by the highly domineering landlady Monica Breedlove. These female rulers are in their turn ruled by their genes, making a pretty mess of it all. The novel tacitly suggests that remorseless serial killing is a specifically feminine accomplishment, as the great majority of the case histories that March included into his novel feature female criminals. The only exception to the proverbial rule is a murderer called Albert Guay. However, March makes it quite clear that he does not even begin to compare to that paragon of vice, Bessie Denker.

Strikingly, the bad seed or evil gene is directly linked to another aberration in the female sex: intellect. Rhoda's grandmother, who is repeatedly referred to as an artist and a genius by Reginald Tasker, is not called Bessie Denker for nothing, her Dutch surname meaning 'thinker'. Obviously, she passed on her astonishing intellect to her granddaughter, who is all brain and no heart. Such intelligence proves to be lethal in women – witness Rhoda. Being forced to deal with these two evil geniuses, even Christine, the epitome of feminine virtue and innocence, becomes something of a 'Denker' herself as she traces her family history, spending long hours on research in the municipal library. This pursuit of knowledge even inspires violence in the loveable Christine, who tries to kill herself and her daughter, thereby making up for the omission of her mother, who failed to slaughter her youngest child in her final killing spree. To top it all off, the bad seed is unfortunately saved and preserved in the end by another female thinker who believes she is the equal of men intellectually, namely the self-styled psycho-analyst and chatterbox Monica Breedlove. This novel is indeed highly misogynistic, and one could say that it enables its reading public to indulge in misogyny under the (pseudo-)scientific pretense of hereditarianism.

While Christian Americanism and Cold War Orientalism set ethnic differences afloat, refining them out of existence, gender differences were firmly anchored in the female body. Anatomy was indeed destiny for most post-war American women, as they were encouraged to concentrate on their reproductive duties and to refrain from a professional career. This focus on female sexuality and fertility also raised fears of and worries about heredity and procreation. The spectacular success of *The Bad Seed* may be explained by the ways in which it caters to these latent fears and preoccupations. One could interpret March's harping on outmoded eugenic ideas as a rhetorical ploy for castigating intellect in women. While racism was increasingly censored, misogyny, it seems, turned into a substitute, although it did remain something of a guilty pleasure that could not be enjoyed out in the open. Given the misogynist subtext of *The Bad Seed*, the burden of fear and loathing does not only rest with Rhoda, but also with the creatures capable of giving birth to such monsters – the maternal body, in short. This comes out quite clearly in a climactic scene in the movie, when Christine hits her womb with her own fists when she has uncovered the full truth. Thus, outmoded scientific theories (eugenics) are revitalized by this Gothic novel as a new source of horror and terror ('hereditary horror'), representing fertile women as walking time bombs.

Conclusion

While Rhoda hardly had any forebears as a literary character, she did produce abundant offspring. From *The Bad Seed* onwards, the irredeemably evil child was here to stay. Rhoda is the mother of these child characters in more ways than one. While evil children come across as monsters, the epitome of monstrosity is summed up by the maternal body that generated them, time and again. In *The Midwich Cuckoos* (1957), for instance, women prove to be an easy prey for extraterrestrial predators, polluting the world by giving birth to a whole spate of aliens nine months later. Strikingly, these 'cuckoos' are only stopped from taking over the human world completely by the heroic self-sacrifice of an elderly man. In *Rosemary's Baby* (1968), the central source of horror is Rosemary's long drawn-out pregnancy rather than the baby itself, who, after all, is only born at the very end of the novel. In Doris Lessing's *The Fifth Child* (1988), it is the smug, self-satisfied complacency of the motherly, ever-pregnant Harriet Lovatt that eventually provokes disaster in the shape of the evil Benjamin. Harriet produces one child after another in an overly confident sort of way, believing herself to be superior as a mother to most of the people she knows. In the end, she is convinced that she has been punished through Ben for her hubris.

Even in Gothic horror movies in which children do seem to take on the full burden of abjection at first, they can only do so because their apparently childlike bodies take on features of mature female sexuality and all that it entails. In *The Exorcist*, the major source of horror is indeed Regan, but only because her prepubescent girlhood is transformed into a sexually active apparatus by the very devil himself. In *The Orphan*, the adoptive mother of the nine-year-old Russian girl Esther seems to be exempt from fear and loathing, while Esther becomes more and more horrifying as the movie goes along. However, it eventually turns out that Esther is only capable of committing crimes because she is not really a child, but a woman in her early thirties, who was stunted in her growth by some rare disease. Esther is starved of (sexual) love and wriggles her way into other people's households as an 'adoptee' in order to gain access to the *pater familias*, killing him off in retaliation if he does not comply with her sexual needs. Eros and Thanatos have indeed joined forces in this woman who merely poses as a girl, and one can only shudder at the thought of what her offspring would be like. In the end, the shape-shifting female body is the ultimate source of abjection again, which becomes quite clear in the concluding scene, when the adoptive mother tries to free herself from the clutches of the murderous Esther by kicking her away, shouting 'I am not your fucking mother!', thereby violently separating herself from the whole abominable institution of (adoptive) motherhood that wreaked such havoc upon her home. Esther strongly confirms and corroborates the rejection of adoption by the former eugenics movement that warned against the dangers of importing low-quality genetic materials (the alien adoptee of unknown family background) into high-quality family surroundings (Esther's wealthy and white adoptive parents). Even in those cases in which the evil child is a boy, such as Damien Thorn in *The Omen* movie series, whose biological mother does not come into the picture at all, the monstrous maternal body nevertheless crops up again when Damien sires a child on his girlfriend in *Omen V: The Abomination* (1985), who has to give birth to her demonic offspring in a horrifying way.

The trade-off between sexism and racism not only goes to explain the success of *The Bad Seed*, but also sheds some light on the writing of cultural history. We are often inclined to conceive of historical periods as monolithic wholes, such as the roaring twenties, the baby-boom 1950s, the swinging sixties, the politically radicalized seventies, the no-future eighties, the money-grabbing nineties and so on. The further we are removed in time from the period under study, the more homogeneous it seems to become. When we assign common denominators to historical periods, we miss out on the controversial, contested nature of the issues that were central to the periods under study. During the 1950s, American citizens certainly shared a common preoccupation with issues of procreation and kinship, but they did not share a common view on the question of what makes a family tick. Rather than submitting to the retrospective illusion of homogeneity, cultural historians should try to recreate the major controversies that beset the crucial issues of any period. Literary historians have a special contribution to make here. Fictional narratives are often out of step with their own day and time because of the polyphonic, multiperspectival nature of narrative. Novels are generally narrated by different narrative voices that present different points of view. Some of these viewpoints may be way ahead of their time, while others may well reiterate perspectives that were already superseded a long time ago by, for instance, the authoritative discourses of various scientific disciplines. This certainly also applies to the Gothic novel, which has a way of counterbalancing the promises of modernization and progress against the values embodied in discarded traditions, practices and institutions, including rejected scientific theories, who often return in the Gothic novel as sources of wonder, horror or terror. The apparently compelling nature of March's retrograde eugenic outlook on kinship as presented by the external omniscient narrator of *The Bad Seed*, reminds us of the basic fact that it was not all pro-natalism, baby boom and Family of Man in 1950s America. Indeed, fantasies about family-making ranged from the roseate optimism of Bertha Holt's transnational family-making in *The Seed from the East* to March's fear of the alien within. Thus, if interpreted with due attention to issues of genre and form, literary works make fascinating sources of cultural history that break through ossified clichés about bygone eras.

Notes

1 In William March, *The Bad Seed*, p. v.
2 Largely, but not quite. If we are dealing with the phenomenon of evil children in general (outside of the context of adoption), then one could argue that Rhoda is preceded by, among others, the child protagonists in Ray Bradbury's 'The Small Assassin' (1946) and 'The Veldt' (1950), Agatha Christie's *Crooked House* (1949), Richard Matheson's 'Born of Man and Woman' (1950), and Jerome Bixby's 'It's a Good Life' (1953).
3 For information about the reception of *The Bad Seed*, see William Paul, *Laughing, Screaming*, pp. 267–86; Showalter in March, *The Bad Seed*; and Perin Gurel, 'A natural little girl'.
4 Murderous mothers also belong to the staple of Gothic characters nowadays. See for instance a novel like Renate Dorrestein's *Heart of Stone*.
5 Fred Botting, *Gothic*, pp. 113–34.
6 See Donald Pizer (ed.), *The Cambridge Companion to American Realism and Naturalism*, p. 12.
7 See Paul, *Laughing, Screaming*; and Gurel, 'A natural little girl'.
8 Irving H. Buchen, 'Emily Brontë and the metaphysics of childhood and love', 63–70.
9 See Ellen Herman, *Kinship by Design*.
10 Bertha Holt was the wife of Harry Holt, an Oregon farmer who played

a central role in organizing the adoption of Korean babies on a large scale. First, they set an important public example by adopting eight orphans into their family in 1955, which already counted six biological children. Feeling this was not nearly enough, they managed to place another 191 Korean orphans with American families in 1961, establishing the Holt Adoption Program. The Holt program placed 55,000 Korean babies between 1955 and 1986. Together with Pearl Buck's Welcome House, it was the first international adoption agency in the United States.
11 See Arissa Oh, 'A new kind of missionary work', 161–88.
12 Carl Doss, a Methodist minister and his wife Helen Doss, set out on the adoption track in the late 1940s because they were unable to conceive children themselves. They first adopted a son according to the 'adoption-by-design' approach. When they started looking for a 'sibling', they discovered that there were virtually no available 'adoptable' (i.e. white) babies in American orphanages. They also discovered that many 'mixed-race' children were waiting in vain to be adopted, because nobody wanted them. They adopted eleven such 'unadoptables', a process that Helen Doss described in her best-selling 1954 memoir *The Family Nobody Wanted*.
13 The Nobel-prize winning author Pearl Buck was the daughter of an American missionary in China, where she grew up. Buck retained a lifelong commitment to improving Asian-American relationships, believing that the adoption of orphaned Chinese and Korean children would greatly enhance American knowledge and understanding of China. Pearl Buck founded Welcome House in 1949. This adoption agency set out with the placement of mixed-race children from American orphanages in American families, but soon broadened its scope to include also orphans from abroad, Korea and China mostly. Like the Holts, Buck also adopted children herself, seven in all.
14 Christina Klein, *Cold War Orientalism*.
15 The Asian trilogy was made up of the musicals *South Pacific* (1949), *The King and I* (1956) and *Flower Drum Song* (1958). Hammerstein also produced a musical about Pearl Buck's Welcome House, called *With the Happy Children* (1950).
16 Klein, *Cold War Orientalism*, p. 143.
17 Elsie Michie, 'From simianised Irish to oriental despots', 125–40.
18 See Doss, *The Family Nobody Wanted*.
19 Joyce Carol Oates, 'Killer kids', 16–20.
20 See Adele Clarke, *Disciplining Reproduction*; and Alexandra Stern, *Eugenic Nation*.
21 The term is Wylie's. See Philip Wylie, *Generation of Vipers*.
22 Gurel, 'A natural little girl', p. 3.

References

Botting, Fred, *Gothic* (London: Methuen, 1996).
Buchen, Irving H, 'Emily Brontë and the metaphysics of childhood and love', *Nineteenth-Century Fiction,* 22:1 (1967), 63–70.
Clarke, Adele, *Disciplining Reproduction: Modernity, American Life Sciences, and the Problems of Sex* (Berkeley: University of California Press, 1998).
Doss, Helen, *The Family Nobody Wanted* (1954; Boston: Northeastern University Press, 2001).
Gurel, Perin, 'A natural little girl: reproduction and naturalism in *The Bad Seed* as novel, play, and film', *Adaptation* (2010), 1–23.
Herman, Ellen, *Kinship by Design* (Chicago and London: University of Chicago Press, 2008).
Klein, Christina, *Cold War Orientalism: Asia in the Middlebrow Imagination, 1945–1961* (Berkeley: University of California Press, 2003).
March, William, *The Bad Seed,* intro. Elaine Showalter (London: Prion Books, 1999 [1954]).
Michie, Elsie, 'From simianised Irish to oriental despots: Heathcliff, Rochester and racial difference', *Novel: A Forum on Fiction,* 25:2 (1992), 125–40.
Oates, Joyce Carol, 'Killer Kids', *The New York Review of Books,* 44:17 (1997): 16–20.
Oh, Arissa, 'A new kind of missionary work: Christians, Christian Americanists and the adoption of Korea GI babies, 1955–1961', *Women's Studies Quarterly,* 33:3/4 (2005), 161–88.
Paul, William, *Laughing Screaming: Modern Hollywood Horror & Comedy* (New York: Columbia University Press, 1995).
Pizer, Donald (ed.), *The Cambridge Companion to American Realism and Naturalism* (Cambridge: Cambridge University Press, 1995).
Stern, Alexandra, *Eugenic Nation: Faults and Frontiers of Better Breeding in Modern America* (Berkeley: University of California Press, 2005).
Wylie, Philip, *Generation of Vipers* (New York: Rinehart, 1942).

5

'Children misbehaving in the walls!' or, Wes Craven's suburban family values[1]

Bernice M. Murphy

'The suburbs dream of violence', observes the narrator of J.G. Ballard's English-set novel *Kingdom Come* (2006).[2] His remark can equally be applied to cinematic and literary depictions of the post-Second World War American suburb, which are even more likely to result in blood-drenched visions of murder and mayhem. What is perhaps most striking of all about these kinds of narrative is the frequency with which the sanctity and supposedly inherent moral worth of the nuclear family is violently rent asunder. In the Suburban Gothic, in other words, you frequently have the most to fear from those you are related to.

In American popular culture, suburbanites are seldom menaced by a terrible 'other'; instead, they tend to be violently despatched by one of their own, usually a murderous family member. The notion that the family *itself* can be a powerful locus of horror is of course nothing particularly new in American literary and popular culture – or, of course, in the Gothic in general. Charles Brockden Brown's *Wieland* (1798), the first significant American Gothic novel, features a delusional madman who butchers his wife and children because he thinks God told him to. Neither does one have to delve too far into the works of Edgar Allan Poe or Nathaniel Hawthorne to find evidence of the fact that one's nearest and dearest can all too often, inadvertently or otherwise, bring about great harm. It is a trope that continues in the work of mid-twentieth-century authors such as such as William Faulkner, Shirley Jackson, Flannery O'Connor and Richard Matheson, and would find further expression in films such as *Psycho* (1960), *Night of the Living Dead* (1968), and *The Texas Chain Saw Massacre* (1974), to name but a few examples.

Over the past 40-odd years, there have also been many films in which the apparently mundane suburban locale becomes the spawning ground for a very human (rather than supernatural) kind of evil, and in which the complex relationship between parents and children in particular becomes a starting point for narratives in which the notion of familial 'togetherness' takes on a much darker perspective than originally intended by the developers and advertisers who promoted the milieu as the ideal environment for the All-American everyman and his family.[3]

It is in the work of one director/writer in particular, Wes Craven, that we can see the 'traditional' Suburban family unit being critiqued over and over again. Craven is the most consistently popular and commercially successful American horror director of the past three decades, and as will become apparent during the course of this chapter his remarkably consistent oeuvre has from the very beginning more often than not dealt with characters and with preoccupations of a very suburban (and familial) nature. From *The Last House on the Left* (1972) to *Scream 4* (2011), Craven's horror movies have depicted brutality and horror at the heart of the American family unit. In addition, more than any other American director he has consistently and effectively undermined the notion that the middle-class, suburban milieu is somehow a particularly safe place for families, and in particular for children and teenagers. Indeed, as we shall see, the threat facing his protagonists most often comes from within the home itself, or indirectly arises from attitudes and actions frequently associated with the so-called 'suburban' mindset.

The Last House on the Left (1972), Craven's horror debut, remains the most controversial film of his career (it would only be passed uncut by the BBFC in 2008). It is, notoriously, a gory, visceral update of Ingmar Bergman's medieval-set drama *The Virgin Spring* (1960), a brutal and notably uncompromising tale of rape, murder and revenge, which set the scene for films such as Tobe Hooper's *The Texas Chain Saw Massacre* and Meir Zarchi's *I Spit On Your Grave* (1978). It is about a comfortable, prosperously middle-class (and middle-aged) couple, John and Estelle Collingwood (Gaylord St James and Cynthia Carr), whose complacent existence is suddenly violated forever by a brutal act of violence that prompts them to commit terrible and irrational acts of their own (a plot development that would be replicated five years later in Craven's *The Hills Have Eyes*).

On her seventeenth birthday, the Collingwoods' daughter Mari and her pal Phyllis (Sandra Cassel and Lucy Grantham) head into the city to see a rock concert performance by their favourite band, the ominously named 'Bloodlust'.[4] However, the girls fall into the clutches of only the first of one of Craven's soon-to-become characteristic antifamilies, a dysfunctional but co-dependent gang of escaped convicts led by the sadistic Krug Stillo (David Hess). The girls are driven to a wooded area, which, by coincidence, happens to be only a short distance from Mari's home. Phyllis makes a desperate bid for freedom, but is soon recaptured, and in one of the most disturbing scenes of the film is stabbed repeatedly. Mari is raped and then shot dead as she wades into a nearby lake. Perhaps even more shocking than the physical violence they endure is the psychological torment and humiliation undergone by the girls at the hands of Krug's gang of misfits. Even the murderers themselves look sickened by what they have done when the violence subsides. In an ironic twist taken from Bergman's original, Krug's gang end up on the Collingwoods' doorstep. Mari's parents are initially quite hospitable to their unlikely guests, but are soon made suspicious by their desperately unconvincing attempts to behave in a 'civilized' manner. Suspicion crystallizes into horrified certainty when they recognize a peace medallion in the possession of one of the killers as that given to Mari just a few hours earlier. The formerly well-mannered suburbanites decide that it is time to get their own back, to kill the gang one-by-one.

For the first, but certainly not the last time in Craven's work, the supposedly civilized, logical, and moral middle-class family carries out acts of great savagery the moment it is threatened. As Kim Newman notes:

> Craven wittily has the carnage stem from each group's desire to emulate its mutual enemy. Krug's maniacs try to pass themselves off as plumbers/insurance salesmen and coo over expensive furnishings, while the middle-aged, well-off Collingwoods prepare to slaughter them.[5]

By the end of the film, the boundaries between revenge and cold-blooded murder, savage and suburbanite have become well and truly blurred.

The white, middle-class suburban family unit again meets its 'uncivilized' double in Craven's follow-up to *The Hills Have Eyes* (1977). In what is essentially a modern take on the legendary Scottish murderer Sawney Beane and his large, inbred family of murderous, cannibalistic bandits, a smug family of affluent suburbanites, the Carters, travel to the Californian desert in their all-mod-cons equipped trailer in search of an old silver mine they own.[6] They find themselves under attack from their opposite numbers, a vicious pack of irradiated, inbred desert dwellers who murder several members of the family (including racist former cop 'Big Bob' Carter, the family patriarch) and steal its youngest member, a baby girl, for food. It is then up to the baby's nerdy father to fight for his child's life, and so another bloody battle between the supposed representatives of civilization and those of primordial savagery is waged.

It is significant therefore that both families are products of the cultural and political contexts of 1950s America, because what the film in effect goes on to dramatize is a war between these two very different representatives of post-war 'Progress'. The Carters are affluent, materially inclined suburbanites who have lost any real sense of connection with the world around them. Their trailer serves, as many critics have noted, as a kind of suburban home on wheels, stocked with all the accoutrements of late twentieth-century life. The fact that they are camped in the middle of the desert does not seem to change their behaviour at all; as John Muir puts it, 'instead of adapting to their new landscape, they try to tame it'.[7]

Their hermetically sealed existence and dependence upon firearms makes them vulnerable to the attacks of the feral clan whose home turf they have unintentionally violated. Yet Jupiter, Mars, Pluto, Ruby and the rest of the desert folk are products of the 1950s: their home is an Air Force Atomic test site, and their regressive behaviour and deformities are at least partially due to radiation poisoning (as well as incest, which makes their existence a kind of queasy extension of the familial 'togetherness' so prized during that decade). Everything we know about the Carters tells us that they have benefited from the economic and technological advances of the Cold War era. Their enemies did not, although their very freedom from the constraints and assumptions of conventional society (and the status quo which Big Bob protected for many years) is what makes them so dangerous.

Significantly, as in *Last House on the Left*, victory for the 'good' family only comes through brutality and animal-like cunning; as Muir suggests, 'It is only when they [the Carters] forsake the tools of twentieth-century life that they begin to succeed in defending themselves. They only defeat Jupiter once they stop seeing their trailer as a shelter, a mobile representation of suburban safety and instead use it as a weapon'[8] Survival against great odds is again only possible when civility and morality is exchanged for aggressive masculinity and ultra violence.

Craven's most famous film of the 1980s, *A Nightmare on Elm Street*, is perhaps the most significant suburban-set horror film since *Halloween* and, like it, focuses upon teenagers who are sorely betrayed by the adults around them. Here, the vaguely supernatural nature of Carpenter's homicidal boy next door is incorporated into the story of a seemingly peaceful neighbourhood in which the wrongs of the adult population are paid for by their teenage children, who are stalked and murdered by a killer who has returned from the dead to stalk their dreams. As in *Last House on the Left*, the decision here by otherwise 'civilized', suburban professionals to take the law into their own hands has devastating consequences. The main difference here is that while the Collingwoods had *already* lost their child, the vigilantism undertaken by the residents of Elm street is aimed at *preventing* harm coming to their children, but, ironically, actually makes it inevitable.

Freddy Krueger is that most feared and hated of suburban bogeymen: the murderous child molester (this important detail, generally left out of the later films in the *Nightmare* series, is highlighted in the dull 2010 remake). *Halloween*'s Michael Myers was, at least initially, a child who kills while Krueger is a killer of children, but the actions of both strike at the very heart of what the suburban neighbourhood is supposed to represent. Krueger, however, as a single, working-class male differs significantly from boy-next-door Myers in that he represents a powerful *outside* threat and fits squarely into the 'untrustworthy janitor' pantheon of Pop Culture villainy, alongside figures like Leroy from *The Bad Seed* (1954) and Lucas Cross in *Peyton Place* (1957). However, had the parents of Elm Street not resorted to vigilante action and murdered him in the first place, their children would have been safe from his nocturnal predations. Though he is most definitely an attacker from outside the suburban sphere, it is the actions of the 'law-abiding' mothers and fathers from within that milieu that give him his power to harm their children while they sleep.

The spectre of the suburban child-murderer/abuser recurs fairly often in the Suburban Gothic, particularly in literary depictions of the milieu. The heroine of Alice Sebold's *The Lovely Bones* is raped and murdered by her next-door neighbour. The release of a convicted child molester and suspected murderer in Tom Perrotta's *Little Children* (2004) leads to violence and vigilantism, while an innocent man suspected of no good is hounded out of a Washington suburb in Suzanne Berne's *A Crime in the Neighbourhood* (1999). Shirley Jackson's *The Road Through the Wall* (1948) is the earliest literary depiction of the suburban community as lynch-mob, one which again seeks to avenge the death of a child.

Linden Peach has observed that 'child murder undermines the fundamental premise upon which the ideal of suburbia is constructed, that the suburban neighbourhood is a safe environment in which to bring up children'.[9] This helps explain why the lynch mob is frequently invoked in order to rid the community of this 'monstrous' aberration. What makes matters worse in Craven's film is that vigilantism represents not the conclusion of the narrative, but rather the starting point. Exonerated on a legal technicality, then burned to death in his own boiler room by the parents of the community, Krueger's evil lives on: he returns as a kind of vengeful ghost, intent on striking at those who killed him in the cruellest way possible, by slaughtering their children.

Craven's leading character in *Nightmare* is teenager Nancy Thompson (Heather Lagenkamp). She quickly distinguishes herself from her more expendable peers Rod, Tina and Glen by dint of her practicality and resourcefulness. While the rest of her cohort are being helplessly picked off one-by-one, Nancy investigates the reasons why they are being targeted, and formulates survival strategies. Significantly, Nancy's faith in the ability of the grown-ups around her to counter Krueger's threat is shaky even before she discovers the real reason for his actions (revenge). This knowledge is invaluable, for it helps her realize that only she can save herself. Her father Don (John Saxon) is distant and evasive, while her mother Marge (Ronee Blakley), is a guilt-stricken alcoholic. Despite the fact that Nancy's father is a law-enforcement officer he can do nothing to help his daughter. Indeed, his position of legal and moral authority means that the fact that Don condoned the vigilante actions of his fellow neighbours makes him even more culpable than they are. Indeed, his initial reluctance to even admit that Krueger existed places Nancy and the other teenagers in even more danger, for it denies them the information that could help them understand the true nature of their attacker.

While Nancy proactively takes steps to save her own life, her booze-addled mother's misguided efforts only make matters worse. She erects bars on all the windows and doors, which means that when Nancy begins to drag Krueger into *her* reality, she is left to battle him alone. Unlike Laurie Strode in *Halloween*, she does not even have a last-minute rescue by a Dr Loomis style-figure to look forward to. As Tony Williams observes, the ineptitude and hypocrisy of Elm Street's adult population makes their children all the more vulnerable to Krueger because:

> Unlike Elm Street's parents he can discipline and definitively punish his teenage victims. The film also indicts the adult world, presenting parents as weak, manipulative and selfish. Nancy angrily reacts to her father, Sheriff John Thompson ... who uses her as a decoy to help capture Rod. He never responds to her appeals for help against Freddy and puts her behind bars at home. Nancy's mother, Marge ... withholds crucial information from her daughter until it is too late. She resorts to alcohol to conceal guilty feelings over her role in Freddy's murder, and she morbidly preserves his knives. *Nightmare on Elm Street* emphasizes the dangerous nature of parental silence. On many occasions it indirectly aids Freddy.[10]

To follow on from Williams's point here, then, it can be argued that in *Nightmare*, Craven advocates a model of parent-child relations defined by honesty and openness, rather than by repression and secrecy. Krueger is of course the greatest monster of all here, but the reluctance of Elm Street's adults to own up to their part in his horrific origin story, and their refusal until late in the narrative to acknowledge his very existence, makes their children all the more vulnerable. Nancy survives (at least until the film's spurious coda) because she has embraced self-empowerment, and separated herself from the parents whose actions, though well-meaning, have had terrible consequences. The parents of Elm Street may not be directly responsible for the deaths of their children, but it is clear that they have much to answer for, not least their attempts to white-wash over the community's darkest moment.

The dangers of poor parenting and adult hypocrisy are even more obvious in *The People under the Stairs* (1991). Here, Craven deals with issues of class and racial politics in his most explicit manner yet, setting the residents of a poor, fundamentally decent black underclass against their deranged, hypocritical and greedy white landlords, the Robesons, who reside in a fortress-like suburban home. The film's fairy-tale-like structure is obvious from the outset, in which a bright 13-year-old known as 'Fool' (Brandon Williams) and his family are evicted from their miserable home so that the Robesons can build condos for 'nice, clean people' instead. When a petty thief named Leroy (Ving Rhames) suggests that Fool help him carry out a burglary at the landlord's house, he therefore feels that he has no choice but to comply. From the moment they arrive at the house, a former funeral home, things go from bad to worse, and like Fool, we soon realize that the real horror here is worse than he could have ever imagined.

'Mommy' (Wendy Robie) and 'Daddy' (Everett McGill), rank among Craven's most bizarre and memorable characters, and represent the ultimate on-screen representation of all of his previous hypocritical parent figures to date. Further compounding their monstrosity is fact that they are not actually a married couple at all, but siblings who live together as man and wife in a set-up that is obviously meant to parody George Bush Senior-era notions of traditional family values. (The fact that the 1991 Gulf War perpetually flickers on television screens in the background of their home helps make their association with noxious notions of conservative morality even more obvious.) The innate perversity of the incestuous, deviant and overtly monstrous 'family' presented here means that Craven's critique goes far beyond the indictment of repression and poor parenting of the conventional family unit seen in *Nightmare*: the Robesons *themselves* are truly monstrous, whereas the parents in Elm Street inadvertently help create the environment in which monstrosity flourishes.

Once Fool, dressed as a boy scout, makes contact with 'Mommy' (who dresses in a style reminiscent of the 1950s), he tries to sweet-talk his way into the house, but the viewer will already have suspected from her odd demeanour and the barred windows that all is not well. It soon turns out that the couple have a sorely abused 'daughter' in her early teens named 'Alice', whom they dress in frilly white frocks and lock in a nursery-like room in which all the furniture is clearly meant for a much younger child (indeed, it rather brings to mind Norman's room in Hitchcock's *Psycho* [1960]). A cross is prominently portrayed on the wall, indicating that twisted religiosity has its own part to play in reinforcing the repressive delusions of Alice's 'parents'. Even more disturbingly, the Robesons also have at least a dozen starved, terribly mutilated 'sons' caged in the basement. The boys are even fed the remains of both their dead brethren and of intruders like Leroy, and so the ceaseless consumerism of the Robesons becomes even more reprehensible: their children are literally nothing but livestock, and human life has no meaning at all.

Once Fool finds himself trapped in the house, the film becomes an amusing succession of ultra-violent and cartoon-like cat-and-mouse scenes in which he scrambles through the unforgiving corridors trying to find a hiding place. In some respects, therefore, the story represents an interesting reversal of *The Last House on the Left*: here, our sympathies lie entirely with the inner-city trespasser, while the weapon-wielding professional couple who are obsessed with protecting the 'honour' of their 'daughter' are the villains.

Fool is aided first by Alice, and then by a skeletal mute boy named Roach, who lives in the walls. Together, the three youngsters scramble to escape 'Daddy', now dressed in a leather gimp suit and brandishing a shotgun. Particularly galling to the Robesons is the fact that a black boy from the ghetto has been in contact with their precious Alice, who has never even left the house: 'He's in there right now, with our little angel!' Again, the powers that be are of little help. Roughly half way through the film, Fool manages to scramble outside to freedom, but Alice, and the injured Roach remain behind. Fool returns to the tenement with enough gold coins to pay for his sick mother's operation and to cover the family's rent, but he cannot rest until he has saved his friends too. He anonymously contacts the police and accuses the Robesons of child abuse, but when the authorities visit the house they are completely fooled by the veneer of middle-class respectability exuded by the couple.

It is up to Fool to creep back in and rescue Alice and 'the people under the stairs' – the boys in the basement – himself. In this he is aided by his own family and by the solidarity of the local community, who assemble outside the Robeson house and demand the return of their stolen children and an end to their economic exploitation. The film ends as Alice finally breaks free of her chains and stabs her supposed 'mother' while the boys in the basement burst into the open, in a scene which strongly evokes the climax of Romero's *Night of the Living Dead* (another film in which the American nuclear family is depicted in decidedly monstrous terms). Fool blows up the house, and in the final moments a long overdue redistribution of wealth takes place as the Robesons' money floats into the hands of those whom they had fed upon for so long. In addition, the obvious friendship between Alice and Fool brings with it the hope that the next generation will not be divided on the same rigidly unequal racial and economic lines as the one before.

Though, unfairly, not generally considered one of Craven's better films, *The People under the Stairs* is nevertheless 'Craven's ultimate exploration of the American middle-class family ... foremost a battle between the "haves" and the "have-nots"'.[11] On one hand, we can see this battle as a kind of parodic indictment of 'traditional' (i.e., socially and culturally conservative) ideas regarding the parent-child relationship. The Robeson household is first and foremost a hierarchy, with 'Mommy' and 'Daddy', naturally, at the top. Most of their parenting seems to be directed towards Alice, who, at least until Fool's arrival, functions as their infantilized, severely repressed and idealized 'good' child, and as such, is permitted to live within the main body of the house. The troublesome 'People Under the Stairs' – all boys, which suggests that they are seen by the couple as more difficult to control than girls, a paranoia which is confirmed by the effect that Fool has upon the family dynamic – are confined to the basement. Their rebellious behaviour means that they are no longer part of the idealized nuclear family, and as such, must be kept out of sight and out of mind.

Both Alice and her disenfranchised 'brothers' are in effect treated as possessions by their 'parents'. She is alternately cosseted and brutalized, viewed as little more than a kind of living doll for her deranged mother figure, while the boys are treated like animals – chained to the walls and used as a means of getting rid of pesky intruders. Liberation from this highly repressive system is only possible when all of the Robesons' much-abused 'children' rebel against the insanely dictatorial 'parents', who have imposed upon them a deranged version of 1950s 'family values'. The film's pointed contribution to the so-called 'Culture Wars' of the early 1990s, therefore, satirizes the folksy hypocrisy of conservatives like President George H.W. Bush, who famously stated at a gathering of the 'National Religious Broadcasters' in January 1992 that

American families should aspire to be 'more like the Waltons and less like the Simpsons'.

Also key to this battle between the 'haves' and the 'have-nots' in the film is the fact that the twisted but recognizably middle-class existence of the Robesons is built upon the exploitation of the poor black community which encircles their privileged enclave. They fear the understandably resentful economic underclass which surrounds them, but as Craven wryly demonstrates, the underclass has much more to fear from *them*. The film ultimately brings to mind observations made by Aviva Briefel and Sianna Ngai in their discussion of one of the few other horror films of the 1990s to actively engage with issues of race and class: Bernard Rose's *Candyman*. They suggest that in slasher films, being frightened is, paradoxically, a sign of empowerment and privilege: the victims are after all consistently white, middle-class suburbanites who are themselves owners or future inheritors of property. In their words:

> The genre itself presents owning a house in particular as a form of proprietorship that automatically entitles the buyer to the experience of fear, as if fear itself were a commodity included with the total package – just as sophisticated alarm systems and security guards have become standard components of the purchase of an upscale home or condominium.[12]

Similarly, while the Robesons live in a fortress, this is built as much to keep the horrors inside from spilling out into the open as it is meant to exclude outside threats. Their fear of intruders, in other words, stems from the fact that they have a great deal to lose, both as representatives of the avaricious middle classes and as the 'owners' of the lower-class children imprisoned in their home. Furthermore, Fool's triumph would have been impossible had it not been for the support of his own deprived but close-knit family, and for the fact that he was able to quickly form sibling-like bonds with Alice. Fool's family, which consists of his mother, sister and grandfather, does not conform to the conventional nuclear-family model, whereas that of the Robesons initially seems as if it does. However, as we have seen, the Robesons are defeated because their much more materially privileged and seemingly traditional 'family' unit was nothing but a hypocritical facade, concealing great horror underneath. Once more therefore, the 'good' biological family triumphs over the 'evil' and decidedly non-biological one – albeit with one important development: perhaps because they hail from the repressed underclass themselves, Fool's family have managed to maintain their innate goodness and integrity, despite considerable provocation.

Given Craven's preoccupation with horror within the nuclear family, it is entirely consistent that the twist in his most-successful post *A Nightmare on Elm Street* film to date, *Scream* (1997), is that the masked killer (or rather, killers) who have been murdering the community's youngsters are themselves spoiled local adolescents and that a conflicted parent/teenager relationship has some part to play. Billy Loomis (Skeet Ulrich) hates Final Girl Sidney Prescott (Neve Campbell) because her mother's adulterous affair with his father broke up his parents' marriage. He wants to destroy her life because her mother ruined his, although the deeply disproportionate nature of his revenge suggests that Billy was something of a psychopath to begin with. He may be tormenting Sidney for what he sees as justifiable reasons but it is clear that while the failure of the Loomis family unit may have precipitated his turn to violence, the potential was there all along.

This trope is continued in all of the later instalments of the series. One of the killers in *Scream 2* is journalist Debbie Salt (Laurie Metcalf), who is actually Billy's vengeful biological mother. It is a plot development that owes much to the last-act-reveal of *Friday the 13th* (1980), which is perhaps hardly surprising, given that Sean Cunningham's influential *Slasher* was referenced in the opening minutes of *Scream*. The suggestion that murderous proclivities can be inherited is also one that owes much to William Marsh's novel *The Bad Seed* (1954) in which evil, like eye colour, is passed down through the bloodline. In *Scream 3*, the villain is Roman, a half-brother Sidney did not even know she had, who was conceived when *her* biological mother Maureen was raped many years earlier. Roman is taking revenge for the rejection he felt when Maureen refused to have anything to do with him as an adult. In a rather laboured spot of plot retro-fitting it is revealed that Roman was responsible for inciting Billy Loomis to commit the murders seen in the first film, thus making the events of *all* of the previous films a result of one man's desire to lash out at his biological family. Though it is presented as a major twist, therefore, it is entirely inevitable that the laboured denouement of *Scream 4* (2011) reveals that the newest spate of grisly slayings in Woodsboro have been masterminded by Sidney's cousin Jill (Emma Roberts).

Interestingly though, unlike Roman, Billy, or Mrs Loomis, Jill does not actively want to punish her own family; her crimes (which include collusion in the murder of her own mother, as well as repeated attacks upon Sidney herself) are rather a manifestation of dispassionate self-interest. Jill does not want revenge: she just wants to be on TV, and if that necessitates killing off her own kin – (which it obviously does, if she wants to inherit her cousin's lucrative Final Girl mantle) – well, so be it. While earlier Craven films therefore indicted the hypocrisy of middle-class parents, *Scream 4* pointedly depicts the celebrity-obsessed modern teen as an amoral psychopath. Though it seems for much of the film as if Jill is merely a younger version of Sidney, a principled, likable survivor-in-training, in fact, she is both her cousin's double and her exact opposite, a calculating villain rather than a pro-active victim, whose in-depth awareness of the ins and outs of the Final Girl trope is one of her most disturbing weapons.

Ultimately it is notable that the only *entirely* positive depiction of the family in Craven's work comes in his post-9/11 thriller *Red Eye* (2005). In this case, the family consists of just a father and daughter. Most of the film takes place on the commercial airliner in which hotel manager Lisa Reisert (Rachel McAdams) is being held hostage by hit man 'Jackson Rippner' (Cillian Murphy) in order to further a plot to assassinate the head of Homeland Security, a regular guest of her hotel. However, in the final twenty minutes the action moves to Lisa's childhood home in the suburbs, and it essentially turns into a slasher movie. Though her bravery thwarts the terror plot, 'Rippner' is ultimately killed by her caring and protective father Joe (Brian Cox). Rippner's attack both vindicates Joe's over-protectiveness – his daughter is indeed in danger, although for most of the film, there's absolutely nothing he can do about it – and to a certain extent negates it, in that by the end of her ordeal, she has shown herself to be fit to handle everything from international terrorists to homicidal maniacs and snotty hotel guests. Unusually for Craven, the parental act of vigilante justice here turns out to have positive rather than negative connotations; perhaps Joe's actions are *directly* responsible for saving Lisa's life, rather than being an act of vengeance carried out after her death.

However, in a thread that again goes back as far as *The Last House on the Left*, the film emphasizes that Joe's nagging concern about his daughter's safety (obvious from the opening minutes of the film) is a result of the fact that she had been raped and assaulted several years previously, by an assailant who, so far as we know, was never caught. Rippner's assault upon the family home, and of course, Lisa herself, means that finally this well-meaning but previously ineffective patriarch can at last take violent action on behalf of his daughter. As well as saving her life, Joe's killing of Rippner symbolically avenges her previous violation.

Red Eye was marketed as a post-9/11 thriller and therefore received by critics as something of a departure from the genre with which Craven is usually associated. However it seems clear that the film's preoccupation with the parent/child relationship is in fact entirely in line with the themes of his horror movies. What differs here, however, is the extent to which the link between America-as-nation and the domestic sphere/family unit is highlighted: in *Red Eye*, an attack on one is essentially the same as an attack on the other. It is no coincidence therefore that the abortive attack upon the head of Homeland Security should culminate in an assault upon a middle-class suburban home. Even international terrorism has consequences for the nuclear family in Craven's characteristically consistent universe. It is fitting too that the terrorist-defying politician being targeted should be depicted as a loving husband and father. If the attack had succeeded, it would have killed not only him but also his wife and two young children. This is clearly not just an assault upon the nation, but upon the family itself.

It is fitting then that it is foiled by Lisa, the resourceful and diligent young manager for whom the hotel – meant to serve as a home away from home, after all – is her own domestic space, to organize as she pleases. The other employees and guests can be seen as her charges, to be accommodated or gently chided, depending on the circumstances. It is telling, though, that Lisa's ability to positively affect events in the film ends once she returns to her childhood home. Although Rippner's final stalk-and-slash-style pursuit of her means that, as his *nom-de-guerre* has telegraphed all along, the suave and dispassionate hit man degenerates into a leering, misogynistic maniac, his rampage through the domestic space is cut short by Joe's well-timed gunshot.

Outside the family home, Lisa may have saved the day, and brought the film's conventional thriller plot to a happy conclusion, but the slasher-style antics of the last twenty minutes are ended by a loving father who just wants to protect his daughter. Unlike the other Craven films in which Gothic kinship is a key preoccupation, there is no suggestion that Joe will be punished for his actions, nor that the relationship that he and Lisa have will be anything but strengthened by their traumatic experience. Lisa has learned to look after herself and Joe has finally been able to protect her in the way that he always wanted to. When combined with the rather pat conclusion to the terrorist-attack plot, this development means that *Red Eye* ultimately presents the viewer with what may well be the most conventional and conservative resolution of any Wes Craven movie to date. Here, the family unit is celebrated rather than critiqued, and the American family and the American nation are seen as one and the same – paragons of unalloyed decency and goodness that need to be protected from irrational and violent external forces. Indeed, it is telling that we never even find out what organization Rippner is working for, as it renders the terrorists merely unapologetically black-and-white bad guys. In this instance at least, patriotism permits no messy grey areas.

As we have seen, therefore, in Craven's films the deceptively idyllic confines of the modern suburban neighbourhood are brutally violated time and time again by irrational forces which usually come from much closer to home than his protagonists would initially care to admit. As a result, the middle-class family is, one way or another, just a hair's breadth away from primal savagery or desperate peril. Given Craven's status as the only American director associated with the 1970s horror boom to have successfully maintained a top-flight Hollywood career, it would seem that this formula is one that continues to resonate with the public as well. His continued box-office success serves as a reminder that Gothic depictions of the middle-class family are certainly nothing if not lucrative, and of the fact that every once in a while, the movie-going audience likes nothing more than to be reminded that it is those we are closest to that we should be most wary of.

Notes

1 This chapter is a significantly revised and updated version of an extract that was first published in *The Suburban Gothic in American Popular Culture*.
2 J.G. Ballard, *Kingdom Come*, p. 1.
3 See L.J. Miller, 'Family togetherness and the suburban ideal'.

4 Interestingly, when the film was remade by Dennis Iliadis in 2009, the suburban setting was jettisoned entirely: the whole film takes place in the countryside. Unlike most modern remakes of well-known 1970s exploitation/horror movies, this one is actually rather more nuanced and effective than the original, mainly because the Collingwoods here are much more sympathetic and three-dimensional, notwithstanding the cartoonish silly coda with which the narrative concludes.
5 Kim Newman, *Nightmare Movies*, p. 55.
6 The premise also owes much to Anthony Boucher's eerie 1943 short story 'They Bite', in which unwary travellers in the desert are attacked and eaten by 'The Carkers', a pint-sized but notably vicious band of supernaturally long-lived and resilient cannibals. Tallant, the arrogant newcomer who meets a nasty end in Boucher's story, is also a prospector – just like the Carters.
7 John Muir, *Horror Films of the 1970s*, p. 66.
8 Ibid.
9 Linden Peach, 'An incident in the neighbourhood', in R. Webster (ed.), *Expanding Suburbia*, p. 113.
10 Tony Williams, *Hearths of Darkness*, p. 228.
11 John Muir, *Wes Craven: The Art of Horror*, p. 167.
12 Aviva Briefel and Sianne Ngai, 'How much did you pay for this place?', p. 71.

References

Ballard, J.G., *Kingdom Come* (London: Fourth Estate, 2006).
Briefel, Aviva and Sianne Ngai, 'How much did you pay for this place? Fear, entitlement, and urban Space in Bernard Rose's *Candyman*', *Camera Obscura*, 37 (1997), 71–90.
Miller, L.J., 'Family togetherness and the suburban ideal', *Sociological Forum*, 10:3 (1995), 393–418.
Muir, John, *Horror Films of the 1970s* (Jefferson, NC: McFarland, 2002).
———, *Wes Craven: The Art of Horror* (Jefferson, NC: McFarland, 2004).
Murphy, Bernice M., *The Suburban Gothic in American Popular Culture* (Basingstoke: Palgrave Macmillan, 2009).
Newman, Kim, *Nightmare Movies: A Critical Guide to Contemporary Horror Films* (Prospect, KY: Harmony, 1989).
Peach, Linden, 'An incident in the neighbourhood: crime: contemporary fiction and suburbia', in Roger Webster (ed.), *Expanding Suburbia: Reviewing Suburban Narratives* (New York: Berghahn, 2000).
Williams, Tony, *Hearths of Darkness: The Family in the American Horror Film* (Madison, WI: Farleigh Dickinson University Press, 1996).

6

Fathers, friends, and families: Gothic kinship in Stephen King's *Pet Sematary*

John Sears

> 'There was something very familiar in this rap, something eerily familiar –' (*Pet Sematary*).

Early in Stephen King's *Pet Sematary* (1983), a neighbourly act of kindness establishes a surrogate family relationship – between a symbolic father and his symbolic son – that will gather in increasingly sinister implications as the narrative develops. Jud Crandall, neighbour to the recently-moved Creed family, offers to help them treat a bee sting suffered by their infant child Gage: 'That would be very kind of you, Mr Crandall', Louis Creed gratefully acknowledges. And his wife Rachel repeats: 'You're very kind, Mr Crandall'.[1] Such acts of domestic kindness establish, at the novel's beginning, notions of compassionate kindness; homonymically, they invoke 'kind' as type, 'being (of a) kind'. These notions structure the narrative of *Pet Sematary*, in which Jud's neighbourly kindness is echoed, for example, in the supernatural conversation between Louis and the recently deceased student Victor Pascow, whom Louis treated as he died earlier that day. Pascow, leading an apparently somnambulant Louis by moonlight to the pet cemetery the Creed family have recently visited, warns Louis: 'The door must not be opened'. As he does so, we see his face: 'A look was on his face which Louis at first mistook for compassion. It wasn't really compassion at all; only a dreadful kind of patience' (75). Pascow's apparent 'compassion', inscribed on his face but already ambivalent, 'mistaken' or misread by Louis, repeats Jud's neighbourly act of kindness, just as Pascow announces that he comes 'as a friend'

(75). The neighbour and the friend, equally apparently displaying, early in this novel, faces of compassion to Louis and his family, also share another feature: the Creeds, and Louis specifically, find them difficult to understand. '"I come as a friend", Pascow said, but was *friend* actually the word Pascow had used? Louis thought not. It was as if Pascow had spoken in a foreign language which Louis could understand through some dream magic ...' (75, italics and ellipsis original). And Jud's Maine accent, as he introduces himself to the Creed family, sounds 'as exotic to their Midwestern ears as a foreign language' (15). Problems of intelligibility and legibility – the difficulty of understanding words and reading faces – thus regulate the relations with others and their 'foreign language' that this novel initially establishes.

'Kind' as '(doing) good' and 'kind' as 'kin' are etymologically connected, sharing a root in the Proto-Germanic *gakundjaz*, 'family' or 'race' (at one point, Louis refers to his family as 'his people' [158]), and *gakundiz*, 'natural, native'. Acts of kindness and compassion, and their misunderstanding or misreading, thread their way covertly through this novel, connecting kindness with likeness, and constituting the key expression of its concerns with ethical relations. Arguably, the entire narrative conceit of *Pet Sematary* relies on different acts of kindness – Louis saving the life of Jud's wife after her heart attack, Louis and Jud helping Louis's daughter to evade facing up to the death of her pet cat, and both attempting in different ways to repay the escalating debts to each other that accrue from these acts – which transform, drastically, into kindnesses of another kind. The word 'kind' inflates in significance, encompassing alternative kinds of meaning through the text. 'Kind' as 'type' works carefully, for example, to distinguish the novel's concern with place. After the family visits the pet cemetery, Rachel points out to Louis that 'It was the first cemetery of *any* kind' for their daughter Ellie (43, italics original). Louis, revisiting the cemetery after his midnight jaunt with Pascow's ghost, thinks of the cemetery's construction: 'Those concentric circles ... as if, all unknowing, the childish hands of North Ludlow's generations had built a kind of scale-model Stonehenge' (86, ellipsis original); and Jud warns him that 'It isn't the kind of place you just tell somebody about' (123). Much later, relating some of the place's mythology, Jud extends this connotation to include 'family and race', warning Louis of the Wendigo, the supernatural creature believed to haunt the American wilderness, which was 'supposed to give those it touched a taste for the flesh of their own kind' (138). And, crucially, Jud also warns Louis about his resurrected cat: 'You've got a different kind of pet now. Not necessarily a dangerous one, but ... different' (143, ellipsis original). 'Kind' and 'kindness' homonymically indicate the novel's play on notions of compassion and generosity, family and belonging. At the same time – as the shared potential foreignness of speech of Pascow and Jud suggests – compassion and kindness might indicate a relation to something (neighbour or friend) outside the family, another 'kind' of kin entirely, coming from and belonging to the 'exotic', 'strange' world beyond the family's purview and demanding, in their 'foreign' speech and 'inscrutable' (124) faces, different kinds of reading. This double potential is indicated in the ways friendship seems to balance familial and foreign relations: Pascow, in asserting his status as *'friend'*, seems also to speak the 'foreign language' of the other that (as revenant) he surely is. Later, this foreignness returns uncannily *within* the family, as Louis ponders his son Gage's infant speech: 'Louis was often struck by Gage's speech, not because it was cute, but because he thought that small children all sounded like immigrants learning a foreign language' (195). Like Pascow, speaking in a seemingly foreign tongue from beyond the grave, Gage (soon to die) expresses in his nascent speech a version of the 'foreignness' of the other, but this otherness signifies now the other within, the otherness *contained* by the family.

This containment, which houses within the space of the family both the familiar and the unfamiliar, is indicated by one of the novel's figures for the family – a circle that marks both its limits and its difference. Louis, pondering the death of Church, his pet cat (the death that initiates the escalating, cyclical, spiralling pattern of death and resurrection that organizes the novel's narrative), thinks (somewhat misogynistically) of the difference between his conjugal sexual relations and those physical contacts that, as a doctor, he regularly encounters. His wife, he concludes, is *'different. Just like your family's different*, he thought now. Church wasn't supposed to get killed because he was inside the magic circle of the family' (106, italics original). This 'magic circle', Louis thinks, should through differentiation protect the family and what it contains; but, in the novel's inexorable logic, it also affiliates it, in ways of which he is not always conscious, throwing out lines of uncanny connection to other circles and other places, and working to include that which it seems also to exclude – making the family's '*difference*' also its difference from itself. In particular, the family circle may contain, rather than protect against, that which threatens the family. Later, at Norma Crandall's funeral (Norma is one of the few living beings in this novel to die a *normal* death), Louis meets Jud's extended family and feels 'a trifle uncomfortable – an outsider in the family circle' (188). He becomes in this moment himself simultaneously contained within and excluded from another family circle, himself an 'outsider', prefiguring the manner in which his own actions will exclude him from his own family 'circle', which he will relentlessly destroy, by becoming precisely that which the family contains and which threatens it. Hélène Cixous, in her discussion of Freud's notion of the uncanny, argues that the uncanny 'is a unit in the "family" but it is not really a member of the family'.[2] Excentric to itself, the uncanny marks the unfamiliar, even as that unfamiliar returns within the spaces of the family as a marker of the difference that confirms and destabilizes the family's shared identity, its assertion of 'being of a kind'. Louis, perceiving himself as 'outsider' within Jud's family circle, personifies, at this moment, the excentric quality of the uncanny. Like his resurrected cat, he is both of the family – Jud's family, but also implicitly his own – and not of it, his ambiguous status rendering him as a kind of other to the Crandall family. It marks his difference, which is also the '*difference*' of his own family – and, in the novel's uncanny twist on this difference, the 'difference' of his family's resurrected pet cat.

The figure of the circle recurs twice more in the novel, first in the structure of the pet cemetery itself, which, to signify the historical process of its construction, comprises 'an almost perfect circle of mown grass' within which lie 'rough, concentric circles' (34). These comprise grave markers bearing inscriptions that, as Louis reads them, have either 'decomposed' (a pointed metaphor in the context of this novel: one inscription has eroded to 'little more than a ghost' [36]), or 'faded away to partial or total illegibility', or 'bore no discernible mark at all' (35). The monuments of the 'concentric circles' of the pet cemetery are thus connected, like the faces and speech of other people, to King's master trope of reading.[3] In *Pet Sematary* the demand of reading such texts, like that of reading the words and faces of others, resides within the tension between inscription and decomposition, conditions of the sign that mark its movement from intelligible to unintelligible or from figuration to disfigurement.

This movement, consequence of an explicitly historical process in the pet cemetery, is, elsewhere in the novel, a result rather of uncanny effacements and disfigurements of signs, confirming Nicholas Royle's assertion that the uncanny itself is an experience 'of reading'.[4] This is reinforced in the significatory potential of the children's misspelling of the word *sema*tary. As Jodey Castricano argues, this misspelling (another kind of disfigurement) works to connote *sema*ntics, from 'the Greek *semaino*, which is to signify, evolved from *sema*, sign or tomb'.[5] The legible, partly legible and illegible inscriptions of the monuments in the pet cemetery also indicate, Louis realizes in another, contrasting, figure, 'a rough timeline extending into the past' (35), a narrative version of the threads of family connection and affiliation that define both Louis's family and the wider community of Ludlow. These are linked to the acts of telling, discerning and reading narratives. Indeed, this community exists in the novel not as real, present actants, but almost completely as a product of Jud's narratives, sketched out in storylines which are also sometimes flows of narrative information ('a constant stream of warm memories and anecdotes' [173]) and comprising a verbal accompaniment to a family visit, fleshing out some of the family storylines connected to the graves in the cemetery.

The pet cemetery is, of course, only the precursor to or taster for the place to which it is most closely affiliated in the novel, the Micmac Indian burial ground, one of the displaced centres of the novel and the other major circular figure in the text. Visited three times by Louis (but only two of these are narrated) it constitutes a figure of displacement, its 'out-of-placeness' quickly perceived by Louis on his first visit, to bury the cat. The narrative describes it as 'a geographical anomaly that would have seemed far more normal in Arizona or New Mexico' (118) than in rural Maine – a place more appropriately sited as far away, indeed, as 'Orlando, Florida' where Louis fantasizes escaping to from his family on the novel's first page (9). The 'geographical anomaly', the out-of-placeness, of the burial ground is described three times in one page by the geological term 'mesa' (118), the Spanish or Portuguese word for 'table' (and thus the momentary intrusion of another foreign language into this text, emphasizing the strange foreignness of this place). 'Mesa' further establishes, in a kind of anagrammatic doubling, a clear line of connection between the Micmac burial ground and the pet *sema*tary. But it is only on his second visit (again implying a difficulty of legibility) that Louis recognizes the circular shape of the burial ground, and, in describing it, personifies it: 'Here on top of this rock table, its face turned up to cold starlight and to the black distances between the stars, was a gigantic spiral, made by what the oldtimers would have called Various Hands' (327). The 'gigantic spiral' both repeats and alters the 'concentric circles' of the pet cemetery. Jud earlier tells Louis that 'the Micmacs believed this hill was a magic place' (120), cementing in the word 'magic' the link between the strange spiral of the burial ground and the ostensibly protective, 'magic', circle of the family. And, of course, the burial ground is, Louis suddenly perceives, 'just like the Pet Sematary' (327), a disturbing likeness for Louis, that asserts through strange but obvious likeness the ex-centricity and out-of-place uncanniness shared between these burial grounds and the systems of doublings and family resemblances that King's novel is establishing.

Metaphors of family circles (figures of containment) and family lines (figures of connection) play across the text. At Norma's funeral, Louis watches Jud's nephews: seeing 'a strong facial resemblance' (188), he notes also that 'They had grown distant from this part of the family' (189). Connectivity and separation define family relations and their historical persistence. In a version of the circle metaphor, Louis shifts the agency of this 'growing distant', thinking of 'Jud's part of the family', childless and reduced, now, to Jud alone, as 'like an eroded planetoid drifting away from the main mass, dwindling, little more than a speck' (189). But this figure of a decaying orbit or declining circle also shifts, as Louis turns attention to his own family: 'the day would come when he would be every bit as unfamiliar to his own blood, the spawn of his brother's children, his own grandchildren, if Ellie or Gage produced kids and he lived to see them. The focus shifted. Family lines degenerated' (189). While family circles extend their orbit before releasing their kin, family lines 'degenerate', children regressing to 'spawn', the familiar (here, the self) becoming potentially 'unfamiliar', having followed a line that has led it beyond the 'magic circle' of the family. Louis's self-consciousness concerning his strange paternal position here is crucial. He is one of several fathers in this novel, and, as such, is both of the family and 'unfamiliar'. He again momentarily recognizes his strangely double position; as noted above, Louis, like the uncanny itself, is both part of and separate from Jud's family and, potentially, from his own. Becoming 'unfamiliar to their own blood' describes the trajectory of fathers in King's novel, and some of the ways this process is explored will be examined below.

As should by now be apparent, *Pet Sematary* deploys a complex and carefully layered network of interconnected metaphors of likeness and unlikeness, containment and foreignness, lines and circles, to indicate an extensive concern with reading and misreading family spaces and lineage, and their relations to the uncanny, labyrinthine structures of Gothic kinship. More specifically, this novel is concerned with how such family structures work both to contain and exclude that which occupies the position of the father, a position that both establishes and interferes with familial relationships and the ethical relations for which they provide a ground – albeit, in this novel, a 'ground' that is, like the ground of the pet cemetery, 'awful stony' and (unlike a circle) 'hard to turn' (36). Jud and Pascow, as different versions of 'neighbour' and 'friend', indicate different potential encounters with the other that Louis and his 'magic' family circle confront, encompass and, inevitably, contain, and which will contribute in different ways to their destruction. Each establishes through their relationship to Louis different kinds of link to the Creed family; Jud becomes, as well as his symbolic father, Louis's 'friend' (when Jud's wife dies, Louis's wife Rachel calls him: 'Could you come, Louis? You're his friend, and I think he needs you' [171]), initiating the narrative sequence and interfering repeatedly in the affairs of the Creed family. Pascow, assuming the paternal role of the revenant sent to advise, warns Louis once, and then warns Ellie: 'He said that he was sent to *warn* but that he couldn't *interfere*' (279). The difference between 'warning' and 'interfering' is the difference between the kinds of paternal friendship signified by Pascow and Jud.

The novel's narrative is superficially simple and originates, Douglas Winter has suggested, in 'the author's interest in funeral customs, an interest seemingly sparked in 1979 by the death of the family cat'.[6] The close-knit, socially isolated Creed family is gradually but relentlessly and violently dismantled by external, supernatural forces which yet find insistent expression *within* the family structure, indeed at its putative patriarchal head, the father who, at the novel's end, survives the deaths he indirectly causes (of cat, son, neighbour and mother), and the sequence of three demonic resurrections he instigates. Louis Creed, introduced to the magical space of the Micmac Indian burial ground by Jud Crandall, develops a compulsive need to use its powers (or to let its powers use him) to resurrect first the family cat, then his infant son, killed by an Orinco oil truck, and finally his wife Rachel, murdered and partially eaten by her resurrected son, who also kills Jud. The escalating horror of this novel is counterpointed by its reliance on the slow-paced, drawling local-historical narratives of Jud, and on the novel's focalization through Creed himself, who offers a convincing mix of perpetrator and victim of the novel's disastrous events. Embedded in the mythically cyclical narrative of death and return and the functions of family rituals of burial and mourning (Slavoj Žižek rightly calls King's novel 'a perverted *Antigone*'),[7] and in the symbolic performance of three resurrections (echoing the three wishes of fairy tale and of W.W. Jacobs' short story 'The Monkey's Paw' [1902]), lurks a complex critique of the repetition compulsions of the contemporary American family, represented as kinds of dysfunctional social performance that radically, perhaps irreversibly, deform those relations and resemblances upon which a notion of the family depends.

Pet Sematary's concerns with Gothic kinship locate it in a complex position in King's extensive oeuvre. Its publication was apparently delayed for contractual reasons; the typescript of the novel's first draft is dated September 1979, and its eventual publication in 1983 enables us to read it as both affiliated backwards with previous and interim texts, and foreshadowing works yet to come.[8] A key connection, for example, lies in King's treatment of children. Ellie Creed, Louis's daughter, who is the only real survivor of the novel's action, displaced as she is for the final third of the narrative to her grandparents in Chicago, displays apparent psychic abilities which link her thematically to other similarly supernaturally empowered children who populate earlier King novels. These include the telekinetic schoolgirl Carrie White in *Carrie* (1974); Danny Torrance in *The Shining* (1977), whose paranormal 'shine' gives the novel its title; and Charlie McGee in *Firestarter* (1980), whose paranormal pyrotechnic skills attract dangerous governmental interest. Each of these 'special' children suggests, in turn, different versions of what Tony Magistrale identifies as one of the key functions of children in King's writing, as 'the nucleus for familial love'.[9] Intra-oeuvre relations are also detectable in *Pet Sematary*; half-way through the novel Louis ponders resurrection and return in a narrative fragment that prefigures the uncanny-family plot of King's *The Dark*

Half (1989): 'I had to buy the concept that the fetus of one twin can sometimes swallow the fetus of the other *in utero*' (177). At another, intertextual level, critics have also explored the ways *Pet Sematary* (typically of King's writing, in which such intertextuality is an 'open secret') reworks and extends a parentage that resides in key texts from the Gothic tradition, like 'The Monkey's Paw' (which is mentioned in King's novel: 226) and Mary Shelley's *Frankenstein* (1818), both canonical Gothic versions of the trope of the return of the dead, and thus key members of a 'family' of narratives sharing that trope. Mary Ferguson Pharr comments that the 'nexus between' King's novel and Shelley's 'occurs in the dream of new life each presents', just as the critical dream of identifying and pursuing familial links and generic resemblances between texts resides in her own use of the word 'nexus' to signify 'connection'.[10]

Critics have focused extensively on exploring the 'connections' between King's writings and the traditions on which they draw. Heidi Strengell's extended reading of King as Gothic writer (her 'tracing' of 'the Gothic line to King') offers no specific attention to the family as theme or trope;[11] but familial tropes (like that of the 'line' of authorial descent) nevertheless insist throughout her text, emphasizing the generic and textual links she explores. So, King is at once 'Like the original Gothic writers in the eighteenth and nineteenth centuries' and 'like most Victorian novelists'; and he 'seems to belong in the category of', while his 'works conform to', and 'can be listed in company with', different aspects of Gothic traditions.[12] Such generic resemblance is also key for Tony Magistrale: 'Like *Rosemary's Baby* and *The Exorcist*, King's world is an easily recognisable one', he argues.[13] Patrick McAleer's recent analysis of King's fiction as an expression of 'Baby-Boomer generation' anxieties and of *Pet Sematary* as an exploration of 'the separation between Creed and Crandall ... as the generational gap' is a further elaboration of these general critical insights.[14] Metaphors of family likeness and resemblance (to a very broadly conceived canon), belonging, and conformity thus structure the major critical responses to King's familial texts, suggesting that critiques of King's writings themselves share familial features, not least their collaborative search for the familial connections that both define King's oeuvre and affiliate it to Gothic literary traditions.

And yet, King's works also resist these affiliations and family resemblances, asserting in crucial ways their differences from these traditions, and from the 'family circle' of Gothic families. In contrast with Fred Botting's assertion that 'There are few families in Gothic fiction', we find hobbled, truncated, abbreviated, distorted or otherwise damaged versions of the family everywhere in King's texts.[15] The family is not absent from these works; instead, it functions as a metaphor, a figure of identity – likeness, kindness – that is relentlessly disfigured, demanding a different kind of reading. *Carrie* offers an incomplete and radically dysfunctional family unit comprising only mother and daughter, the father long since killed off; and later, *Lisey's Story* (2006) redefines the 'family' as simply the bereaved widow of dead writer Scott Landon who, it is revealed, has murdered his own father. *Firestarter* reconfigures this parental incompleteness as a more effectively functional pairing of father and daughter. *'Salem's Lot*, establishing an insistent trope in King's works, draws heavily on the 'crew of light' (and on many other features) of Bram Stoker's *Dracula* (1897) to redefine the various familial structures of conventional small-town America into networks of group interdependency and resistance to a different, monstrous-archaic family formation, that of the victims of 'the Master' vampire Barlow, a version of the primal, all-consuming monstrous Father. *The Shining* (as most critics of the novel have noted) deconstructs the nuclear family by displacing, and then destroying, the father as locus of violently asserted patriarchal power. Later, King experiments with family structures as products resulting from different kinds of effacement: of the potential future in *The Dead Zone* (1979), in which Johnny's relationship with Sarah is interrupted and closed off by his coma, his potential paternity curtailed and erased from the futures he can now predict; of children in the degree-zero parodic 'romance-couple' of *Misery* (1987) (although Paul Sheldon still manages to produce, in his novels, surrogate 'children' – as implied in the title of his putative last romance work, *Misery's Child*);[16] of parents in the child-centred extravaganza of *It* (1986), where the potential motherhood of 'It', in the seeming absence of any father-figure, affirms a strange horror of the maternal and the parental; and of both parents and siblings in the punitive, isolated wilderness endured by Trisha McFarland in *The Girl Who Loved Tom Gordon* (1999). Or, occasionally, the family is presented as a structure of cloying domestic (and apparently autobiographical) bliss, threatened in *The Dark Half* (for example) by the impossible resurrection of a ritually-interred fictional creation, the strangely doubled alter ego of its creator, the writer-father.

In every case, the (ideal, nuclear) family exists (or persists) in King's texts as a trace, a desired but absent structure, effaced yet present (or excessively present, overdetermined, its 'uniqueness' threatened by uncanny doubling), an empty frame deprived of (at least one of) its centre(s). The family as a structure with the father at its head is frequently only a residue, a remainder, a reminder of a unit of social organization perceived, in King's Gothic, to have been eroded beyond repair, yet still desired, postulated as unattainable, or at best perpetually threatened, merely a fragile ideal, relentless different to itself and, at extreme moments, containing within itself the difference that destroys it. Indeed the intimate structural grasp of how families work – as systems of interdependence, co-reliance, mutual inter-definition, as well as structures of repression and suppression, undesired persistence and repetition, and relentless re-enactment – insists throughout King's works, suggesting that the processes of construction of the 'family romance', and its inevitable deconstruction, are recurrent, wholly integral themes in his brand of Gothic.

Magistrale has discussed (and connected to other, American Gothic, traditions) King's representations of 'non-traditional' families, and his construction in their lieu of narratives in which 'the only hope for moral survival is within a small group that sustains its identity against those forces in the world that stand in opposition to it' – that is, in a familiar but disfigured version of the family that replaces the 'traditional' family structure.[17] As noted above, this trope of the group struggling for survival characterizes many of King's works, from *'Salem's Lot* through to *Cell* (2006). More recently, critics like Steven Bruhm have shifted attention away from the problems of establishing connections between King's writings and other Gothic texts, or locating them *within* a family tradition, or identifying familial concerns *within* his texts, towards instead applying theoretical insights into his representations of family structures as ways of accounting for some of the unsettling effects King's writings consistently produce. Bruhm's reading of *The Shining* argues for the novel's construction of 'a place of knowledge that is different from that of the Oedipal spectacle and of the panicked heterosexual father' – a place, that is, outside the conventional family romance that novels like *The Shining* (and, in different ways, *Pet Sematary*) both establish and disfigure, a place in which, for example, the effects of secrecy may be revealed and the abuses of paternal authority challenged.[18] Bruhm notes how, in deconstructing the paternally centred family and exposing its secret tensions, *The Shining* locates the father in a variety of places, including, as the novel's possessed father Jack Torrance batters his own face with a mallet, 'the place of [the] mother'. Through this dislocation, Bruhm reads what he defines as King's 'queer Gothic' as a displacement of the paternal into 'the position of the feminine maternal destroyed by the very mirror other of himself'.[19] But dislocation is also self-destruction, figured in this novel as a form of disfigurement: as Bruhm notes, Jack 'turn[s] his murderous roque mallet upon himself and smash[es] his own face in'.[20] Resisting paternal violence leads, in *The Shining*, to the disfigurement (the 'smashed face') of the father. *The Shining*'s restless troping of face, place and displacement indicates how family structures, far from providing stable, reassuring sites of social agency, afford instead a disturbing, Gothicized mobility in which 'family' itself is not stable and reliable, but fugitive, placeless, figured repeatedly by its own disfigurement.[21] Bruhm is right to locate this disfigurement in the figure of the father; *Pet Sematary*'s analysis of the family, deploying similar disfigurements, (dis)locates the father as a kind of mobile function, a figure always already disfigured by ambiguity (Louis's potential to become 'unfamiliar to his own blood') or by its displacement or replacement by another father-surrogate. Fatherhood is one version of the novel's many displaced centres; the two circular cemeteries might be read as extended metaphors for different kinds of paternal spheres of influence, the beneficent and the demonic. Each is a sign, constantly misread in the novel, for a different kind of fatherhood.

The insistent, violent, Gothic redefinition of the family in King's works can, then, be read as a series of radical disfigurements of its ideologically conventional appearance, centring on a subversion of paternal authority in which fatherhood itself is repeatedly disfigured. Family, as a recurrent and recognizable set of features, of shared qualities, is, in King's works, repeatedly effaced, mobilizing his Gothic explorations of ideological and historical disfigurements related to, affiliated with and yet beyond, excluded from, the family's domestic spaces. Disfigurement here carries the multiple resonances invested in it by Paul de Man's analysis of Shelley's *The Triumph of*

Life, which traces in the poem 'a trajectory from self-knowledge to disfiguration'. Such a trajectory is characteristic also of King's narratives and of *Pet Sematary* in particular, in which Louis's possessed pursuit of 'a different kind of knowledge' is also a version of this 'trajectory', a movement away from 'self-knowledge' into an experience of disfiguration. 'The erasure or effacement is indeed the loss of a face', de Man insists:[22] the disfigured 'face' of the family and of the face of the father at the family's head, we might summarize, is a sign of the family's failure, of its loss of significatory agency in the social and ethical worlds that King's narratives construct. This failure is, in *Pet Sematary*, a product of the disfiguring distortions of paternal 'self-knowledge' (failures of paternal self-recognition and of reading the paternal self's reflections in its doubles and alter egos) that intersect with the novel's exploration of Bruhm's 'different place of knowledge'. This place – figured as the faces of others, as the 'face' (327) of the Micmac burial ground itself) – is also the place in which the otherness contained within the family is revealed, in the forms of Louis's 'different kind' of resurrected pet and, eventually, the 'Gage-thing' (342) that had been his son.

The father's disfigurement, literal and metaphorical, is everywhere in *Pet Sematary*, both a signifier of the violent effacement of social cohesion that results, in King's ideological universe, from the shattering of family structures, and a coded version of the disfigurement of the family itself. The deformation of the family finds expression, for example, in kinds of paternal disfigurement displaced (like the visiting of sin) onto sons. In Jud Crandall's narrative of Timmy Baterman, a historical parable told to Louis the night before his own son's funeral as a warning not to consider attempting to resurrect Gage (a parable from which Louis, of course, fails to learn anything), we read a graphic example of the novel's insistent encounters with the disfigured face of the other. Timmy's body, after he is killed in the War, is returned to Ludlow, where his father secretly re-inters it in the Micmac cemetery. Resurrected, he is found 'staring up at that red, bloody sun as it went down. His whole face was orange with it, like he'd been flayed alive … You could see the red marks across his face, like pimples or little burns' (238–9). Timmy's 'red' face punningly bears the readable inscription of the truth of his own uncanny persistence, a warning text demanding to be read; its warning echoes the novel's insistent prohibitions that go unheeded. It offers an external expression not only of Timmy's corruption, but also of that of his father, who, Jud tells Louis, 'looked like he was dead inside and just waiting for his soul to stink' (234) – that is, he resembles the dead son he has resurrected.

This face of paternal otherness is reflected back to Louis throughout the novel. In the early stages of the schizoid delusions that disfigure his own paternal authority, Louis imagines the consequences for his domestic help, Missy Dandridge, of bringing back his own dead son: '*Can't you see her harrowing her own face with her fingernails?*' (256–7). In the act of killing the thing his son has become, Louis witnesses the mobility of the disfigured face of paternal otherness as he watches its face 'ripple and change …; its was Jud's face, dead and staring; it was the dented, ruined face of Victor Pascow, eyes rolling mindlessly; it was, mirrorlike, Louis's own, so dreadfully pale and lunatic' (359). And, seen by his colleague Steve Masterton carrying Rachel's corpse towards the Micmac burial ground, Louis's own disfigurement is finally revealed: 'Louis's hair had gone white' and his 'face was that of an old, old man' (364). Steve can read in his disfigured face the signs of Louis's insanity (and Jud can read the marks on Timmy's face) in a way that Louis earlier fails to read Jud's 'inscrutable old man's eyes' (124): the ethical failure in the relation between father-figures who are 'friends' and 'neighbours' is indicated in Louis's transformation by disfiguration, at the novel's end, into a version of Jud, his symbolic father.

The relation between Louis and Jud is ambiguous from the novel's first sentence, in which Louis, the father in the Creed family, 'finds' his 'lost' father in his new neighbour (9). The word 'father' is repeated three times in this opening sentence, establishing paternal authority at the novel's head and at the family's, but also locating a putative, symbolic patrilinear line of descent at the narrative's origin, a line into which *Pet Sematary*'s potential historical allegory can be placed. Arriving in New England from Chicago to start his new job, Louis's family enacts a kind of reverse, disfiguring narrative of American origins and displacements nevertheless akin to that of the Founding Fathers, a reversed repetition of the 'founding' of America by the Pilgrim Fathers that involves, not the founding of a nation, but the finding of a father. Finding and founding (and, eventually, foundering) and their relations to paternity thus organize the opening of a novel that is, strangely, replete with fathers, and link the novel in different ways to the American history with which several critics have connected it.[23] Louis and Jud are simply the first and principal occupants of a role shared with Rachel's father Irwin Goldman, who offers a strangely anti-Semitic portrait of malign paternal beneficence; Timmy Bateman's 'daddy' (229) Bill; and, briefly, Victor Pascow's nameless father, who appears only via a reported telephone conversation: 'Louis had spoken to the tearful, mercifully faceless voice of Pascow's father on the telephone; the father had only wanted assurance that Louis had done everything he could' (91). Mr Pascow's 'faceless voice', like his namelessness in the novel (he is just 'Pascow's father'), indicates his performance of a role, a paternal function potentially, but not in this instance, in conflict with the symbolic place (and face) reserved throughout this novel for Louis Creed; Mr Pascow's facelessness contrasts, for example, with the 'dead' look of Bill Bateman. Fatherhood in this novel is a performed role, a symbolic identity like a kind of mask passed from one father to another. Its mobility repeatedly draws attention to the fragility of the family as a structure reliant on the masquerade of paternal authority.

This mobile paternal role is reinforced by the insistent trope of facial resemblance, a version of the family 'likenesses' and 'of-a-kindnesses' that, as discussed earlier, organize *Pet Sematary*. Jud's face, the face of the neighbour, friend and other, and, above all, the face of the symbolic father, becomes, in this reading, the master trope of the novel's concerns with resemblance and family likenesses. Louis's newly white hair and his prematurely aged face at the novel's end resemble those of Jud, just as his possessed son's corpse momentarily wears Jud's face; and Rachel, resisting her father's entreaties not to return to Ludlow in response to Ellie's psychic nightmares, sees her father anew: 'At that moment he looked very old, and it suddenly occurred to Rachel that her father looked like Jud Crandall' (290). Kinship between different personifications of the father is thus established through facial resemblance between father-figures, in which ageing signifies a premature disfigurement of youthful paternity. Fatherhood, in *Pet Sematary*, involves a specific kind of disfigurement of the self, the developing of a facial resemblance to the father figure whose face, at crucial moments, is the location of the novel's deceptions and concealments.

Jud's face is a recurrent image in the text, nearly always under Louis's scrutiny or, more pointedly, its failure. Louis's (mis)readings of Jud's face reflect back onto Louis himself, indices of his own drastic failure of self-knowledge, his movement into disfiguration, and his failure to establish a place of knowledge in which his family can be protected. On the way to bury the cat, Louis 'thought he saw something bright and not completely pleasant in the old man's eyes' (114). Realizing the nature of his debt to Jud after Church's return, Louis 'now saw something in Jud's eyes that told him the old man knew it' (142). And, confessing the extent of his own near-addiction to the Micmac burial ground, Jud's face is first concealed – 'Jud covered his face with his hands' (148) – and then uncovered to reveal 'eyes that seemed incredibly ancient, incredibly haggard' (148). Jud's 'ancient' features connect him to the burial ground itself, which, he tells Louis, 'is old' (121). His face constitutes the obscured, encrypted or otherwise disfigured face – a kind of monstrous warning, connecting him to another of *Pet Sematary*'s key tropes, that of the face of the monster – that Louis must learn to interpret in order to understand his own relation to the power of the Micmac burial ground, a relation he fails to regulate just as he fails, inevitably, to read Jud's face.[24] This failure to read is, of course, a failure of self-recognition and of recognition of the potential different place of knowledge, and results in Louis's own disfigurement, as he comes inevitably to resemble Jud, Irwin Goldman, and the burial ground itself.

Amid all these real and surrogate, similarly disfigured and defaced fathers, a notable absence from King's novel is a real, extra-familial figure of authority, a sign of paternity's expression at the social, rather than familial, level. *Pet Sematary* provides no equivalent to paternal police officer Alan Pangborn (of *The Dark Half* [1989] and *Needful Things* [1991]), or to authorities and agencies like the governmental White Commission in *Carrie* or the military forces that arrive to help resolve the alien invasion at the end of *The Tommyknockers* (1988). The police officers who question Louis at the end of the novel are ciphers, easily diverted from his disfigurements by his 'hat' and 'gardening gloves' (368). The novel's one effective external figure of authority can be found in Jud's narrative of Timmy Baterman – a War Department lieutenant whose job it was 'to sort out malicious mischief from plain old tomfoolery' (237). In a final telling encryption of this novel's extensive concern with the uncanny structures of Gothic kinship, the name of this figure of authority is Kinsman.

Notes

1. Stephen King, *Pet Sematary*, p. 15. Subsequent page numbers are cited parenthetically in the text.
2. Hélène Cixous, 'Fiction and its phantoms', 525–48.
3. See John Sears, *Stephen King's Gothic*, pp. 1–27.
4. Nicholas Royle, *The Uncanny*, p. 16.
5. Jodey Castricano, *Cryptomimesis*, p. 66.
6. Mary F. Pharr, 'A dream of new life', p. 119.
7. Slavoj Žižek, *Looking Awry*, p. 26.
8. Stephen Edwin King papers, box 1014: *The Pet Sematary*.
9. Tony Magistrale, *Landscape of Fear*, p. 75.
10. Pharr, 'A dream of new life', p. 116.
11. Heidi Strengell, *Stephen King*, p. 103.
12. Ibid., pp. 30, 104.
13. Magistrale, *Landscape of Fear*, p. 15.
14. Patrick McAleer, '"I have the whole world in my hands … now what?"', 1218.
15. Fred Botting, *Limits of Horror*, p. 33.
16. Stephen King, *Misery*.
17. Magistrale, *Landscape of Fear*, p. 105.
18. Steven Bruhm, 'Picture This: Stephen King's Queer Gothic', p. 276.
19. Ibid., pp. 272–3.
20. Ibid., p. 272.
21. See Sears, *Stephen King's Gothic*, pp. 156–81.
22. Paul de Man, 'Shelley disfigured', p. 46.
23. See Jodey Castricano, *Cryptomimesis*; Kevin Corstorphine, '"Sour ground": Stephen King's *Pet Sematary* and the politics of territory'; and Rebecca Janicker, 'The horrors of Maine: space, place and regionalism in Stephen King's *Pet Sematary*'.
24. See Sears, *Stephen King's Gothic*, pp. 182–208.

References

Botting, Fred, *Limits of Horror: Technology, Bodies, Gothic* (Manchester: Manchester University Press, 2008).

Bruhm, Steven, 'Picture this: Stephen King's queer Gothic', in David Punter (ed.), *A Companion to the Gothic* (Oxford: Blackwell, 2000), pp. 269–80.

Castricano, Jodey, *Cryptomimesis: The Gothic and Jacques Derrida's Ghost Writing* (Montreal/Kingston: McGill/Queen's University Press, 2002).

Cixous, Hélène, 'Fiction and its phantoms: a reading of Freud's *Das*

Unheimliche (The Uncanny)', *New Literary History*, 7:3 (Spring 1976), 525–48.

Corstorphine, Kevin, '"Sour ground": Stephen King's *Pet Sematary* and the politics of territory', *Irish Journal of Gothic and Horror Studies*, 1 (October 2006). At http://irishgothichorrorjournal.homestead.com/kevin.html (Accessed 30 December 2011).

De Man, Paul, 'Shelley disfigured', in Harold Bloom (ed.), *Deconstruction & Criticism* (London: Routledge & Kegan Paul, 1979), pp. 39–74.

Janicker, Rebecca, 'The horrors of Maine: space, place and regionalism in Stephen King's *Pet Sematary*', *U.S. Studies Online*, 11 (Autumn 2007). At http://www.baas.ac.uk/index.php?option=com_content&view=article&id=157%3Aissue-11-autumn-2007-article-2&catid=15&Itemid=11 (Accessed 30 December 2011).

King, Stephen, *Pet Sematary* (London: Hodder & Stoughton/Book Club Associates, 1984).

——, *Misery* (London: Hodder & Stoughton/Book Club Associates, 1988).

——, Stephen Edwin King papers, box 1014: *The Pet Sematary*. Special Collections at the Raymond H. Fogler Library, University of Maine at Orono.

McAleer, Patrick, '"I have the whole world in my hands … now what?": power, control, responsibility, and the baby boomers in Stephen King's fiction', *Journal of Popular Culture*, 44:6 (December 2011), 1209–27.

Magistrale, Tony, *Landscape of Fear: Stephen King's American Gothic* (Madison, WI: Bowling Green State University Press, 1988).

Pharr, Mary F. 'A dream of new life: Stephen King's *Pet Sematary* as a variant of *Frankenstein*', in Gary Hoppenstand and Ray B. Browne (eds), *The Gothic World of Stephen King: Landscape of Nightmares* (Madison, WI: Bowling Green State University Press, 1987), pp. 115–25.

Royle, Nicholas, *The Uncanny* (Manchester: Manchester University Press, 2003).

Sears, John, *Stephen King's Gothic* (Cardiff: University of Wales Press, 2011).

Strengell, Heidi, *Stephen King: Monsters Live in Ordinary People* (London: Gerald Duckworth & Co., 2007).

Žižek, Slavoj, *Looking Awry: An Introduction to Jacques Lacan through Popular Culture* (Cambridge, MA: MIT Press, 1992).

7
Sisterhood is monstrous: Gothic imagery in Dutch feminist fiction

Agnes Andeweg

How do feminists deal with monsters? The feminine as monstrous has become a familiar object of analysis ever since second-wave feminism. Feminists have explored 'the technology of monsters', to use a phrase coined by Judith Halberstam, in various ways. Some have posited that the monstrous-feminine has subversive qualities, while others have claimed it confirms the status quo. Either the monster functions in a feminist revision of hegemonic gender constructions, or the monstrous outsider is a necessity to define the insider.[1] Although its political potential is disputed, one thing about the monster is clear: it is a marker of difference. As Kim Toffoletti notes, feminists have noticed 'that difference, deviance and monstrosity are often conflated',[2] while Rosi Braidotti jokes that the monstrous body is an 'indicator of the register of difference, which is why the monster has never been able to avoid a blind date with women'.[3] Braidotti makes clear, however, that the conflation of different differences (into ethnicized, gendered, extra-terrestrial and/or technological monstrosity) only happens when seen from the perspective of the masculine, white, heterosexist norm: 'Only in His Gaze are [...] respective differences flattened out in a generalized category of 'difference'.[4] Braidotti calls into question this idea of the monster as a screen onto which negative qualities are projected, and instead proposes a feminist revaluation of the monster by reading difference positively. Her reading of the monstrous-feminine stresses the aspect of becoming, the expression of emerging (female) subjectivities. The monster's liminality and inherent ambiguity feature in Braidotti's argument, yet it is *difference* that receives most attention in her analysis.

In this chapter I will discuss *Het perpetuum mobile van de liefde (The Perpetual Motion Machine of Love*, 1988), a novel by Renate Dorrestein, in which Gothic monstrosity is perceived from a feminist subject-position, but turns against feminism itself.[5] Renate Dorrestein is known as the queen of Dutch Gothic. Her work comprises more than twenty novels, many of which have been translated into a dozen or more foreign languages. Several of her novels have been adapted for the screen. *Heart of Stone*, the English translation of *Een hart van steen* (1998), was well received in the USA. In the 1980s, Dorrestein became a renowned feminist in the Netherlands, famous for her sharp-witted columns in the feminist magazine *Opzij* (Move Over). In 1986 she co-founded the Anna Bijns Prize, a literary award for 'the female voice in Dutch literature'.

Dorrestein's *Perpetual Motion* is an intriguing mix of Gothic fiction, feminist pamphlet and autobiography. Clearly autobiographical episodes about Dorrestein and her sister are interspersed with raging feminist monologues and fictional, surreal passages featuring larger-than-life characters like Godelieve Ochtendster (which translates as 'God's love Morningstar'). *Perpetual Motion* gives a hilarious yet tragic account of Dorrestein's painful struggle to become a writer. Before she can claim her work as her own, Renate – the narrator and Dorrestein's fictional self – must liberate herself from the vampire shadow of her deceased sister and various other monstrous women in her environment.[6]

Perpetual Motion shifts attention from the monster as a sign of *difference* to the monster as a threat because of its *resemblance* between Self and Other. I will argue that it is sameness rather than difference that is the source of Gothic monstrosity in *Perpetual Motion*. This can be seen in Renate's relationship both to her dead sister, who casts her vampire shadow over Renate's work, and to the fictional character of the feminist Godelieve, whom Renate calls her 'Frankenstein'. In both relationships, with her biological and her metaphorical sister, the monstrous body is the site of struggle. I will show that it is precisely the kinship between Renate and her Others – i.e., the sisterly relationship defined by a shared identity – that constitutes the monstrosity in these Others.

Perpetual Motion depicts (feminist) sisterhood as monstrous and artistic failure as liberating. In order to explain how the novel achieves these two outcomes – quite paradoxical for a feminist whose ambition is to be a writer – I will examine links between second-wave feminist discourse and Gothic narrative strategies, taking my inspiration from Nancy Armstrong's observations on these connections in her *How Novels Think* (2005). Armstrong argues that the Gothic, a natural habitat for monsters, is a cultural narrative eminently equipped for dealing with transgressions and ambivalence, especially with regard to the nuclear family. I will argue that Dorrestein explores the feminist notion of sisterhood through both the autobiographical narrative about her sister's suicide and the fictional story of Godelieve, revealing the ambivalences that constitute (second-wave) feminism. By using the Gothic, Dorrestein finds modes to express the unspeakable rivalry and competition between sisters – including sisters in the feminist sense.

Perpetual Motion is a hybrid novel, if indeed it can even be called a novel. It has been called a 'fictional autobiography' by Maaike Meijer (1993), which she characterizes as a literary, politicized life narrative of the type that abounds in second-wave feminism, the most famous of which are probably Lisa Alther's *Kinflicks* (1976), Erica Jong's *Fear of Flying* (1973), and Marilyn French's *The Women's Room* (1977). International examples include Verena Stefan's *Häutungen* (Germany, 1975), Marie Cardinal's *Les Mots pour le Dire* (France, 1976), and Anja Meulenbelt's *The Shame is Over* (The Netherlands, 1976). It is fair to say that these fictional autobiographies constituted the genre that exemplified second-wave feminism by both representing the confessional gesture and describing the process of consciousness-raising, thereby inviting readers to identify and liberate themselves. Despite the ambivalences these feminist novels sometimes voice, they read like liberation narratives. As feminine *Bildung* narratives describing the long road towards self-discovery and self-realization they are usually written in a realist mode.[7]

Dorrestein's *Perpetual Motion* was written about a decade later than the novels just mentioned and to a certain extent follows the feminist liberation genre, but also departs from it in significant ways. Like its feminist predecessors, *Perpetual Motion* has an autobiographical narrative strand. Narrator Renate recounts her sister's suicide at the age of 20, when Renate was 27. Her sister, who suffered from anorexia and bulimia, received psychiatric treatment and was even admitted to a psychiatric ward. Despite the medical attention, she took her own life by jumping off a tower block. Like Renate, the sister had wanted to be a writer, as Renate's recollections of her youth and later life reveal. In the autobiographical parts of the novel, Renate mourns the loss of her sister and tries to understand why she chose to end her life. She also tries to deal with her own feelings of guilt, both as a survivor and as an established writer. At the same time, the autobiographical narrative covers the process of writing and the reception of the narrator's previous four Gothic novels. While the first two novels were received fairly well, the third met with criticism. In her story, Renate tries to come to terms with this unexpected blow.

Perpetual Motion is not only an autobiographical account; it is also a feminist pamphlet. Renate rages against what she calls the 'perpetual motion machine of love'.[8] By this she means the regime that keeps women in their subordinated place, as 'minders and feeders'[9] of men and children, which imprisons them in the nuclear family and denies them a life of their own. The perpetual motion machine of love equals the ideology of romantic love, which according to Renate is usually followed by familial love. Needless to say, she is very suspicious of both. Her sister seems to be the ultimate victim of the ideology of romantic love. As a bulimia patient she was the victim of the beauty ideal imposed upon women, yet her death is not ascribed entirely to this patriarchal form of oppression as Annelies van Heijst has argued.[10]

These first two narrative strands are in line with the genre of feminist life narratives in the sense that they are non-fictional and explicitly political accounts of women's quest for autonomy. Renate's rejection of any form of dependence on men or family is reminiscent of the radical feminist slogan 'don't sleep with your oppressor' which gave rise to political lesbianism in the 1970s. Fifteen years after the heyday of consciousness-raising groups and feminist separatism, Renate does not advocate such radical steps. She is ambivalent about the path to women's liberation that many 1970s novels propose, that of sharing experiences with other women and joining the women's movement. Renate has to find her own answers to the questions of how to be connected and how to be independent (and from whom).

In addition to the autobiographical and feminist strands, the novel also contains clearly fictional elements. The two narrative strands are interwoven with absurd allegorical stories about two female characters who fall prey to the perpetual motion machine of love. The characters also serve to embody and magnify some of the narrator's sister's characteristics. The first one is Mad Lydia, Renate's neighbour who is desperately looking for love. Lydia is so eager to please a man that she goes mad. He wants an 'airhead', so in order to please him Lydia is willing to 'lose her mind'. She ends up on a psychiatric ward. While Lydia loses her mind, the second fictional character literally loses her face. This is Godelieve Ochtendster, whose story is most interesting in the context of this chapter.

Godelieve is described as 'the World's Ugliest Woman', a judgement shared even by her parents in her childhood. Thanks to her homely looks, she is rather unaffected by the perpetual motion machine of love; men are simply not interested in her, so she is free. This changes when her employer – a notary for whom she works as a secretary – decides she has to project a more presentable image and forces her to undergo cosmetic surgery, after which she embodies the Ideal Woman. However, she is deeply uncomfortable with her new looks; she runs away and starts working as a transvestite at a nightclub, where 'she pretends to be a man pretending to be a woman'[11] (121). Godelieve is the star of the show until her former employer, who is in the audience, 'unmasks' her as a woman. He accuses Godelieve of fraud ('that woman was a woman!'[12]) and she is kicked out of the club. When Renate, the narrator and feminist journalist, hears about the case, she writes a searing article about the injustice done to Godelieve, who is pilloried for being a real woman. The article causes an uproar; in the end Godelieve is rehabilitated and embraced by the public as their darling feminist. And this is where matters take a Gothic turn.

By publicizing the unfair treatment Godelieve suffers, Renate is responsible for her emergence as a martyr and a feminist. Godelieve acknowledges Renate's role as her creator when she says 'You opened my eyes'[13] (152). But Renate despises her creation: 'Godelieve Ochtendster was my Frankenstein, and I forcibly suppressed any thought of her'[14] (96). The narrator's antipathy is caused by the public support Godelieve receives, the very support Renate herself lacks. While Renate's own feminist views constantly meet with resistance, Godelieve enjoys the image of the Ideal Feminist in the public's perception. And while Renate's opponents cry 'Off with her head, off with her head!'[15] (100), just like the Queen of Hearts in *Alice in Wonderland*, Godelieve is revered by both men and feminists. She, so people say, has made feminism 'respectable'. When she is given a warm welcome by a feminist splinter group called the Johannas, Renate feels betrayed.

Godelieve embodies two different types of monstrosity. Seen from the hegemonic perspective, she was a monstrous woman when she was a misfit because she did not conform to the perpetual motion machine of love. In Renate's view, however, Godelieve only became monstrous after she was turned into a feminist. With a body that after plastic surgery suddenly fits the beauty ideal all too well, and accepted as a feminist by the general public, Godelieve is too close for comfort to Renate.

The second Gothic moment in *Perpetual Motion* occurs when Renate describes the relationship between herself and her dead sister as vampiric. Increasingly tormented by feelings of guilt about her sister's death, Renate senses that she is beginning to transform into a vampire at night. She feels a diabolical agitation and her teeth and jaws hurt as if something is cutting through them: 'my jaws were alight with thunder and lightning like in a horror movie'[16] (88). Her fingers are 'bent, clawed around the pen'[17] (87), and when, after a night of hellish toothaches, she bites her lip, a trickle of blood runs down her neck. When she looks at her dead sister's picture on her desk, it literally feels as if Renate can suck the inspiration out of her, and her head 'presses against the head of my dead sister, like the teeth of a vampire sink into a white neck, irresistibly attracted by the content: the missing half of my talent. I suck with such vigour!'[18] (109) Feeding on her dead sister, keeping her undead, does not give Renate peace of mind. She is tormented by a mad frenzy. This changes only after seeing a Dr Stephen Kaplan from New York, 'head of the world's only Vampire Research Centre' on TV, and addressing him in her mind in a therapeutic monologue. At that point she finally manages to get rid of her sense of being a vampire.[19]

There is a link between the two appearances of female monstrosity in this novel, between Godelieve as Renate's Frankenstein, and Renate as a vampire in relation to her sister. Although both monsters are female, it is not their femininity that makes them monstrous – after all Renate is a woman herself. Nancy Armstrong's *How Novels Think* (2005), which locates the Gothic novel's cultural work in establishing kinship relations, provides a way of understanding the monstrous relationships between these female characters.

Armstrong reads the history of the novel in terms of the relationship between the modern individual and society. In fact, she equates the two: 'The history of the novel and the history of the modern subject are, quite literally, one and the same'.[20] She attributes to the genre of the novel a mediating role in the central tension of liberalism: how striving for maximum individual freedom always runs up against the limits of what the community can allow. Novels attempt to channel that tension productively: 'The novel ... was born as authors gave narrative form to this wish for a social order sufficiently elastic to accommodate individualism'.[21] Armstrong analyses the novel's ways of narrating how the social order incorporates the protagonist's 'individualistic energy'.[22] Does society manage to include 'deviant' individuals? In other words, does it become more inclusive or does it force these individuals to conform? Armstrong argues that while eighteenth-century protagonists managed to both realize themselves as individuals and stretch the social order, the Victorian novel took a conservative turn. In the Victorian novel, protagonists learn that they must accept reality and reconcile themselves to social inequality and the impossibility of true change. Instead of having society become more flexible and inclusive, the Victorian novel expects the protagonist to have 'a change of heart'.[23] This shift from utopianism to realism makes the Victorian novel essentially a conservative genre, Armstrong argues. The nuclear family becomes the model for society as a whole; crudely put, society is built on expanding the number of nuclear families and allowing more and more new citizens to be born. There is a growing intolerance for individuals who deviate from that norm.

Armstrong is disappointed in the novel, because the genre did not achieve its utopian potential of representing a society which is increasingly inclusive. Here, Armstrong draws a surprising parallel with strategies employed by second-wave feminist literary academics. They, too, strove to widen the social order (to include women), but failed to transcend the liberal paradox of increasing individualistic expression within an ever more inclusive community. Surprisingly enough, Armstrong blames this on the fact that feminist literary scholars put too much emphasis on women authors and their protagonists acquiring a voice of their own:

> This move convinced a generation of readers that acquiring a voice – access to print, or what might be called cultural agency – could

compensate for the forms of property that traditionally authorized the rights-bearing citizen.[24]

Rhetorical power (of the character, or of the author) was expected to compensate for the lack of political and economic power/authority. In this strategy, literature served as a model for a utopian struggle in reality. There, too, it sometimes seemed that claiming one's own voice was the most important goal.

Armstrong's ideas are relevant when analysing Dorrestein's Gothic novel. Dorrestein operates on the edge between feminism and the Gothic, both of which Armstrong links to an unrealized utopia. Additionally, the voice of women is an explicit theme in *Perpetual Motion*. Armstrong blames feminists for having made the 'madwoman in the attic' the symbol of their own (suppressed) position as women and scholars. This madwoman, the Gothic monster, is an individual that society cannot accommodate. She represents the rage of every woman trapped in a masculine culture; this is how the madwoman became the female voice par excellence. This 'politics of difference', based on emphasizing gender difference, had certain risks, of which feminists began feeling the disadvantages in the early 1980s. By using the exclusion of women (the lack of economic and political power) symbolized by the madwoman as a source of rhetorical power ('the female voice'), power itself became tainted.

While feminists such as Ellen Moers (1978) read the Gothic as a 'female voice' in literature, Armstrong introduces a more inclusive reading. Rather than emphasizing the 'madwoman', she focuses on the utopian potential of the Gothic in a fascinating chapter on Bram Stoker's *Dracula*. Armstrong sees something utopian in the radically inclusive way in which social links are established in *Dracula*. For vampires (Dracula and his victims), collective desire and individual desire are one and the same. When you become one, you become them all, so there is no conflict between individualistic energy and collective interest. Vampires represent a different mode of reproduction: not by creating a family, but by including new vampires. The vampire marks the end of individualism, of individual desire.

The novel now ceases to function as a way to protect the community against excessive individualism. The vampire creates a radically inclusive community that eradicates the gender differences naturalized by the nuclear family. The Gothic renders the nuclear family and the liberal, autonomous individual obsolete. In other words, Armstrong sees the Gothic as a possible alternative to the ideology of modern individualism and to the logic of the 'natural' nuclear family as a model for society. The Gothic subverts that logic by imagining alternative forms of kinship.

Keeping Armstrong in mind, it is clear that Dorrestein's *Perpetual Motion* is all about the tension between 'individualistic energy' and the (in)flexibility of the collective. Every character is driven by the struggle for individual autonomy: Renate's sister, unattractive Godelieve, mad Lydia and Renate herself. All but Renate fail in their struggle. Their individual desire and agency are crushed by the perpetual motion machine of love, the collective norm. Renate's sister commits suicide, Godelieve is first forced to have plastic surgery and is then incorporated into the feminist collective, and Lydia goes mad. Only Renate, the narrator, survives thanks to her voice as a writer and feminist: '[I] have a voice ... that let me escape from the obligation to be seen but never heard, a voice that enabled me to escape the fate of my body ...'[25] (144). Her voice is what has enabled Renate to resist the perpetual motion machine of love, to claim agency and an autonomous position in society. By stressing the importance of her voice, she runs the risk of identifying with the 'female voice', a danger she is well aware of. Renate feels that speaking as a woman and showing solidarity with other women is suspect because the female voice is all too easily categorized as a madwoman's voice. In *Perpetual Motion*, that makes sisterhood sinister.

The slogan 'sisterhood is powerful' gained currency during second-wave feminism. *Sisterhood is Powerful* was the title of a popular anthology of the women's liberation movement.[26] 'Sisterhood' functioned as the shorthand term for the idea or the ideal of solidarity among women. Defining the relationship between women as one of kinship evoked a metaphorical family. In the late 1960s and early 1970s, consciousness-raising groups served to solidify this idea. Women telling each other their life stories created the sense of a shared experience. Rooted in personal life, a collective was formed and political aims were formulated. The concept of 'women's voice' was instrumental in this. By speaking up and using their voice, women made themselves heard. The key importance of 'voice' is evident in the numerous books from that period that include the phrase 'women's voice' (or some variation on it) in their title.[27]

In the 1960s and 1970s, women's personal narratives were seen as a means to expand the collective of women, achieve a more inclusive society and support women in their self-expression. But the women's movement soon fell victim to Armstrong's paradox of liberal society as well. An inevitable tension surfaced between maximizing individual expression and strengthening the collective. For whom could 'the female voice' speak? The metaphor of sisterhood stressed the similarities between women but was soon criticized, by black feminists for instance, for masking the differences between them.[28]

In *Perpetual Motion*, Dorrestein's narrator not only fulminates against (male) society, which is governed by the ideology of romantic and familial love, but also against a collective of feminist women called 'the Johannas'. To her dismay, Renate sees that Godelieve is welcomed by and included in the Johannas, '... one of the many obscure sects in the women's movement. This society, which seemed to consist of women who were invariably called Johanna, kept itself busy revaluating feminine values'[29] (134). Although Renate agrees that the female contribution to history and culture has always been underestimated, she does not see the point in the Johannas' strategy of singing the praises of feminine qualities: 'they confirmed ... the old lie that always made both sexes toe the line: that men and women are different, each other's complementary halves, each with their own duty' (135). Renate's summary of the Johannas' activities is laced with sarcasm: 'I always regarded them as a bunch of scatterbrains, with their afternoons of origami-for-peace, their seaweed tampons and their deep insights in yin, yang and Jung. The menstrual dance! The homemade wheat bread! Communication with the womb! That's sure to bring about change!'[30] (135)

The Johannas is a feminist collective ruled by the idea of female solidarity. They form an alternative to patriarchal society that is ruled by the perpetual motion machine of love. The Johannas consider Godelieve their martyr, and she basks in their attention. Renate realizes she is so angry with the Johannas because they have proclaimed Godelieve their feminist figurehead, while she was Renate's feminist heroine too: 'I had recognized ... my own issues in Godelieve's history'[31] (136).

The Johannas are a collective with no room for individual differences. They are always referred to in the plural and they all look identical. This collective of sisters all share the conviction that 'the gentle powers' will conquer. They work like vampires. Godelieve is literally 'annexed' (134) when she joins them. Her appearance changes. 'She [started wearing] her hair parted in the middle, Johanna-style, and dressed in the uniform of the sect ...'[32] (137). These Johannas can be read as a vampiric collective. They reproduce, not by means of nuclear families, but by annexation, and all members of the collective become identical beings with identical desires.

Renate's relationship with her sister is also vampiric. The two of them form the smallest thinkable collective, but they are indistinguishable as individuals. Renate speaks in terms of 'we' when she describes how she and her sister used to tell each other stories when they were young, dreaming of a future as writers. Even when Renate accompanies her sister to the bulimia treatment centre, she speaks of 'we': 'We get out. We gather courage. We start putting one leg in front of the other. We do not flee. We go inside'[33] (72–3). In this particular instance, the use of 'we' may sound absurd, but Renate cannot imagine how a psychiatrist would have been able to see the difference between them.

These sisterhoods – Renate and her sister, and the Johannas – signify a new reproductive strategy analogous to Armstrong's alternative to the ideology of romantic love: 'just like the vampire itself, her victim will also be so-called undead, and therefore in perpetual motion ... The vampire not only takes her prey's life, she also steals her victim's death; she prevents her from finding eternal, undisturbed peace'[34] (104). The concept of the perpetual motion machine pivotal to the novel acquires a different meaning here. The vampire collective forms an alternative to the machine of romantic love. The vampire's victim becomes part of the collective, just as Armstrong read in *Dracula*, 'and therefore in perpetual motion'. The perpetual motion machine of love is aimed at reproducing the social order by creating new families, or, as Renate sarcastically puts it, with a 'crowning of your love'. Renate resists that 'crowning': she dumps her lover the moment he expresses the wish for a child. The vampire-like perpetual motion machine is an alternative means of creating a community. But however strong Renate's aversion is to the nuclear family, the Johanna collective evokes just as much loathing in her. The vampiric community springs from an evil act, and 'the curse of this evil deed is that it will continue to bear evil'[35] (104); it prevents the dead from resting in peace. And this is what leaves Renate feeling possessed. While Armstrong sees the utopian potential of the community of vampires, in *Perpetual Motion* things work out quite the opposite.

The night when Renate thinks she is a vampire marks the moment that she acknowledges her feelings of guilt about her sister's death. Until then, she had denied feeling any guilt at all, 'because if I, I, I was not capable [of saving her sister, AA], then no one could have'[36] (106). In other words, her sister's death was unavoidable and her guilt irrelevant. Renate's feelings consist not only of 'standard survivor's guilt', or guilt over the fact that she was the one to admit her sister to a psychiatric hospital. Because of her success as a writer Renate is possessed by the thought that she has benefited from her sister's death and is living off her talent: 'And this is the crown on my guilty conscience: I'm not just whispering to my sister night after night for nothing ... What I am really doing, is keeping her awake ... As long as my blood-thirst for recognition has not been quenched, she may not rest. I keep her undead'[37] (109). Renate realizes that her writerly voice is 'the same voice, to come to the point, that my sister had wanted to have one day'[38] (144), because her sister had wanted to be a writer as well. Renate feels guilty because sharing her voice with her deceased sister feels as if she has in fact appropriated her sister's voice, or is tapping her sister's talent to fulfil her own ambitions.

The vampiric relationship between Renate and her sister, where Renate has trouble discerning her own motives, her own voice, can be read as an allegory of feminist sisterhood. For Renate, this sisterhood has none of the utopian qualities Armstrong attributes to it. Renate is glad to get past her vampiric episode, just as she is happy to escape the sisterhood as conceptualized by the Johannas. Renate has difficulty maintaining her independence in relation to the Johannas, just as she had trouble distinguishing her individual self from her sister's. She has to acknowledge that her attempts to save her sister (and her neighbour Lydia) spring from a sense of superiority she also feels towards the Johannas. She has behaved as a 'minder and feeder', as a saviour: '[I]n all earnestness I considered myself capable of preventing death and madness, and like a megalomaniac, I held myself responsible when life decided differently'[39] (153). In other words, she has behaved like a Johanna:

What was I but a housewife wanting to believe that without her eternal mopping and tidying up, everything would go awry ... In what sense did I differ from the Johannas, I who had turned my own frustrated powerlessness, my inability, my *wish* to influence and to bring about, into an indispensable tool for someone else's salvation or doom? Chalk up a point for the Johannas![40] (154)

Renate realizes she was driven by the same sense of female superiority as the Johannas. She felt she could save her sister, just like they believed they could save the world. She is unable to distinguish her own effort from that practised by the Johannas, despite her aversion to them. She unwittingly behaved like a Johanna – as if she had become a part of the feminist collective. She became a victim of Johanna thinking, as if she had been bitten by the vampire.

The moment Renate acknowledges that she is thinking like a Johanna, she can finally let go of her sister. She can reclaim her individuality when she realizes she never had the power to save her sibling: 'But perhaps, if I can see both of us as separate individuals, without any power over each other's fate; if I dare to let myself be separate from her, then maybe I no longer have to push her away like a demon, or pull her in like prey ...'[41] (155–6).

Only after the bad reception of her third novel can Renate acknowledge that this book is really her own work: 'my sister would definitely not have wanted to write a book which was run into the ground in a way that cuts through the soul'[42] (p. 144). If the book is this bad, it has to be her own work. This realization restores her sense of authorship and agency. The unfavourable reception of her novel is crucial to her sense of individuality. While at the beginning of *Perpetual Motion*, she writes: 'I am a writer, I have the power to rewrite the usual script'[43] (37), at the end of the book it is liberating for Renate to realize that her power as a writer is limited. Paradoxically, she is confirmed in her authorship when she fails as a writer. When she loses, she can finally abandon her authorship competition with her sister. Ironically, individuality is confirmed by a failure of voice. The voice is what matters to Dorrestein – her woman's voice, her feminist voice, but ultimately: her own.

Nancy Armstrong shows how the novel as a genre mediates in the conflicts between the modern individual and the collective social order. Dorrestein adds an extra collective layer to this individual-versus-collective model: the collective of sisters; both feminist and familial. In a sisterhood, it is hard for an individual to find her own voice and it is difficult to break away from the community. This is true of sisterhood both in a familial sense and in a feminist context. In both cases, Renate's struggle to break free is a struggle *contre coeur*. She thereby reveals the deep ambivalence that forms the foundation of second-wave feminism: on the one hand, 'we women' – the alternative collective – was a great mobilizing force for realizing societal reforms. On the other hand, feminist sisterhood calls up new conflicts between individual and collective, as history shows. In *Perpetual Motion*, the Gothic does not offer a wide view on a new type of collective, as Armstrong would have it. The Gothic turns against the community of women itself. In *Perpetual Motion*, the Gothic is a cultural strategy to represent Renate's struggle for autonomy. The most threatening monster is the monster that most resembles the Self, that is most akin. This Other is the sister: the vampiric community of sisters forms a threat to the female individual. Renate cannot regard 'her' monsters positively because she cannot see them for what they are: different from herself. Only when Renate acknowledges her sister as a separate, different being does she manage to find her uniqueness as a writer.

Notes

1. Key publications in the field of monsters, feminism and the feminine include Julia Kristeva, *Powers of Horror* (1982); Bram Dijkstra, *Idols of Perversity* (1986) and *Evil Sisters* (1996); Barbara Creed, *The Monstrous-Feminine* (1993); Judith Halberstam, *Skin Shows* (1995); Margrit Shildrick, *Embodying the Monster: Encounters with the Vulnerable Self* (2002); Rosi Braidotti, *Metamorphoses* (2002). Kim Toffoletti's *Feminism, Popular Culture and the Posthuman Body* (2007) provides a useful overview. I'd like to thank Louis van den Hengel for his valuable advice on monster theory.
2. Kim Toffoletti, *Feminism, Popular Culture*, p. 94.
3. Rosi Braidotti, *Metamorphoses*, p. 191.
4. Ibid., p. 197.
5. Henceforth referred to as *Perpetual Motion*. Unfortunately, this novel has not yet been translated into English. Translations of quotations are my own. Page numbers refer to the Dutch edition *Het perpetuum mobile van de liefde* (1988; Amsterdam: Contact, 2002). Subsequent page numbers are cited parenthetically in the text.
6. Although the first-person narrator Renate resembles the author Renate Dorrestein, I want to maintain the distinction between narrator and

author, because *Perpetual Motion* clearly contains fictional elements. Therefore, I use 'Dorrestein' to refer to the author, and 'Renate' when writing about the novel's narrator.
7 For a discussion of American examples, see Jane Gerhard, *Desiring Revolution*, Chapter 4.
8 'het perpetuum mobile van de liehiefde'. Dorrestein consequently writes 'liehiefde' instead of 'liefde', the Dutch word for love; thus giving it a melodramatic or even exalted character.
9 'hoedsters en voedsters'.
10 Van Heijst, *Leesbaar lichaam*.
11 'waar zij net deed alsof ze een man was die net deed alsof hij een vrouw was'.
12 'die vrouw was een vrouw!'
13 'Jij hebt me de ogen geopend.'
14 'Godelieve Ochtendster was mijn monster van Frankenstein, en met kracht verdrong ik elke gedachte aan haar.'
15 'Haar kop eraf, haar kop eraf!'
16 'Het donderde en bliksemde in mijn gebit als in een griezelfilm'.
17 'De vingers om de pen gekromd, geklauwd'.
18 'maar het andere deel drukt zich tegen het dode hoofd van mijn zusje, zoals de tanden van een vampier in een blanke hals glijden, onweerstaanbaar word ik aangetrokken door de inhoud: de ontbrekende helft van mijn talent. Hoe ik zuig!'
19 As it happens, a Stephen Kaplan has published two hard-to-find books on the subject: *In Pursuit of Premature Gods and Contemporary Vampires* (Long Island, New York: Vampire Research Centre, 1976) and *Vampires Are* (ETCC publications, 1984).
20 Nancy Armstrong, *How Novels Think*, p. 3.
21 Ibid., p. 139.
22 Ibid., p. 39.
23 Ibid., p. 142.
24 Ibid., p. 140.
25 '[I]k [bezit] een stem ... die mij heeft doen ontkomen aan de opdracht alleen maar gezien en nooit gehoord te worden, een stem die het mij mogelijk heeft gemaakt te ontsnappen aan het lot van mijn lichaam ...'
26 Robin Morgan, *Sisterhood is Powerful*.
27 Two well-known examples are Carol Gilligan's *In a Different Voice* (1982) and Claire Kahane's *Passions of the voice* (1995).
28 See Carby, 'White Women Listen!'
29 '... een van de obscure sekten waaraan de vrouwenbeweging rijk is. Dit gezelschap, dat leek te bestaan uit vrouwen die altijd allemaal Johanna heetten, hield zich bezig met het opwaarderen van vrouwelijke waarden.'

30 'Ik bezag ze altijd als een troepje warhoofden, met hun middagjes kraanvogels-vouwen-voor-de-vrede, hun van zeewier gevlochten tampons en hun diepe inzichten in yin, yang en Jung. De menstruatiedans! De zelfgebakken tarwebol! Het communiceren met de baarmoeder! Bracht me dat even schot in de zaak!'
31 'ik had in Godelieves geschiedenis ... mijn eigen speerpunten herkend'.
32 'Zij droeg haar haren nu in gordijntjes, in Johanna-trant, en ging gekleed in de uitrusting waarin de sekte zich uitdoste ...'
33 'Wij stappen uit. Wij verzamelen moed. Wij beginnen het ene been voor het andere te zetten. Wij slaan niet op de vlucht. Wij gaan naar binnen.'
34 'evenals de vampier zelf wordt haar slachtoffer namelijk een zogenoemde ondode, en zo perpetuum mobile ... De vampier beneemt haar prooi dus niet alleen het leven, zij ontneemt het slachtoffer ook diens dood; zij maakt het onmogelijk dat men tot in alle eeuwigheid ongestoord rust.'
35 'De vloek van deze boze daad is dat die verder kwaad zal baren'.
36 'want als ik, ik, ik, dat niet had gekund, was dat dus een aperte onmogelijkheid.'
37 'En dat zet de kroon op mijn schuldgevoel: niet zomaar lig ik nachtenlang te fluisteren tegen mijn zusje ... Wat ik werkelijk doe is haar wakker houden, ... Zolang mijn bloeddorst naar erkenning niet is gestild, mag zij niet rusten. Ik houd haar ondood.'
38 'dezelfde stem, om nu ter zake te komen, die mijn zusje op een dag had willen bezitten.'
39 '[I]n alle ernst achtte ik mezelf in staat dood en gekte te voorkomen en, megalomaan, hield ik mezelf verantwoordelijk wanneer het leven anders besliste'.
40 Wat was ik anders dan een huisvrouw die graag wil geloven dat zonder haar eeuwige gedweil en geredder alles in het ongerede zal raken? ... In welk opzicht verschilde ik nou helemaal van de Johanna's, ik die mijn eigen gefrustreerde machteloosheid, mijn onvermogen, mijn *wens* te beïnvloeden en te bewerkstelligen, had verheven tot een onmisbaar instrument voor andermans heil of onheil? Punt voor de Johanna's!'
41 'Maar misschien ... als ik ons beiden kan zien als separate individuen zonder macht over elkaars lot, als ik het aandurf van haar gescheiden te raken, misschien dat ik haar dan niet langer als een demon van me af hoef te stoten, of als een prooi naar me toe hoef te halen.'
42 'Mijn zusje had zeker geen boek willen schrijven dat werd neergesabeld op een wijze die van links naar rechts dwars door de ziel sneed.'
43 'Ik ben schrijfster, ik heb de macht het bekende scenario te herschrijven.'

References

Armstrong, Nancy, *How Novels Think: The Limits of Individualism from 1719–1900* (New York: Columbia University Press, 2005).

Braidotti, Rosi, *Metamorphoses: Towards a Materialist Theory of Becoming* (Cambridge: Polity, 2002).

Carby, Hazel V., 'White women listen! Black feminism and the boundaries of sisterhood', in *The Empire Strikes Back: Race and Racism in 70s Britain* (Birmingham: Centre for Contemporary Cultural Studies, 1982), pp. 211–35.

Creed, Barbara, *The Monstrous-Feminine* (London: Routledge, 1993).

Dijkstra, Bram, *Idols of Perversity: Fantasies of Feminine Evil in Fin-de-siècle Culture* (New York and Oxford: Oxford University Press, 1986).

——, *Evil Sisters: The Threat of Female Sexuality in Twentieth-Century Culture* (New York: Henry Holt and Company, 1998 [1996]).

Dorrestein, Renate, *Het perpetuum mobile van de liefde* (1988; Amsterdam: Contact, 2002).

Gerhard, Jane, *Desiring Revolution: Second Wave Feminism and the Rewriting of American Sexual Thought, 1920 to 1982* (New York: Columbia University Press, 2001).

Halberstam, Judith, *Skin Shows: Gothic Horror and the Technology of Monsters* (Durham, NC: Duke University Press, 1995).

Heijst, Annelies van, *Leesbaar lichaam: Verhalen van lijden bij Blaman en Dorrestein* (Kampen: Kok/Agora, 1993).

Kristeva, Julia, *Powers of Horror: An Essay on Abjection*, trans. Leon Roudiez (New York: Columbia University Press, 1982).

Meijer, Maaike, 'De tweede feministische golf en de literatuur. 15 oktober 1976: Anja Meulenbelt publiceert De schaamte voorbij', in M.A. Schenkeveld-van der Dussen (ed.), *Nederlandse literatuur: Een geschiedenis* (Groningen: Martinus Nijhoff, 1993), pp. 819–25.

Moers, Ellen, *Literary Women* (London: The Women's Press, 1978).

Morgan, Robin (ed.), *Sisterhood is Powerful: An Anthology of Writings from the Women's Liberation Movement* (New York: Vintage Books, 1970).

Shildrick, Margrit, *Embodying the Monster: Encounters with the Vulnerable Self* (London: Sage, 2002).

Toffoletti, Kim, *Feminism, Popular Culture and the Posthuman Body* (London: I.B. Tauris, 2007).

8

The political uncanny of the family: Patricia Duncker's *The Deadly Space Between* and The Civil Partnership Act

Anne Quéma

In the twenty-first century, the nomos and practices of the family in Western culture are characterized by contradictions and paradoxes. On the one hand, cultural practices attest to the diversification of the nuclear family.[1] From single-parent families and reconstituted families following divorce to same-sex and transsexual parenthood, the postmodern family has emerged from a process of implosion which the law has sought to regulate in its own terms. On the other hand, political discourse and cultural representations keep constituting a family sociodicy harking back to what Martha Fineman has dubbed the family metanarrative, whose prevalent normative definition rests on the assumption that 'the appropriate family is founded on the heterosexual couple – a reproductive, biological pairing that is designated as divinely ordained in religion, crucial in social policy, and a normative imperative in ideology.'[2] Similarly, Davina Cooper argues that 'in Britain at the turn of the twenty-first century, the reinforcing of inequality is articulated to the predominance of norms of belonging, familialism, and home, that is to private norms over the public ones, within civil and political life … [t]hus we can see the institutional pervasiveness of private norms in the popular discourse of social inclusion, which is largely about incorporating people within community – as belonging – the good stranger reinscribed in the familial trope of kin.'[3] The persistence of this narrative is all the more paradoxical as it coexists with the development of technology-assisted reproduction, which has effected a major historical transition from a procreative account of the family to an account that foregrounds the precedence of social relations over biological origins.[4] Furthermore, the family narrative has been disrupted by the emergence of an LGBT public discourse queering cultural, biological and legal assumptions concerning the constitution of a family. In the early days of the same-sex marriage debate, gay and lesbian writers saw in matrimony the occasion to foster cultural heterogeneity and transformation by creating gender and sexual trouble for family culture and the institution of family law. For instance, Didi Herman cautiously argued that 'the legal recognition of lesbian and gay families does not so much approve a mimicking of the idealized "norm" as "trouble" the norm itself.'[5] At the same time, the terms of the debate were not solely underwritten by a political belief in radical difference in that the desire to make trouble coexisted with the conviction that extension of the right to marry to same-sex couples would blaze the way to social recognition. This discourse of recognition, which still persists today, oscillates between tropes of affective recognition, whereby same-sex couples *feel* recognized, and tropes of civic recognition, whereby same-sex couples are recognized as full *citizens*.[6]

So we have three narratives in the social web of family discourses: one is ideological and shores up a nomos with the family as its natural foundation; another is scientific and severs sexual reproduction from conjugal family; and the third seeks to appropriate the traditional nomos of the family in a double desire for difference and sameness, radicalism and assimilation. In all cases, we see the cultural sphere renaming and unnaming the norms of kinship and affiliation through their practices and symbolic power. The definition of the family in matrimonial, para-, or quasi-matrimonial terms becomes a ground for competition: at stake is the socio-political desire for recognition and for maintaining terms of identification in the polis. Contradictions are generated whereby the conception of the family grounded in a historical discourse of natural sexuality and reproduction clashes with social patterns of family and technological practices that point to other ways of telling the family. It is in this context that I propose to analyse the legitimation of same-sex union in the Civil Partnership Act (2004) and the exploration of gender, sexuality and kinship in Patricia Duncker's *The Deadly Space Between* (2002).[7] If the legal meaning of the Act derives from its intertextual relation to other texts of family law, and if Duncker's novel is inscribed in a literary genealogy of representations of desire and identity, their significance is accrued when cross-examined as part of the vast cultural and discursive constitution of the family, desire and gender identities. From this cultural intertextuality between different fields of knowledge, regulation and representation emerges a performative process of social poiesis that seeks to maintain but also prod social norms, and that leaves in its wake a historical narrative characterized by contradictions, dissent and uncanny patterns, each of which marks a struggle for political power.

Duncker's novel presents itself as a journey towards origins: the origins of Toby's existence and his family; the origins of Gothic tales of family, which shared with fairy tales a fascination for the unfamiliar, the forbidden and sexual violence; the origins of the Western, bourgeois family whose matrimonial heteronormativity was legitimated in 1753 in English family statutory law, and theorized by Freud in his writings on the Oedipal complex; and the origins of that which could be but has been spectralized by proscription. A site of aberrant performativity, the novel queers the family as a cultural, psychic and sexual legacy regulated by heteronormative principles of social organization.[8] The novel presents itself like a Gothic disfiguration of kinship, which gives the literary genre of the *Bildungsroman* renewed significance: Toby's first-person narrative builds and unbuilds the traditional terms of gender identification and sexuality within a matrix where queer desire jostles with heteronormative desire. As the eighteen-year-old narrator, he seems destined to reproduce the Oedipal script to the extent that he experiences incestuous desire for his mother, Iso, and displays the normative signs of parricidal jealousy towards a mysterious father figure who appears out of nowhere and ravishes his mother, and whose identity remains enigmatic until the last page. Woven in this narrative is the naming and unnaming of this father figure, Roehm, whose name is elusive if not spurious, whose sexual identity oscillates between straight and gay, and who as a Gothic revenant straddles the past, present and future.[9]

In their reviews of the novel, commentators have noted the predictability of the Oedipal plot, which they have identified as a weakness of Duncker's writing.[10] I suggest that the reading, interpreting and rehearsal of the Oedipal complex is precisely the central concern of the novel whereby Toby's account presents itself as a performative rewriting of Western foundational texts that, like speech-acts, have authorized and reiterated the Oedipal narrative.

These include writings by Freud but also by Sophocles (*Oedipus Rex*), Shakespeare (*Hamlet, Othello*), Melville (*Billy Budd*), Carl Maria von Weber (his opera *Der Freischütz*, also translated as *The Marksman*), Thomas Mann ('Mario and the Magician'), and Mary Shelley (*Frankenstein*), all of which are cited in more or less explicit terms in Duncker's text, with a particular emphasis on Shelley's novel. However, the novel is not a pure exercise in intertextual virtuosity; instead, it reads as a dizzying and dangerous experiment that, through the citing and reinterpretation of Oedipal scripts, participates in a poiesis of kinship that erodes binary structures of identity and relationships. David Punter argues that vestment and the ceremonial characterize Gothic narratives.[11] The novel takes this Gothic vestism one step further by developing a narrative transvestism whereby in his narrative performance Toby dons on and off the different accounts of the Oedipal myth that were produced throughout history. Spectacles of desire and performances of kinship are enhanced through intertextual references to opera, painting, hypertext, literature, psychoanalysis and music, which all constitute an archive of Oedipal culture. This Gothic vestism is reinforced by a sartorial motif that underlines gender and sexual identifications through a cultural process of fashioning.[12] Different characters resort to dressing, fashion, crossdressing and other media of representation to manifest both their socialization into dominant norms of gender and their deviation from them. Thus Duncker draws on the ornamental texture of Gothic fiction where sexual excess is matched by a metamorphic narrative that queers the telling and retelling of identity and desire with fluctuation. However, this Gothic travesty is held in check by the political uncanny haunting the social regulation of Oedipal kinship. Trapped by the very cultural narratives his account seeks to queer, Toby becomes progressively immured in conflicting and predatory discourses inherited from the past. In this sense, the novel is profoundly Gothic: while Gothic language can be used to stage and describe social, psychological or political situations of confinement and paranoia, Duncker's novel flips language upon itself by staging a narrative in which political and historical performatives of kinship, sexuality and gender identification relentlessly haunt the protagonist.

The novel is characterized by performatives of sexual desire that circulate from one cultural template of gender identification to another, and that in the process dislodge and scramble dominant norms of sexual regulation. While in Oedipal logic the desiring subject is summoned to substitute an external object of desire for the originary parental object of love, in Duncker's novel this logic of substitution is superseded by one of permutation and repeated displacement beyond established gender binaries. The characters' relations revolve around triangles of desire that take their cue from the Oedipal script but that also reformulate it by unmooring it from its heteronormative origins. The novel opens with the depiction of a queer network within which Toby grew up. What Toby calls the 'Amazonian triangle' of desire consists of the fashion designer and great-aunt Luce, the lawyer Liberty as the great-aunt's lesbian partner, and the painter Iso as Luce's niece and Toby's mother. Toby's narrative participates in the reconfiguration of kinship not only through his description of lesbian kinship but also through the citing and appropriation of symbolic representations from the cradle of Western culture. Thus, in an oblique reference to the dramaturgic origins of Oedipus, Toby states that '[t]his triangle of women … was like a companionable Greek chorus' (9). The Amazonian triangle is therefore governed by a social and psychic performance entangling reproduction with deviation, sameness with difference. Similarly, the relation between Toby and his mother derives from a process of gender fusion instead of heteronormative differentiation. Toby and Iso are said to look alike, and through mimetic desire swap conventional gender characteristics: 'short, straight, blonde hair, like a couple of Nordic heroes, pale freckled skins which burn easily, and the same grey-blue eyes. I looked into her face and saw the reassuring mirror of my own … my hands were smooth and untouched. I had the hands of a rich, spoilt woman. She had a man's hands' (11). The irruption of Roehm as Iso's mysterious lover establishes a contrast between the Amazonian triangle of desire and kinship and a heterosexual triangle, and triggers the narrative of Oedipal rivalry between father and son. The regulatory dimension of the Oedipal complex is conveyed by Toby's translation into English of a French text on geometry. This geometric representation of the triangle becomes the symbolic means of transforming Toby into an Oedipal subject at both discursive and affective levels. From a geometric figure, the triangle becomes the means of describing the affective space from which Toby observes his mother's meeting with the man who appears at night to pick her up in a heavy black car: '[Iso] walked past her own car, peering briefly into the back seat. Then she looked up and quickened her stride. I followed the line of her gaze. From the angle of the window I was secure at the apex of the triangle, watching her flicker across the void, converging on the obscure point, fixed, unseen. There was a slight movement, a hand descending. And my gaze came to rest on the figure in the coming dark' (25). By the end of the first chapter, Toby predictably exhibits the signs of parricidal jealousy towards the mysterious man he identifies as his unknown father. In this configuration, Roehm as the name-of-the-father is the manifestation of an Oedipal cultural script that is 'thousands and thousands of years old' (107). Toby's narrative is in the grips of a cultural destiny which he apparently cannot but rehearse.

Seduced by the Oedipal narrative of kinship, Toby cites it, seeks approval from it, but also deviates from it. For a third triangle of desire emerges as Toby competes for Roehm with Iso. Shadowing the Amazonian triangle and the Oedipal triangle is the unfolding of the unpatterned side of things where the object of desire is also the father, an ambivalent figure all at once irresistible and dreadful, a source of pleasure and annihilation. The formula of casino games, '*Faites vos jeux. Rien ne va plus*' (218), captures the paradox of Toby's account, which both reproduces and deviates from the cultural patterns of telling identity and sexuality. As desire circulates through the different configurations of kinship, Toby's appearance undergoes metamorphoses, alternately displaying masculinity at school when he jabs a bully's hand with the sharp leg of his compasses, or displaying the femininity of an 'Aryan Cleopatra' (7) when he wears a crown of flowers. This process of fluidity and resignification courses its way through the novel whose function is to create a site of impropriety, 'a deadly space between' that appears whenever Toby crosses cultural thresholds through acts/phantasms of sexual transgression.

Running through the different triangles of desire is the transgression of the incest interdict that does not differentiate between same-sex and heterosexual desire, young and old, and that in fact unlocks gender identities from the dominant heteronormative pattern of identification.[13] In Toby's account, the infraction of the interdict is common to the three triangles of desire and migrates from one set of relations to the next. The reader is never in a position to ascertain whether actual transgression occurs, or whether the transgression is phantasmal. Incestuous desire is full-fledged in the description of the love-making between Iso and Toby when she is thirty-three and he eighteen. Toby accounts for their encounter in the following terms: 'she accepted me back into her body, whenever I leaned against her belly, her thighs, her breasts. She was the open door. She had never pushed me away, forcing me to leave her, find someone else, grow up. The silk twist she had let down for me had never frayed or broken' (116). It is no accident that the incestuous encounter between Iso and Toby should be heralded by an initial ritual of cross-dressing between the mother and the son. While Iso is cross-dressed as a hunter in a green costume, Toby is fantastically cross-dressed 'as a lesbian boy in one of Liberty's dashing tuxedos with a lilac bow tie and a green carnation made of silk' (111–12). The gender trouble created by the infraction of the incest interdict coincides with a disrobing and redressing of Toby's and Iso's gender appearances while fostering a chimaera of normative permutation and mobility.

Incestuous forms of desire reappear in the relation between Luce and Liberty, who is said to be even younger than Toby's mother and at least twenty-five years younger than Aunt Luce. In other words, the maternal relation between Luce and Iso establishes age as a norm for a proper relation and identifies Luce as a transgressor. Furthermore, Toby's incestuous desire for the mother does not reproduce the logic of the Oedipal complex to the extent that the phantasm not only thwarts the displacing of desire onto another woman but is also shadowed by the equally incestuous desire for Roehm as the paternal figure. A third incestuous triangle shadows the Amazonian and Oedipal triangles, and plays out among Toby, Roehm, and Iso. Toby's incestuous desire for Roehm leads to yet another reconfiguration of the meaning of Greek mythology. When he describes his first encounter with Roehm, he calls upon the Greek myth of the minotaur but reverses its terms of gender references: 'His outline suggested the Minotaur, metamorphosed completely into man, irrefutably male, yet unequivocally bestial. She dwindled into pathos behind him … I felt him watching me creep down the staircase, reading my body rather than my face. My mother took my arm and led me down to him as if I was a virgin bride' (33–4). Toby's account reveals a desire for the father through the mother, and a desire for the son through the mother. As Eve Sedgwick long ago argued, 'Oedipal schematics to the contrary, there is no secure boundary between wanting what somebody else (e.g. Daddy) has, and wanting Daddy.'[14] While Toby states that he wants his mother's place, he ascribes a similar incestuous desire to Roehm: 'I remembered all the nights lying awake, waiting for her to come home, all the sly prying which had turned me into a spy, the sexual Charybdis of triangular desire, the moment when he had offered her to me, the moment when he had made me long for him. But above all I remembered the uncanny sensation, which came and went like a flutter of a moth, that it was not the woman that he wanted but the boy, and that he had seduced the mother to possess the son' (179).[15] The scandalous significance of the novel does not lie in Toby's phantasmal or physical enactment of incestuous desire, but in the revelation through incestuous desire of the contiguity of heteronormative regulation of kinship to queer identification. The co-presence of the three triangles of desire in Toby's narrative indicates a narrative logic of exchange through the transference and volatility of desire. Rattling the Oedipal pattern of kinship, gender identification and proper expressions of sexual desire, Toby's narrative inherits normative patterns from the cultural past and submits them to a drag show of metamorphosis, twisting terms of symbolic representation of kinship. His account creates a space for creativity and reproduction, transformation and reiteration.

At the same time, his narrative remains outside the pale of normative legitimacy, not only because it infringes on cultural and legal norms of kinship, but also because his first-person account remains invalidated, unreliable and phantasmal. In particular, his account is characterized by a fundamental narrative absurdity, as it is driven by a diabolical logic resting on the notion that, as a spectre, Roehm does not actually exist yet is the object of Toby's and Iso's desire. Indeed, representatives of the law undermine either the existence of Roehm, or the validity of Iso's and Toby's reference to Roehm. When Toby confides in Liberty the lawyer and enlists her help to investigate Roehm's identity, she announces that Roehm is nowhere to be located and that there is no legal proof of his existence, scientific activities or academic affiliation. At the end of the novel, when a frantic Iso, who thinks she has spotted Roehm walking towards her and her son on the glacier in Chamonix, tells her story to a *gendarme*, the latter tells her off, asserting that the body she has seen is in fact the frozen body of a nineteenth-century Swiss botanist, which the melting of the glacier has uncovered. In other words, twice the law intervenes to erase any evidence that would substantiate Toby's account, rendering it erroneous. Therefore, the novel revolves around a narrative malapropism that is signified by the ghostly presence/absence of the character, and that disturbs the relation between the reader and the text, as the reader is at the beck and call of a hermeneutics of suspicion and indeterminacy.[16]

That Toby's account of his incestuous fantasies should occupy the public space of literature, yet be transcribed in phantasmal terms, seems to indicate that the narrative is still governed by a logic of interdict and transgression.[17] His narrative remains fundamentally spectral, the effect of normative regulation and proscription orchestrated by the oxymorons of a cultural narrative: Oedipal yet natural. In other words, the cultural narrative turns on a political unconscious to the extent that its arbitrary and historical origins have evaporated to make room for a customary account of the way things are. The fact that some critics have responded negatively to the novel's indirection and unreliability highlights the notion that Toby's narrative remains beyond normative reception because it cannot be authorized. Ceaselessly shuffling the cards, Duncker has created a baffling, queering and profoundly satisfactory Gothic narrative that begins to explore in Butler's words 'what happens when we begin to understand Oedipus outside the exchange of women and the presumption of heterosexual exchange'.[18] The impropriety of desire in Duncker's novel designates a 'deadly space between' that cultural terms and practices cloister to contain what is deemed unnatural desire within kinship. And this cloistering is no more evident than in the Civil Partnership Act whose political unconscious shadows family law's endeavour to legitimize same-sex union.

Although this Act contributes to the fashioning of new rights and obligations, its textuality also resists this pattern of historical transformation and, through statutory language, seeks to regulate excess and deviation. This ambivalence stems from the fact that the Civil Partnership Act is governed by an intertextual cross-reference to the 1949 Marriage Act, and is thus determined by an analogical type of thinking. A comparative analysis of the way in which analogy governs the relation between the Marriage Act and the CPA indicates that legislators wavered between granting similar rights to different social agents and maintaining normative boundaries between these social agents, both liberating and colonizing same-sex unions.

The Gothic tropes of Duncker's novel speak to the ways in which a narrative of sexual transgression and incestuous desire throws a system of kinship into disarray, turning the family into the unfamiliar and unsettling cultural norms. In contrast, the statutory language of the CPA remains governed by the master narrative of sexual reproduction through biological pairing, which functions as the terms of a political uncanny and creates the conditions for the spectralizing of same-sex sexuality and for the delegitimizing of same-sex terms of kinship.[19] Rhetorically speaking, the law's containment of the transformative effects of same-sex union is enacted by the use of analogical thinking relying on a trope of assimilation, which is none other than the simile.

The analogical relationship between the CPA and the Marriage Act is not exclusive to these two Acts, as it has a precedent in the relationship between religious marriage and civil marriage in English family law. The Marriage Act is divided into three parts. Part 1 addresses specific restrictions on marriage. Part 2 regulates religious marriage, while Part 3 regulates civil marriage. The creation of the last two parts speaks to the cultural notion that religious marriage and civil marriage are mutually exclusive. Thus section 45 (4) states that 'no religious service shall be used at any marriage solemnized in the presence of a superintendent registrar'. At the same time, a close reading reveals that, through a process of performative mimesis, the Act establishes a series of equivalences between religious marriage and civil marriage. Therefore statutory language negotiates cultural difference by establishing equivalence through analogy while maintaining boundaries between a secular culture and a religious.

The CPA is based on a twofold strategy: on the one hand, it establishes a boundary between civil partnership and civil marriage with religious marriage as its foundation. Thus the relation between the two Acts is based on a cordon sanitaire, which ensures that same-sex individuals cannot marry, and that heterosexual individuals cannot enter a civil partnership. On the other hand, the statutes establish an analogical relation between civil marriage and civil partnership. So the same double relation of segregation and functional mimesis governing the relation between religious marriage and civil marriage obtains between civil partnership and marriage. Just as civil marriage is functionally like religious marriage but the two are not the same, civil partnership is functionally like marriage by registration, but the two are not the same. This analogy is established through the use of a terminology allowing for equivalence but not identity. Marriage becomes partnership; the superintendent registrar becomes the civil partnership registrar. Or, the marriage certificate becomes a partnership schedule (s 14), which is granted if there is no impediment to the partnership.

The objective seems to have been the establishing of universality and equality by degendering the language of the Marriage Act. However, at the heart of the language of the Marriage Act and the CPA lies a mimetic device of kinship reproduction that indicates that English family law regulates same-sex partnership by superimposing on it a heteronormative governance of kinship and identification. To this extent, family law exercises symbolic violence by legitimizing the dominant cultural pattern of things, and by sealing this pattern through acts of institutional power. The proscriptive effects of heteronormative principles of social organization constitute the political uncanny of the CPA. The unconscious effect of this mode of knowing the social world and shaping gender and sexual norms of identification does not lie in psychological repression; instead, it lies in the masking of the historical and arbitrary origins of this mode of shaping the terms of the social nomos. The paradox of the CPA derives from its intention to maintain heteronormative preponderance while seeking to authorize and legitimize same-sex unions in a language pruned of its heteronormative lexicon. The progeny of this paradox is a fundamentally euphemistic statute in that it creates pockets of silence and elusion about the sexual specificity of the union and its implications for kinship.

The silencing of the sexual body in the CPA has been noticed by two major commentators in two separate analyses published the same year. Carl Stychin observes that consummation and adultery, historically central to the institution of marriage, are noticeably absent from the CPA under the pretext that the two concepts are irrelevant to same-sex relationships. According to Stychin, '[t]his absence in the legislation – and the coy explanations that accompany it – provide a useful illustration of the continuing centrality of penetrative intercourse in the way in which the law constitutes heterosexual relationships'.[20] To this must be added Stephen Cretney's shrewd analysis of the transition from the wording in the Marriage Act to that of the CPA. Cretney remarks that, unlike the Marriage Act, the CPA does not include marriage vows, whose tradition dates back to the 1836 Marriage Act, and which 'involves an *exchange of spoken words* in the presence of a Registrar and witnesses. In contrast, a civil partnership can apparently be created in complete silence.'[21] Only the signature of the civil partnership schedule is required. In other words, civil partnership is constituted by law through silence whereby the sexual nature of the union is omitted.[22] In contrast, and as Cretney reminds us, 'marriage is founded on the principle that (save in exceptional cases) a sexual relationship is of the essence: "with my body, I thee worship" as the Book of Common Prayer puts it. But the same is apparently not intended, as a matter of law, to be true of civil partnership.'[23] Further, Cretney comments on the fact that 'in the relation between same-sex couple and child, legally (and genetically) the sperm donor will be the child's father.'[24] In 2006, the only option was to seek an adoption order to establish the relation between civil partners and child. Nestled in the apparent neutrality of the CPA language are modes of sexuality incompatible with the belief in matrimony as the cornerstone of a heterosexuality geared towards sexual reproduction. This incompatibility culminates in an aberrant utterance which Cretney identifies and on which I will expand.

Indeed, if we re-examine section 3 (Eligibility) of the CPA and its appended schedule 1 in light of section 1(Restrictions on Marriage) and schedule 1 of the Marriage Act, we discover a language that regulates degrees of affinity as a means of establishing the types of union that do not infringe upon the incest interdict. In other words, when one opens the Marriage Act and the CPA, the first items one comes across is a legitimation and codification of what Freud conceptualized as the Oedipal complex. The reproduction of these Oedipal terms of kinship is brought out in the comparative table of prohibited degrees of affinity appended to this chapter (p. 151). Throughout the three Parts the first two columns on the left stem from the Marriage Act, while the column on the right stems from the CPA. While the heteronormative terms such as mother, father, daughter and son have been replaced in the CPA with neutral terms such as parent, child or adopted child, and sibling, the same device securing the gender distinction between man and woman shadows the regulation of same-sex relationships. This shadowy presence of heteronormative gender identity is revealed by the statement that '[i]n the list "sibling" means a brother, sister, half-brother or half-sister' (CPA, Schedule 1, 1 (2)).Therefore, governing the CPA is a premise that maintains a heterosexual reading of kinship. From a rhetorical standpoint, the integration of the prohibited degrees presents itself as a non sequitur whereby euphemized same-sex sexuality is hitched onto a lexicon of reproductive sexuality. This non sequitur is the express sign that the CPA remains caught in the time warp of a kinship system that rests on the family governed by concepts of biological closeness and continuity.

The heteronormative premise of the CPA also hits at the heart of gender reconfiguration and cancels out the possibility for heterogeneity which earlier commentators had associated with same-sex marriage. The heteronormative significance of the legal schedule in the Marriage Act becomes clear when one highlights the terms mother/father/daughter/son as the four poles of Western kinship. The remaining terms of the two columns result from a systematic scaffolding upon these four foundational terms of affinity. The statutory language used to interpret the schedule leaves no doubt as to the partitioning effect of matrimonial law, which traces firm boundaries between the licit and the illicit, man and woman, kin and non-kin. In transposing this social engineering of gender and family to the CPA, the law blurs out a fundamental contradiction: on the one hand, it legitimizes the deletion of binary gender differences by same-sex union; on the other, in applying an interdict that reinstates the Oedipal logic of binary relations, it undoes the acknowledgement of same-sex union. The outlandish language of the statute reveals how the incest interdict as a discursive tool to regulate practices both bans and enlists the subject of kinship, excluding those who do not do their gender and kinship right. This constitutes the power effects of the political uncanny at the heart of English family law whose mimetic reproduction of the heteronormative incest taboo betrays a rejection of what it regulates, pushing it back into the closet. The CPA functions as the ground on which the state through law reasserts exclusionary terms of identification and citizenship. In an act of *regia potestas*, the state through the law maintains kinship as the privileged nexus where nation, nativity and naturalness meet and where private and public spheres collide.[25] In regulating degrees of affinity, the CPA slips into sovereign power over bare life, phantasmatically seeking to appropriate the symbolic agency of queer bodies. Appropriating a discourse of kinship as a site of privacy in order to regulate the public legitimation of a not very productive same-sex desire, the CPA manifests itself as a sovereign power reducing citizenship to reproductive biology, and civic identity to a 'naturally' prescribed and gendered body.

While English family law asserts its legal intentionality through the fashioning of same-sex kinship through civil partnership, Toby presents himself as the narrative agent developing his account of family origins and destiny. While the CPA seeks to regulate same-sex desire through silence and a heteronormative scheme of affiliation, Toby's account disturbs Oedipal boundaries by dislodging the name-of-the-father from its monological meaning. At the onset of his narrative, Toby searches for Roehm's origins by googling his name on the internet. In this virtual universe, Roehm becomes a shape-shifter, an embodiment of public and historical figures such as a homosexual Nazi chief of staff, a French film director and interpreter of the Marquise of O, and an eighteenth-century Swiss Alpine explorer and botanist. This phantasmal destabilizing of the name-of-the-father accounts for the complexity of the narrative, which in fact should be approached as a network of para-narratives defusing the claim to a central narrative of kinship. The novel is first and foremost a hologram displaying on one and the same surface contradictory meanings, which are manifested through the deployment of different discourses of kinship, what they entail and what they mask. Toby's phantasmal identification with Roehm deregulates degrees of affiliation, throwing the heteronormative family into disarray, as conveyed by his account of a dream:

> I dreamed about him that night ... And in my dream I see myself as if I am two people. One is pressed, sweating, terrified, against the damp slab of heat and the other supple, erotic, a boy sure of his power to entice and possess ... I see myself, erect and untouched, pushing towards him through the ensnaring green. Roehm does not move, but he smiles, eerie, suggestive, ambiguous, triumphant. And then I know that I love this man, that he has come back for me, that he has never forgotten me. It is my desire that you should come for me. And I am unafraid. (69–70)

Toby is enthralled, and it is no accident that, in an allusion to *Paradise Lost* and *Faust*, Roehm should be the Satanic apologist of excess and transgression. Out of this economy of desire under proscription emerges a figure of demonization described as the 'erotic green cadaver of the Demon Huntsman' (125), a protagonist in Weber's *The Free Shooter*, which Toby, Iso and Roehm discover on a night at the opera. The Demon Huntsman operates like a mobile trope of excess transiting from Iso to Roehm. While Roehm's physical appearance is associated with the Demon, Iso makes him the subject of her painting: 'His cape swept the floor, and with a meticulous attention to detail she had drawn the giant hollowed chest and the ghostly ribcage of his living corpse' (125). The Demon Huntsman is the Gothic trope at the heart of the narrative of heteronormative kinship: excessive, incestuous, improper desire pounding in the ribcage of the living corpse.

In this demonization of excess, Toby names transgressive desire through his reading of Freud's story of the Wolf Man. His identification with the Freudian script occurs at the same time as his incestuous encounter with Iso, as if the transgression of the incest interdict laid bare the violence inaugurating the emergence of the desiring son: 'There in the mirror she stood, framed and fixed in red and green as if she was a nineteenth-century portrait of an aristocrat in hunting costume. She was the Wolf Man's mother, ready for the forests and the great sweep of snow. The figure in the mirror bowed low before me' (116). In identifying Iso as the mother of the Wolf Man, Toby identifies himself as the Wolf Man, Iso as the object of sexual aggression and Roehm as the bestial copulator of the mother. Toby's narrative retells the archetype of the Freudian primal scene of desire as a nocturnal staging of sado-masochistic heterosexuality between Iso and Roehm on which, he tells the reader, he spied from the garden while raking leaves. Here is the *mise en scène*: 'Behind them rose [Iso's] latest project, a huge canvas, six by four, representing a procession of grey and white pillars, in which the white dominates ... She had her arms around [Roehm's] neck. It was as if he covered her completely, his darkness bearing upon her puckered flesh, the two of them framed by the almost white canvas towering behind them. They became part of her painting ... She leans her head against his chest. I see her naked face for the first time. She is in pain. Her mouth is open, her eyes closed, her cheek a terrible unearthly shrieking white' (89–91). Toby's identification with the Oedipal script coincides with the narrative rehearsal of a genealogy of phantasmal tropes of kinship.[26] At the same time, his parasitic identification with the sexual maternal body and vicarious enjoyment of Roehm's sexual penetration queers the tableau so that the meaning of the Wolf Man functions according to a different register and context. Recollecting the scene, Toby's feeling of horror morphs into pleasure and desire for the father figure: 'I was no longer angry, humiliated, ashamed, but strangely excited. The worm of pleasure had entered my skin and begun to burrow and turn' (100).[27] As a configuration of desire, the trope of the Wolf Man ignores cordons sanitaires and propagates, its meanings varying exponentially with each and every different narrative context.

However, Toby is not master of his narrative terms, as those are steeped in textual precedents, be they psychoanalytical, literary, musical or painterly, as well as in social precedents, be they political and/or legal. To put it in Butler's terms, Toby remains unaccountable even as he persists in accounting for his origins: 'If I try to give an account of myself, if I try to make myself recognizable and understandable, then I might begin with a narrative account of my life. But this narrative will be disoriented by what is not mine, or not mine alone. And I will, to some degree, have to make myself substitutable in order to make myself recognizable. The narrative authority of the "I" must give way to the perspective and temporality of a set of norms that contest the singularity of my story.'[28] Just as the CPA makes queers law's subjects, past narratives of kinship author Toby's desire. Toby gets lost in a maze of textual indices of subjectivity and narratives of kinship that all at once illuminate and obscure the identities of the characters and their interaction. As a family subject, he is undone if not outdone by this maze of cultural and artistic intertextuality. Analysing the textual intricacies of the Gothic, Halberstam states: 'The monstrosity of *Frankenstein* is literally built into the textuality of the novel to the point where textual production itself is responsible for generating monsters.'[29] In *The Deadly Space Between*, this monstrous textuality is in the grips of the political uncanny secreted by the cultural narratives which Toby absorbs like a sponge. In particular, if Toby's account of incestuous desire creates an aberrant and transgressive space of kinship, it also remains haunted by a spectral textuality casting a shadow on his interpretations while exposing him to both the symbolic violence of normative injunctions and Roehm's sovereign power.[30] For, in tapping the archives of the Oedipal family, Toby's account also brings back from the dead the patriarchal bogeyman.[31] Roehm as the Wolf Man functions as a trope of historical revenance, and exhibits signs of sovereign power over bare life in the space of kinship.

The first hint of this sovereign power is conveyed in Toby's earlier account of his visit to Roehm's scientific laboratory located in the basement of a hospital in central London where he apparently experiments with species and climate change. Toby describes an eerie progression in a labyrinth through which like the minotaur Roehm leads him by unlocking a series of secret doors, descending further and further into a primeval world of vegetation and animals. In this subterraneous space, both scientific and fantastic, Toby perceives Roehm as a murderous threat as he hears 'his shoes clicking like dog's claws on the polished floors' (62), and as he reads signs of panic in the animals' fretting. Roehm leads the young man to a heterotopic space of power over caged animals, separated from the social world and functioning as a space of exception where violence is deployed and where Toby deciphers in Roehm a threatening Frankenstein wielding sovereign power over all forms of life.[32] Toby identifies this sovereign power as that which lies outside normality: 'To pass from a normal nature to [Roehm] one must cross "the deadly space between." And we had passed that delicate snow bridge. He was in our blood, our bones ... He was always there. We had become his creatures' (246). The father figure as intruder and violator is indissociable from Toby's perception of his own familial origins, which he recounts at the end of the novel. At this point, the first-person narrative becomes an exercise in ventriloquism through which the reader assumes to be hearing Iso's first-person account of her encounter with Roehm on a school trip to Austria when she was fifteen. According to this account, a Rapunzel-like Iso left her parental home the daughter of a religious couple, disciplined into a flat-shod, long-haired and docile body. As Roehm pays for a haircut and a new wardrobe, Iso emerges as a figure of desire, while the age difference between her and Roehm identifies him as a father figure and Iso as the daughter of his incestuous desire. Iso's sexual awakening follows the path of a symbolic process that includes a reconfiguration of her body and a sartorial transformation, but the sexual initiation veers to an act of subjugation through violation reducing Iso to silence and bare life: 'When he pushed inside me I felt as if I was being torn open with a giant iron bar ... All I could feel was his brutal weight and the unhesitating accuracy of the pain that rose into my intestines, my stomach. He intended to hurt me. I was being ripped open, laid to waste' (204). We are also led to believe that Toby was born out of this one sexual act. The latter took place at the Austrian *Gasthof*, which is also the place to which Iso as a mature woman and mother takes refuge after escaping Roehm, and where Toby finds her. From a seductive and enchanting figure showering Iso's family with Christmas gifts, the figure progressively turns into the Gothic patriarchal villain, perpetrator of violence against mothers and little red riding hoods – male or female. This switch in characterization sets in motion the archetypal plot of the villain stalking mother and son. Initially fascinated by Roehm, Iso and Toby eventually dread him and flee first to Austria, then to the ski resort of Chamonix in the French Alps.

By the end of the novel, Toby is left stranded in a spectral zone where the process of destabilizing and reinventing gender identification is frozen into stasis. In a rewriting of *Frankenstein*, Duncker chose the icy universe of the Mer de Glace in Chamonix to create the landscape of the psychic life of power. The significance of this wintry heterotopia, which Toby discovers while on a Christmas holiday with his great-aunt, lies in its ambivalence. The glacier's potential liquidity signifies transformation and flow; its solidity threatens with stasis and containment. Both depth and surface, solid and fluid, inside and outside, masculine and feminine, animate and inanimate, geological and animal, this icy universe embodies the polysemic and metamorphic principle undergirding this queer narrative: 'I am wandering across the surface of the Mer de Glace … I am walking the dragon's spine. There are no markers in the snow. To my left and right a muscle of rock is thrown up from the white flesh of this living thing moving beneath me. The creature is carefully, surreptitiously, flexing its length, white as a dove, subtle as a serpent. Its white hood is spread out before me. The skin of the glacier moves more swiftly than the braided ice far beneath' (147–8). An expression of Toby's estrangement from Iso – a mère de glace who spends a weekend in Paris with Roehm – the scape reappears in Iso's earlier paintings, and is further associated with the father figure, as Roehm's spectral body is said to be made of cold. The uncanniness of the iceworld increases when the narrative switches from Toby's sensorial perception of the glacier to his exploration of a website documenting the geological properties of a glacier. Stepping into these virtual surroundings, Toby wanders in a space that is neither static nor mobile, neither dangerous nor hospitable – but all at once. In deciphering Toby's account, the hypertextual scientific description, and the allusions to Shelley's narrative, the reader wanders on the white pages of a narrative fissured by crevices between phantasm and perception, chaos and normative scripts, alertness and hallucination.[33]

From this point onward, the paranoid plot of Gothic tradition leaps into action, and the uncanny iceworld ceases to operate as a potential site of transformation. Toby and Iso are fleeing from Roehm whose apparitions at the casino, in the ski lift and on the glacier vampirize their mental energy. The initial attraction for the father's body has become an object of uncanny representation, relegated to a spectral zone of homoeroticism. The construct of the father as bogeyman works at the expense of the son's queer desire, which remains crippled by narratives of kinship through which sexual and gender identification historically took place. Toby's expeditions to Chamonix are repeated voyages towards this father figure, but the desire is foreclosed when Roehm is revealed as the Swiss botanist whose body lies frozen in the Mer de Glace: proscribed desire reappears in the form of the cryogenic body of the father. Through police intervention, the body is returned to where it belongs: the site of phantasmal, obsessive grotesqueries – a solipsistic theatre for 'a sombre gust of queer fantasies' (70) shorn of their potential for the social and historical resignification of gender, sexuality and kinship.

MARRIAGE ACT 1949/CIVIL PARTNERSHIP ACT 2004

Part I. Prohibited degrees of relationship/Absolute prohibitions

Mother	**Father**	Adoptive child
Adoptive mother or former adoptive mother	Adoptive father or former adoptive father	Adoptive parent
		Child
Daughter	**Son**	Former adoptive child
Adoptive daughter or former adoptive daughter	Adoptive son or former adoptive son	Former adoptive parent
		Grandparent
Father's mother	Father's father	Grandchild
Mother's mother	Mother's father	Parent
Son's daughter	Son's son	Parent's sibling
Daughter's daughter	Daughter's son	Sibling
Sister	**Brother**	Sibling's child
Father's sister	Father's brother	
Mother's sister	Mother's brother	
Brother's daughter	Brother's son	
Sister's daughter	Sister's son	

Part II. Degrees of affinity referred to in section 1(2) and (3)/qualified prohibitions

Daughter of former wife	Son of former husband	Child of former civil partner
Former wife of father	Former husband of mother	Child of former spouse
Former wife of father's father	Former husband of father's mother	Former civil partner of grandparent
Former wife of mother's father	Former husband of mother's mother	Former civil partner of parent
Daughter of son of former wife	Son of son of former husband	Former spouse of grandparent
Daughter of daughter of former wife	Son of daughter of former husband	Former spouse of parent
		Grandchild of former civil partner
		Grandchild of former spouse

Part III. Degrees of affinity referred to in section 1(4) and (5)/qualified prohibitions

Mother of former wife	Father of former husband	Former civil partner of child
Former wife of son	Former husband of daughter	Former spouse of child
		Parent of former civil partner
		Parent of former spouse
		Relevant deaths
		The child; the child's other parent
		The former civil partner; the former civil partner's other parent
		The former spouse; the former spouse's other parent

Notes

1. On the fragmentation of the family, see Richard Collier, *Masculinity, Law and the Family*; J. McCandless, 'Recognising family diversity'; and Richard Collier and Sally Sheldon, *Fragmenting Fatherhood*.
2. Martha Fineman, *The Neutered Mother*, p. 145.
3. Davina Cooper, 'Like counting stars?', p. 85.
4. On the reconfiguration of kinship generated by technology-assisted reproduction, see M. Strathern, 'Displacing knowledge'.
5. Didi Herman, *Rights of Passage*, p. 145.
6. For a critique of the disciplinary costs of sexual citizenship, see Brenda Cossman, *Sexual Citizens*; and Michael Warner, 'Beyond gay marriage'.
7. Patricia Duncker, *The Deadly Space Between*. Subsequent page numbers are cited parenthetically in the text.
8. On Gothic narratives contesting constructs of sexuality and the power deriving from these constructs, see Steven Bruhm in 'Gothic sexualities'.
9. On recurrent Oedipal patterns of kinship in the Gothic, see Eve Kosofsky Sedgwick, *Between Men*, p. 91. On Poppy Z. Brite's *Lost Souls* as a narrative transgressing the heteronormative family based on blood ties, inheritance and property, see William Hughes,'"The taste of blood meant the end of aloneness"'.
10. On the characters' lack of credibility, see Laura Fraser in 'Frankenstein as a modern monster'. On the novel's lack of distinction between fantasy and narrative facts, see H. Stevenson in '*The Deadly Space Between* by Patricia Duncker'.
11. David Punter, *Gothic Pathologies*, p. 11.
12. Duncker's novel is inscribed in a queer tradition that Kathy Gentile traces to *The Castle of Otranto* (1764) in which 'an assemblage of rhetorical effects ... coalesce into the granddaddy of Gothic drag', in 'Sublime drag', p. 17.
13. The transgression of the incest interdict constitutes a topos of the Gothic. In her analysis of Horace Walpole's *The Mysterious Mother* (1768), E.J. Clery identifies the mother as not only a sexual but also a social trouble-maker when, on her husband's death, she trumps her son's right of inheritance, a dislocation redoubled by her wilful, incestuous desire for him, in 'Horace Walpole's The Mysterious Mother and the Impossibility of Female Desire'. For a Lacanian interpretation of the incest motif from *The Castle of Otranto* to Eliza Parson's *The Castle of Wolfenbach*, *The Monk* and *Matilda*, see Dale Townshend, *The Orders of Gothic*. On the sublime of incestuous desire in *The Castle of Otranto*, see Donna Heiland, *Gothic and Gender*. On Daphne du

Maurier's and Iris Murdoch's use of incest in their writings, see Avril Horner and Sue Zlosnik, 'Keeping it in the family'. For the centrality of incestuous transgression in queer Gothic and its challenge to patriarchal heteronormativity, see George E. Haggerty, *Queer Gothic*.

14 Sedgwick, *Between Men*, p. 106. As Sue-Ellen Case argues, '[t]he queer is the taboo-breaker, the monstrous, the uncanny', in 'Tracking the vampire', p. 3.
15 On this trope of 'queer Gothic recognition' through enthralment to a powerful and dangerous figure, see Mair Rigby, '"Do you share my madness?"', p. 41.
16 On the ghost as a prosopopoeia, see Eric Savoy in 'Spectres of abjection', p. 162.
17 For the phantasmal significance of the lesbian figure, see Terry Castle, *The Apparitional Lesbian*, p. 63.
18 Judith Butler, 'Is kinship always already heterosexual?', p. 128.
19 For a more detailed critique of the CPA, see my article 'Kinship, sexuality, and citizenship in The Civil Partnership Act 2004'.
20 Carl Stychin, 'Not (quite) a horse and carriage', p. 83.
21 Stephen Cretney, *Same Sex Relationships*, p. 23.
22 On law and silence in former laws on sodomy, see Leslie Moran in 'Law and the Gothic imagination'.
23 Cretney, *Same Sex Relationships*, pp. 33–4.
24 Ibid., p. 33.
25 On nationalism, discourses of kinship, and social recognition in France, see Butler, 'Is kinship always already heterosexual?' On New Labour's recentring of the family in a modernized and civil national space, see Carl Stychin, *Governing Sexuality*.
26 Duncker's novel is part of a novelistic, psychoanalytical, and critical corpus that includes Peter Brooks's claim that *Frankenstein* anticipates Freud's narrative of the Wolf-Man, in *Body Work*, p. 216.
27 For Gina Wisker's analysis of the Gothic discourse of lycanthropy as proscribed sexuality, see 'Love bites', p. 128.
28 Judith Butler, *Giving an Account of Oneself*, p. 37.
29 Halberstam, *Skin Shows*, p. 31.
30 On the Gothic and hauntology, see Punter in *Gothic Pathologies* (p. 14). On phantomatic textuality, see Julian Wolfreys, *Victorian Hauntings*; and Paulina Palmer, *The Queer Uncanny*, pp. 77–8.
31 On the ghostly form of the spectral phallus in contemporary culture, see Benjamin A. Brabon in 'The spectral phallus', p. 58. On phallocentricity as the spectre of heterosexism, see Stéphanie Genz in '(Re)making the body beautiful', p. 71.
32 On heterotopia and the uncanny, see Fred Botting, 'In Gothic darkly, pp. 3–14.

33 On the ice world in Shelley's *Frankenstein* as the space of queer desire, see Rigby in '"Do you share my madness?"', p. 46. For a queer reading of *Frankenstein*, see Sedgwick, *Between Men*; Brooks, *Body Work*; Halberstam, *Skin Shows*; and Michael Eberlé-Sinatra, 'Readings of homosexuality in Mary Shelley's *Frankenstein* and four film adaptations'.

References

Botting, Fred, 'In Gothic darkly: heterotopia, history, culture', in David Punter (ed.), *A Companion to the Gothic* (Oxford: Blackwell, 2000), pp. 3–14.

Brabon, Benjamin A., 'The spectral phallus: re-membering the postfeminist man', in Benjamin A. Brabon and Stéphanie Genz (eds), *Postfeminist Gothic: Critical Interventions in Contemporary Culture* (Basingstoke: Palgrave Macmillan, 2007), pp. 56–67.

Brooks, Peter, *Body Work: Objects of Desire in Modern Narrative* (Cambridge, Mass.: Harvard University Press, 1993).

Bruhm, Steven, 'Gothic sexualities', in Anna Powell and Andrew Smith (eds), *Teaching the Gothic* (Basingstoke: Palgrave Macmillan, 2006), pp. 93–106.

Butler, Judith, 'Is kinship always already heterosexual?', in *Undoing Gender* (New York: Routledge, 2004), pp. 102–30.

——, *Giving an Account of Oneself* (New York: Fordham University Press, 2005).

Case, Sue-Ellen, 'Tracking the vampire', *Differences: A Journal of Feminist Cultural Studies*, 3:2 (1991), 1–20.

Castle, Terry, *The Apparitional Lesbian: Female Homosexuality and Modern Culture* (New York: Columbia University Press, 1993).

Clery, E.J., 'Horace Walpole's *The Mysterious Mother* and the impossibility of female desire', in Fred Botting (ed.), *The Gothic* (Woodbridge: D.S. Brewer, 2001), pp. 23–46.

Collier, Richard, *Masculinity, Law and the Family* (London: Routledge, 1995).

—— and Sally Sheldon, *Fragmenting Fatherhood: A Socio-Legal Study* (Oxford: Hart, 2008).

Cooper, Davina, 'Like counting stars?: equality and the socio-legal space of same-sex marriage', in Robert Wintemute and Mads Andenaes (eds), *Legal Recognition of Same-Sex Partnerships: A Study of National, European and International Law* (Oxford: Hart, 2001), pp. 75–96.

Cossman, Brenda, *Sexual Citizens: The Legal and Cultural Regulation of Sex and Belonging* (Palo Alto, CA: Stanford University Press, 2007).

Cretney, Stephen, *Same Sex Relationships: From 'Odious Crime' to 'Gay Marriage'* (Oxford University Press, 2006).
Duncker, Patricia, *The Deadly Space Between* (New York: HarperCollins, 2002).
Eberlé-Sinatra, Michael, 'Readings of homosexuality in Mary Shelley's *Frankenstein* and four film adaptations', *Gothic Studies*, 7:2 (2005), 185–202.
Fineman, Martha, *The Neutered Mother, the Sexual Family, and Other Twentieth Century Tragedies* (New York: Routledge, 1995).
Fraser, Laura, 'Frankenstein as a modern monster: secrets, incest and intrigue enter a boy's life with a mysterious stranger', *SF Gate* (7 July 2002). At http://articles.sfgate.com/2002–07–07/books/17555065_1_patricia-duncker-roehm-tobias (Accessed 7 July 2002).
Gentile, Kathy, 'Sublime drag': supernatural masculinity in Gothic fiction', *Gothic Studies*, 11:1 (2009), 16–31.
Genz, Stéphanie, '(Re)making the body beautiful: postfeminist Cinderellas and Gothic tales of transformation', in Benjamin A. Brabon and Stéphanie Genz (eds), *Postfeminist Gothic*, pp. 68–84.
Haggerty, George. E., *Queer Gothic* (Urbana: University of Illinois Press, 2006).
Halberstam, Judith, *Skin Shows: Gothic Horror and the Technology of Monsters* (Durham, NC: Duke University Press, 1995).
Heiland, Donna, *Gothic and Gender: An Introduction* (Malden: Blackwell, 2004).
Herman, Didi, *Rights of Passage: Struggles for Gay and Lesbian Legal Equality* (Toronto: University of Toronto Press, 1994).
Horner, Avril and Sue Zlosnik, 'Keeping it in the family: incest and the female Gothic plot in du Maurier and Murdoch', in Diana Wallace and Andrew Smith (eds), *The Female Gothic: New Directions* (Basingstoke: Palgrave Macmillan, 2009), pp. 115–32.
Hughes, William, '"The taste of blood meant the end of aloneness": vampires and gay men in Poppy Z. Brite's *Lost Souls*', in William Hughes and Andrew Smith (eds), *Queering the Gothic* (Manchester: Manchester University Press, 2009), pp. 142–56.
McCandless, J. 'Recognising family diversity: the "boundaries" of re G', *Feminist Legal Studies*, 13 (2005), 323–36.
Moran Leslie, 'Law and the Gothic imagination', in Fred Botting (ed.), *The Gothic*, pp. 87–109.
Palmer, Paulina, *The Queer Uncanny: New Perspectives on the Gothic* (Cardiff: University of Wales Press, 2012).
Punter, David, *Gothic Pathologies: The Text, the Body and the Law* (Houndmills: Macmillan Press, 1998).
Quéma, Anne, 'Kinship, sexuality, and citizenship in The Civil

Partnership Act 2004', *Contemporary Issues in Law*, 10: 4 (2010), 313–29.

Rigby, Mair, '"Do you share my madness?" Frankenstein's queer Gothic', in William Hughes and Andrew Smith (eds), *Queering the Gothic* (Manchester: Manchester University Press, 2009), pp. 36–54.

Savoy, Eric, 'Spectres of abjection: the queer subject of James's "The Jolly Corner"', in Glennis Byron and David Punter (eds), *Spectral Readings: Towards a Gothic Geography* (Houndmills: MacMillan, 1990), pp. 161–74.

Sedgwick, Eve Kosofsky, *Between Men: English Literature and Male Homosocial Desire* (New York: Columbia University Press, 1985).

Stevenson, Helen, '*The Deadly Space Between* by Patricia Duncker: this Oedipus is too complex', *The Independent* (16 April 2002) at www.highbeam.com/doc/1P2-1684282.html

Strathern, Marilyn, 'Displacing knowledge: technology and the consequences for kinship', in Faye D. Ginsburg and Rayna Rapp (eds), *Conceiving the New World Order: The Global Politics of Reproduction* (Berkeley: University of California Press, 1995), pp. 346–63.

Stychin, Carl, '*Governing Sexuality: The Changing Politics of Citizenship and Law Reform* (Oxford: Hart, 2003).

——, '(Not quite) a horse and carriage: The Civil Partnership Act 2004', *Feminist Legal Studies*, 14:1 (2006), 79–86.

Townshend, Dale, *The Orders of Gothic: Foucault, Lacan, and the Subject of Gothic Writing, 1764–1820* (New York: AMS Press, 2007).

Warner, Michael, 'Beyond gay marriage', in Wendy Brown and Janet Halley (eds), *Left Legalism/Left Critique* (Durham, NC: Duke University Press, 2002), pp. 259–89.

Wisker, Gina, 'Love bites: contemporary vampire fiction', in David Punter (ed.), *A Companion to the Gothic* (Oxford: Blackwell, 2000), pp. 167–79.

Wolfreys, Julian, Victorian Hauntings: Spectrality, Gothic, the Uncanny and Literature (New York: Palgrave, 2002).

9

Violent households: the family destabilized in *The Monk* (1796), *Zofloya, or the Moor* (1818), and *Her Fearful Symmetry* (2009)

Joanne Watkiss

The nuclear family is exposed as an unhomely, violent site in Gothic literature. Far from a familiar unit held secure by lineage, the nuclear family does not remain a unit by the end of the text. Concerned with disrupting and perverting the norm, Gothic literature refuses straightforward, linear succession to its families. In the texts under observation here, events do not proceed as they should; these are families that are 'out of joint', redundant in their ability to sustain themselves and future generations. In addition, qualities aligned with the institution of the family such as the familiar, the domestic and the homely are exposed as unstable foundations. As that which revels in the destabilization of foundational signifiers, narratives and values, Gothic fiction is particularly suited to deconstruction. As Mark Wigley suggests in *The Architecture of Deconstruction: Derrida's Haunt*, 'deconstructive discourse unearths the representative mechanisms by which other senses are hidden within that traditional figure, senses that are already threatening in their very multiplicity'.[1] For the Gothic, the nuclear family acts as a fertile stage to expose uncanny forces that are concealed in its construction as a sustainable, secure unit, 'identify[ing] the undecidables that uncannily intimate violence within the familiar domain'.[2] The undecidable is where the Gothic repeatedly locates itself in its ability to disrupt, to challenge and to pervert. Through an analysis of three families, this chapter demonstrates how, in Wigley's words, 'that which supposedly lies outside the familiar comfort of the home turns out to be inhabiting it all along'.[3] The Gothic has always been concerned with bringing inside what should remain outside, and so presents the reader with unsettled, destabilized familial households. This chapter charts the development of the Gothic family through early texts, *The Monk* (Lewis, 1796) and *Zofloya, or the Moor* (Dacre, 1818), before turning to Audrey Niffenegger's *Her Fearful Symmetry* (2009), to explore the Gothic family in a contemporary context. In all of the families explored here, the familiar, the linear and the domestic are revealed to be fragile constructions, demonstrating that the family unit is based on insecure foundations. For the family unit to function, 'instability must always be concealed to produce the effect of unambiguous stability'.[4] The Gothic delights in disturbing such stability by offering households that are violent and unhomely.

As Freud has explored, the etymological origins of the *unheimlich* relate to a simultaneous unfamiliar familiarity, where the Latin *familiaris* is clearly the root for both the familiar and the family. Therefore, the family by definition should be that which is familiar and known, and not what is unfamiliar and unknown. This is clearly the case in Matthew Lewis's *The Monk* where the uncertain origins of a family have disastrous consequences for the villain of the title, Ambrosio. As narrated by Don Christoval: 'The late Superior of the Capuchins found [Ambrosio] while yet an Infant at the Abbey-door. All attempts to discover who had left him there were vain, and the Child himself could give no account of his Parents ... No one has ever appeared to claim him, or clear up the mystery which conceals his birth.'[5] In contrast to the institution of the family as a known space, the Gothic presents the dramatic impact of a family that is not securely located or known. As Freud states, the uncanny is evident when secrets have been concealed for a period of time and then come to light. Such secrets clearly constitute the core of the Gothic family, as Ambrosio's Aunt, Leonella, indicates: 'A young Nobleman fell in love with [Ambrosio's mother, Elvira], and married her unknown to his Father. Their union remained a secret near three years' (13). This Gothic family is unfamiliar, and therefore, based on insecure foundations. Because of this, Ambrosio's only home is the Abbey, whose unhomeliness is evident in an extreme censoring of life experience. As Leonella explains, 'he is now thirty years old, every hour of which period has been passed in study, total seclusion from the world, and mortification of the flesh' (17). This strict upbringing as a result of uncertain origins severely restricts Ambrosio's life. Because Ambrosio's origins are so unclear, he has no idea that the girl he subsequently desires, rapes and murders is his sister, nor that her mother – whom he smothers with a pillow in an attempt to possess her daughter – is his mother also. Such restriction also applies to Ambrosio's sister, Antonia, who is described by her Aunt Leonella, as 'a young Creature who is totally ignorant of the world. She has been brought up in an old Castle in Murcia; with no other Society than her Mother's, who, God help her! has no more sense, good Soul, than is necessary to carry her Soup to her mouth' (12). Because of her over-protective mother, who attempts to censor her environment (even the Bible is subject to her revisions), Antonia falls victim to the violence of her own brother: 'the world was composed only of those who resembled her, and that vice existed was to her still a secret' (249). The original secrecy of Elvira's marriage is repeated in the upbringing of her children, just as original sin is revisited upon the offspring: the next generation are the victims of such an uncertain origin. Despite being removed from his family and being unaware of his origins, Ambrosio is still shaped by them.

On hearing of his daughter's marriage, Ambrosio's grandfather, a Marquis, 'had the cruelty to take from us my Sister's little Boy, then scarcely two years old, and whom in the abruptness of her flight, She had been obliged to leave behind her. I suppose, that the poor little Wretch met with bitter bad treatment from him, for in a few months after, we received intelligence of his death' (13). The secret of his parents' cross-class union (his mother was the daughter of a Marquis, his father the son of a young Nobleman) resulted in the orphaning of Ambrosio, and hence, his path towards vice. For the Gothic family, uncertain origins destabilize the individual, exposing a reliance on the familiar that is extremely precarious and fragile. Through the concealed marriage of his daughter, the Marquis's family is also rendered unfamiliar to him and therefore he cannot welcome their offspring. As the product of a secretive union, Ambrosio is tainted with secrecy also, and as a result, is shunned by both his immediate family and his wider family. Although the instigators of the scandal escape, the sins of the parents are revisited on the offspring: both Ambrosio and his sister Antonia pay for their parents' behaviour. Because of his daughter's transgression, the Marquis abandons his grandson at the Abbey door, halting the lineage of such a union by ensuring their child will remain within the Abbey walls. By removing her child, the Marquis attempts to halt a transgressive lineage by punishing Elvira's offspring. Through the actions of the Marquis, Ambrosio becomes symbolic of the debt his parents must pay for their transgressions, and so his understanding and experience of the homely is bound by his religious hosts. However, because the Marquis places his grandson in a convent, he also punishes himself in his attempt to halt his own family line. As with the familiar, Gothic families disrupt the necessary linearity of traditional inheritance that is the foundation for the family as a self-sustaining unit.

Although Antonia is clearly a victim of her parents' secret marriage and a censored upbringing, she does not act violently. As evident in early Gothic fictions, she (as the Gothic heroine) is a stage for violence rather than the instigator of such violence, as indicated by her death at the hands of her brother: 'without allowing himself a moment's reflection, He raised [the dagger] and plunged it twice in the bosom of Antonia' (391). As in *Her Fearful Symmetry*, Ambrosio's desires are achieved through an elaborate plan involving the 'faking' of Antonia's death so that he can possess her in the tombs where she will be laid to rest. As Matilda advises him: 'receive this constellated Myrtle ... breathe upon it thrice, pronounce her name, and place it upon her pillow. A death-like slumber will immediately seize upon her ... Sleep will hold her till break of morning' (278). After her funeral has taken place, Ambrosio 'lifted her still motionless from the Tomb: He seated himself upon a bank of Stone, and supporting her in his arms, watched impatiently for the symptoms of returning animation' (379). Uncannily, his sister is rendered undead by her brother, who waits for her to come back to life, in order to ravish and then kill her: 'gradually he felt the bosom which rested against his, glow with returning warmth. Her heart throbbed again; Her blood flowed swifter, and her lips moved' (380). As the act of procreation necessary to ensure the lineage of the family is a perverse one, the incestuous union of brother and sister must result in the termination of the family line. As one child is the instrument of transgression, the other is the site for such violence; the next generation effectively cancels itself out. Both children, therefore, are victims of a destabilized, unhomely, family unit. This is also the case for Leonardo in *Zofloya, or the Moor* as he also exerts violence on the body of his sister Victoria, wounding her with a poignard: 'the point of the dagger entered the shoulder of Victoria ... the eyes of the wounded and fainting Victoria were riveted upon a countenance that memory immediately identified as her brother!'[6] Victoria's realization demonstrates the horror of the simultaneous familiarity of a brother with an unfamiliar stranger who trespasses into her home and causes violence. In this way, both Ambrosio and Leonardo act out the violence of a destabilized family unit on the bodies of their siblings, causing the nuclear family unit to collapse further and ensure lineage is halted.

The violence of the unhomely household is similarly evident in Charlotte Dacre's *Zofloya, or the Moor*. This text witnesses the immediate breakdown of the nuclear family as Laurina, the mother figure of the Loredani family, abandons her husband and two children, Leonardo and Victoria, to be with her lover, Count Ardolph. Because of Laurina's actions, 'Leonardo, the pride and heir of the house, had, soon as the flight of his mother became known, rushed from his home and never since returned' (82). Ashamed to admit to his family name, Leonardo effectively abdicates his title as heir to such a contaminated lineage: 'to remain longer on the spot where his mother had heaped disgrace upon her ruined family, would be vile and unworthy' (86). Like Ambrosio, the heir to the estate is denied a sense of belonging as his family are destabilized through the removal of the mother. After his mother's transgression, the house, estate and title become tainted by the acts committed there. '"My name," he replied, "is Leonardo, – that which is subjoined to it, I must be excused from revealing"'(88). The corruption of the family name causes Leonardo to distance himself from his origins and, like Ambrosio, his ancestry is censored. Although it is his mother who has brought shame onto the family, it is the name of his father which holds the weight of such scandal, as this signifier is invested with the authority of lineage. In this instance, however, this authority is undermined by the mother figure, whose actions destabilize the family unit in her disruption of the family home: 'blast[ing] the doting husband with conviction of his dishonour – plung[ing] his offspring in eternal ruin and disgrace, and despoil[ing] them of the protection and tender services of a mother' (12). The unhomeliness that results from her desertion exposes the link between the home and the domestic; ideals which form the foundations of the family. As Wigley writes, 'the house is always first understood as the most primitive drawing of a line that produces an inside opposed to an outside, a line that acts as a mechanism of domestication' and so the house is 'not just a domestic space, it is a space in which a certain idea about the domestic is sustained and protected'.[7] The domestic is the lens through which the family and the home are sustained. Such an overlap demonstrates how the concept of domesticity is undermined in Gothic families, revealing the homely to be a construction, a myth, a hidden violence as: 'to constrain the unruly play of representations is to house them, to domesticate them'.[8] As that which should determine the homely but has the potential to destabilize it, the domestic is revealed as a controlling force that can impact violently on family members, especially offspring. Therefore, as the 'paradigmatic mechanism of domestication', the supposedly secure space of the home 'becomes the site of the most radical insecurity – indeed the very source of insecurity'.[9]

Lacking a family name and a sense of origin, Leonardo is, like his sister, driven to illegal acts and incessant wandering in an effort to locate himself securely. Due to his mother's exposure of the violence of domesticity, Leonardo is drawn to similar sites of disruption, such as the home of Megalena Strozzi: 'they soon reached the villa, and a smothered sigh, as he entered it, was the last tribute paid to the memory of his neglected home' (104). The home Megalena offers to Leonardo, however, is one of seduction and vice: 'she spared no artifice or allurement to induce him to protract his stay beneath her roof' (105). His sense of belonging and homeliness is, as with Ambrosio, dependent on fulfilling the requests of the host who demands that he murder an old rival, Theresa, and her ex-lover Berenza (in which he fails, injuring his sister instead). Therefore, as Wigley suggests, 'the alienating space of the home veils a more fundamental and primordial homelessness. To be at home in such a space is precisely to be homeless'.[10] To be subject to the law of the host is to be contained in a domestic economy of exchange that perverts the homely. In Wigley's words, 'the philosophical economy is always a domestic economy, the economy of the domestic, the family house, the familiar enclosure'.[11] Leonardo also occupies the home of the bereaved Nina, whose stay there depends upon his performance as her deceased son Hugo. As Leonardo suggests to Nina: 'what if I could supply to you the place of your son, would you allow me to remain under your roof?' (97). As a substitute son, Leonardo is subject to a violent domesticity that relies upon some kind of exchange to sustain the homely. His debt to the mother figure persists into this home. As he muses to himself after arriving at Nina's: 'this is the second time that the heir of Loredani has been indebted to the benevolence of strangers for shelter' (97). As he feels indebted, his sense of the homely is bound up with the language of exchange. Perversely, his only inheritance is from this substitute mother figure, an act that transcends the boundaries of the familial line: '"All I have is thine", she murmured, making an effort to open her eyes, and fix upon him her last look' (101). His stay at the Zappi household is similarly bound to obligations, as the mistress of the house demands his affections before rendering him homeless once again. As he refuses her affections, her husband rescinds his offer of hospitality: 'quit instantly a roof which has sheltered you too long, and never let me more behold your face' (93). Ultimately, Leonardo ends the text as leader of the nomadic Banditti, a criminal group which functions as a substitute family unit: 'some sat cross-legged, some reclined, talking over deeds of bloody outrage, while the red fire-light cast upon their marked features an additional tinge of ferocity' (249). As with Ambrosio and the Abbey, Leonardo's belonging also depends upon the censorship of his origins: 'the chief, still masked ... looking the wild genius of the terrible abode' (249). It is only through an illegal, violent sense of the domestic that Leonardo locates a sense of belonging.

Like her brother, Victoria struggles to seek belonging after her mother's disruption of the homely. She witnesses in her mother, 'the flagrant violation of a most sacred oath' of her marriage and the 'baleful effects of parental vice upon the mind of a daughter' (28). Laurina is a 'perjured wife' (26) whose behaviour pollutes the family name but also the reputation of her daughter. As Victoria's lover and subsequent husband Berenza suggests, 'there was a certain stigma in his idea attached to her, through the misconduct of her mother, which it was impossible for his delicate mind to overlook' (80). Although the act of betrayal was committed by her parent, Victoria, like Ambrosio, is rendered guilty by association, tainted by the corrupt family name. This is effected through the bloodline that parent and child share, akin to a vampiric relationship in the parasitic corruption of the child by the parent. Laurina's relative, the religious Signora di Modena, is fearful of such a contamination after shaking hands with Laurina, as she 'withdrew her hand, as from pollution' (42). In this way, Victoria, like Leonardo and Ambrosio, is a victim of a destabilized, immoral family unit. As she admits to Leonardo, her mother '*first* corrupted and allured my mind' (259, author's italics). The corruption of the family is symptomatic of a poisonous infection, a pollution which extends to 'the contaminated roof under which [Laurina] presided' (29). For Derrida, 'it is the violence of the "household" that produces the family'.[12]

Like her brother, Victoria is also bound to unhomely households. At seventeen, she is taken to the home of her relative, the Signora di Modena, and left there by her mother and her lover. Like Ambrosio, Victoria is abandoned in a religious house by her family and subject to the 'varied and unworthy artifices [that] the pious Signora di Modena had recourse to, for the torment and annoyance of her charge' (51). She is, like her brother, subject to the authority of her host, with the unhomely imposed on her due to her contaminated lineage. As Modena states to Victoria: '[you are] the contaminated offspring of one who is immersed many fathoms deep in guilt and shame' (51). Therefore, after her marriage, Victoria's own home is determined by a perverted sense of domesticity. Paralleling her mother, she desires a man other than her husband, Berenza's brother Henriquez, who loves the young Lilla. By poisoning Berenza in his own home, Victoria renders their domestic sanctuary unhomely. 'Whatever she willed, right or otherwise, was law to the fond, the dying Berenza ... with treacherous hand but looks of love, she held towards him the life destroying draught' (171). Like her mother, Victoria removes her husband who stands in the way of her desire, and so the husbands of both mother and daughter are murdered. After her various illegal acts and subsequent pact with the demon-figure Zofloya, Victoria and her brother are destroyed before they can reproduce, halting the trajectory of the family line and rendering the family name redundant. Like Ambrosio, Victoria's death is sited as a moral necessity in the text: the conclusion of the novel must also be the conclusion of the family. Through such conclusive narratives, early Gothic fiction ensures that these Gothic families cannot continue by halting their linear trajectory. Conclusions to contemporary Gothic families however, are not so resolute.

Her Fearful Symmetry clearly inherits its portrayal of the Gothic family from earlier Gothic fictions. As before, we are presented with siblings whose relationship is particularly fraught with violence. Significantly though, there is no male heir present in this text, as the sibling rivalry is between twin sisters, Julia and Valentina, who inherit their Aunt Elspeth's flat overlooking Highgate Cemetery. Uncannily, Julia and Valentina's mother Edie is also part of a twinship with Elspeth. Both twinships are characterized by sibling rivalry rather than affection: Valentina admits that Julia 'tries to hit me'[13] just as their mother and aunt were regularly violent with one another: 'watching [the twins] come unglued is too much like whatever happened to [Elspeth] and Edie' (237). As Freud has posited, twins are uncanny in their doubling of the same, a repetition of the familiar: 'these themes are all concerned with the phenomenon of the "double", which appears in every shape and in every degree of development. Thus we have characters who are to be considered identical because they look alike'.[14] Two sets of twins however, are even more disturbing as Julia and Valentina are doubles of their own mother and aunt: 'Elspeth saw in Julia and Valentina the strangeness, the oneness that had always so discomfited people in herself and Edie' (88). For Freud, there is between twins a literal 'doubling, dividing and interchanging of the self'.[15] This is a Gothic family that is notably female, with uncanny similarities between mother, aunt and daughters. As with *The Monk* and *Zofloya, or the Moor*, Niffenegger's text is concerned with the disruption of the family as a secure, familiar unit.

The ritual of inheritance results in the revelation of secrets as the twins realize 'there's some big secret about Elspeth and Mom' (235). Instead of hidden paternity, the unique position of twins permits hidden maternity: because Edie and Elspeth have identical DNA and both slept with the same man, either Edie or Elspeth could biologically be their mother. As it turns out, it is Elspeth, and not Edie who is their mother as the twins switched identities shortly after Julia and Valentina's birth. As Elspeth (Edie before the switch) admits:

> I lived with Jack for almost a year, though it was Elspeth he had married. I had the twins, worked out like a maniac to lose the baby weight, cooked and kept house and almost went mad with boredom and rage and a sense of having been trapped in a farce ... it was Elspeth (now Edie) who returned to Lake Forest a few months later with the twins. (305)

The ability to deceive both their children and Edie's husband suggests a duplicitous relationship which hints towards the deceitful nature of the inheritance. As Edie suggests to her husband 'She's not just leaving it to them, she's prying them away from us' (40). Therefore, the inheritance of the flat is from mother to daughter and not from aunt to niece, which renders the events that occur later on all the more horrific. Crucially, however, this secret remains cryptically concealed from the twins throughout the text as, rather unusually, they do not know who their mother is. Like Ambrosio, the lack of familial knowledge through censorship has extreme consequences as the family unit is not based on familiar foundations.

In a letter from Elspeth (just before her death) to Edie, she writes: 'I didn't leave you anything. You got to live my life. That's enough. Instead I'm experimenting – I've left the whole lot to the twins. I hope they'll enjoy it' (6). By offering her property to the twins, Elspeth ensures that they inhabit her property (where she remains as a ghost) for a certain period of time, and so, her malicious intentions are masked as gain. The will reads:

> You are her residuary legatees; that is, she has bequeathed to you her entire estate ... on the following conditions: 1) ... She bequeathed this apartment to you on the condition that you both live in it for one year before you may sell it. 2) The entire bequest is given on the condition that no part of it shall be used to benefit Ms Noblin's sister, Edwina, or Edwina's husband, Jack (your parents). Also, Edwina and Jack Poole are forbidden to set foot in the flat or to inspect its contents. (37)

However, as the text reveals, the moment of inheritance is fraught with debt: the twins are manipulated into their mother's power, as although she is deceased, her spirit haunts the flat and influences the twins throughout their stay there. As is indicated in the will, Elspeth ensures the twins' parents cannot enter the property, refusing them entry and knowledge of her malevolent intentions. Such restriction is symptomatic of the secrets between Elspeth and Edie kept from the twins (and their father) throughout their lives. Although Elspeth has given her daughters her home, she demands Valentina's life – or more specifically, her body – in return. Therefore, inheritance in this novel is an unethical transaction, a contract that the daughter is bound to without her knowledge. This debt dislocates what should be a linear process of inheritance, as the deceased remains in control of the descendants to such an extent that Elspeth controls their domestic realm and, ultimately, their lives. The will permits Elspeth ownership over her children: only in death can she reverse the secret and become a mother to her children. She is, however, a destructive mother who gains her children for her own purposes; first to watch them, secondly to influence them, and thirdly to kill Valentina and inhabit her body with her (Elspeth's) own spirit. In this text, inheritance is revealed as a perverse, non-linear exchange, where the dead gain more than the beneficiary.

As the twins move into their new home, they are subject to an uncanny welcoming: 'the front hall was full of umbrellas and mirrors. The twins were reflected eighteen times in as many mirrors, and their reflections were reflected, and on and on. They were startled by this; both stood perfectly still and were each unsure which reflection belonged to which girl' (82). Such reflections represent the corrupt domesticity of the contract with their mother: instead of gaining a welcoming home, the unhomely hallway suggests the debt they are now subject to. Through the multiple layers of reflection, their new home forces them to witness an overwhelming, uncanny confrontation with the familiar. Through such a visual confrontation, the twins are forced to see themselves not as individuals, but as part of a multitude; an ancestry that threatens their very existence as beings. The oppressive home they have inherited is apparent as they walk into the living room: 'as Julia stepped into the front room behind Valentina, she had a sensation of being underwater, as though the room were at the bottom of the pond' (83). Such a sensation exposes the autonomy of Elspeth to trap the twins in the space. Her presence is so strong that the twins 'looked at the doorway as though expecting to be caught intruding on the silence of the flat' (83). Elspeth's offering of the domestic, therefore, is an oppressive one that reinforces her authority within. As Wigley suggests, 'to dominate is always to house ... Domination is domestication'.[16] Such an experience equates to Derrida's understanding of the homely, as 'the most familiar becomes the most disquieting. The economic or egological home of the *oikos*, the nearby, the familiar, the domestic, or even the national (*heimlich*) frightens itself. It feels itself occupied, in the proper secret (*Geheimnis*) of its inside, by what is most strange, distant, threatening'.[17] Although the flat is their home, it is occupied not only by the presence of their mother's spirit, but by the secret foundations of such an inherited contract, revealing 'the apparent innocence of the familiar [as] a mask that alienates'.[18] Elspeth's presence is so strong that traces of her existence remain; 'on the desk sat a scruffy computer, heaps of papers, more books, a credit-card processing machine, a delicate white-and-gold teacup with long-evaporated tea at the bottom and apricot lipstick staining the rim' (84). Although the twins own the property, the authority of the space remains with the matriarch, ensuring that she remains host in their home. The home offered to the daughters is based on a violent exchange.

The twins are, however, unaware that Elspeth was their mother, though they quickly embrace her spirit and communicate with her through a variety of methods. Valentina confides in Elspeth about her relationship with her twin stating that 'I'm frightened of her,' (238) and 'I have to get away from Julia' (265). Although they are twins, Julia is the source of Valentina's fear, rendering her uncanny in her 'fearful symmetry'. Like Ambrosio and Antonia, and Leonardo and Victoria, these siblings are destructive in their closeness. Because Julia is the dominant twin, she makes many decisions that attempt to control Valentina's life: 'Julia won't do anything that would let me be independent. I'm stuck' (237). By doing so, Valentina allows Elspeth to develop a plan for her escape, which is to stage her own death. Like Antonia, Valentina is victim to her actual death (through a family member) by performing it first. The plan relies on Elspeth's lover, Robert (who lives in the same building) to ensure Valentina's body is frozen and not embalmed. After Elspeth has removed Valentina's spirit, she promises her daughter she will return her spirit to her body after the funeral has been performed. Valentina asserts that, 'I'll die, Julia will be forced to go on without me, she'll get over it. And you'll put me back in my body and I'll live happily ever after' (278). In order to escape her violent twin, Valentina makes the mistake of turning to another family member who is much more malicious in her intentions. As Robert declares to Elspeth, 'you were sending the twins here as a sort of substitute for yourself' (228). Instead of placing Valentina's spirit back into her body, Elspeth takes the body for herself. As Freud's essay 'The Uncanny' explores, 'the primitive fear of the dead is still so strong within us and always ready to come to the surface on any provocation. Most likely our fear still implies the old belief that the dead man becomes the enemy of his survivor and seeks to carry him off to share his new life with him'.[19] Because Elspeth is dead, Valentina makes the fatal mistake of assuming the saintly nature of the deceased and therefore allows Elspeth to claim ultimate ownership by hosting her body: such an act is the ultimate demand from mother to daughter.

Like a nineteenth-century body-snatcher, Robert sneaks into

the Noblin family tomb at night: 'Valentina's body lay ensconced in white silk ... Robert reached into the coffin with both arms and scooped Valentina up' (344). After Robert has removed Valentina's body from the tomb, he returns to the flat where the spirits of 'Elspeth and Valentina stayed in the drawer together' (321). In a macabre fashion, he combs her hair, ready for her return to life: 'he caught sight of the two of them in the mirror, an image out of a horror film: the candlelight flickering from below, dark shadow cast across his face, Valentina's head thrown back, her neck offered up, her arms and legs dangling. *I am the monster* [he thought]' (249, author's italics). Ironically, on her first arrival at the flat, her twin Julia 'thought of Sleeping Beauty, and the palace, still for a hundred years, full of motionless courtiers' (83). Valentina is positioned as a perverse Sleeping Beauty in that she will not wake; her mother will take her body and wake instead. In a macabre fashion, Robert attempts to maintain her body as she comes back to life: 'her hair was tangled. To distract himself Robert began combing her hair. Very delicately, so as not to tug at her scalp, he began to work the tangles out' (347). He has also 'filled the bedroom with flowers' (346) in an attempt to reaffirm an idea of the domestic and cover the smell of decay: 'her breath smelled wrong, like spoiled food, like the hedgehog he'd found dead in the heating system of the cemetery's office' (353). Like Antonia in the tombs of the Abbey, Valentina's body is trapped in the flat for Elspeth to possess herself. As Elspeth is reborn in her daughter's body, she becomes monstrous, akin to Frankenstein's monster: 'the body opened its mouth and took a jagged, asthmatic breath ... it lurched sideways and Robert caught it ... something like electricity wracked her body; her limbs contracted; her head swerved violently back and forth, once' (350). As an unnatural creation, the body is scarred by its violent birth. Similarly, Victor Frankenstein's creation of his monster is through 'a spark of being' resulting in a 'convulsive motion [that] agitated its limbs'.[20] In Elspeth's new body, Robert notices that 'something about her expression was different' (351) and 'her voice cracked; she sounded like a ventriloquist's dummy, off kilter, high, raspy and stressed wrong' (352) just as Victor's monster 'muttered inarticulate sounds'.[21] As Elspeth's soul is in Valentina's body, there is a discord between the inside and outside resulting in an uncanny Gothic body. As a ventriloquist, the control Elspeth has over Valentina's body is evident, uncanny in that this control should not be apparent: one's ownership over a body should be seamless, yet there is clearly a delay between Elspeth's intentions and the body's response which indicates the duality of its foundation. The reference to 'Valentina's hands like badly wired robots' (353) is suggestive of the electricity that 'wracked her body' as she was reborn in an unnatural fashion. The uncanniness of the switch is clear when Elspeth looks in a mirror: 'when she got to the footboard she stood swaying, regarded herself in the mirror. Oh. Oh … There was Valentina … she stared at her reflection that was not herself; this was a consummately impressive costume which she would now wear as her body' (355). The Gothic family has gone to new lengths as the mother inhabits the body of her daughter who, as a foetus, once inhabited hers. Such a horrific switch doubles the initial switch between Edie and Elspeth that triggered such a perverse inheritance to take place. As Freud suggests, repetition of familiarity is uncanny as it makes clear how 'the repetition of the same features or character-traits or vicissitudes, of the same crimes, or even the same names [can recur] through several consecutive generations'.[22] Like the multitude of mirrors on the twins' arrival at the flat, the repeated image of the familiar distorts the comforting nature of such a construct, rendering it unfamiliar.

After her 'birth', Elspeth and Robert immediately engage in sexual activity, as she demonstrates her ownership of the body of her daughter: 'he undressed her. She tried to help, but seemed too weak' (353). At this point, Robert does not know that Elspeth inhabits Valentina's body while Valentina's spirit looks on. Such a discord between inside and outside challenges conventional understandings of body and soul, resulting in the horrific realization that mother and daughter are one. Such horror is signified by the partial decay, and subsequent reanimation, of the body: 'Robert wasn't quite sure if he could bring himself to kiss her mouth … some parts of her body seemed more alive than others' (353). Like Ambrosio's arousal on Antonia's awakening, their union is necrophilic: 'he ran his hands over her thighs; they were like meat from the refrigerated case at Sainsbury's' (353). Like Ambrosio's incestuous union with his sister, this act also suggests the distinction between natural and unnatural, and the living and the dead. Therefore, both Ambrosio and Elspeth violate the bodies of their relatives through acts that are transgressive in their collapse of cultural distinctions. Later in the text, Julia bumps into her mother (in Valentina's body) in the street:

'she was like Valentina, and she wasn't. There was an extraordinary resemblance and none at all: the girl had Valentina's features, and none of her expression ... Julia saw that the girl was pregnant' (376). Through her occupation of Valentina's body, Elspeth permits another occupant as Valentina's womb now holds a foetus who is perversely, both her brother and her son. Therefore, the Gothic family now inhabits one body as three generations – mother, daughter and son/grandson – occupy the one body, undermining the secure positions of individuals within a family unit. Generational boundaries are transgressed when Elspeth becomes pregnant and gives birth to her own son/grandson, whose simultaneous position echoes that of Elspeth as both Aunt and mother to the twins. Through such a perversion of the singular body, the family unit and the linearity that should compose it, the Gothic 'attempt[s] to articulate the unspeakable'.[23] In contrast to earlier Gothic fiction, the lineage of this immoral family will continue through a perverse, non-linear family line.

In conclusion, it can be noted that Gothic fictions demonstrate how the family unit is based on insecure foundations such as the familiar, the linear and the homely. The Gothic family destabilizes such conventional understandings of the unit, rendering the household unfamiliar, unhomely and violent, permitting 'access to the endlessly strange structure of the family'.[24] Similarly, the Gothic texts explored here expose the overlap between the home and the family, by disrupting the notion of the domestic as a secure space. Like deconstruction, the Gothic 'is no more than a rethinking of inhabitation'.[25] Unlike early Gothic texts such as *The Monk* and *Zofloya, or the Moor*, whose Gothic families are denied lineage, Niffenegger's *Her Fearful Symmetry* allows the Gothic family to continue through the non-linear; a perverse rendering of familial relations that accumulates three generations into one body. Gothic families also destabilize binaries such as natural and unnatural, self and other, and body and soul that determine acceptable actions of those within the family unit. Like the house, the family is determined by the distinction between inside and outside, a constructed division that the Gothic destabilizes through violence, necrophilia, haunting and the uncanny. As Wigley writes, the Gothic highlights 'the irreducible strangeness of [the family] that must be concealed by a range of institutional practices'.[26]

Notes

1. Mark Wigley, *The Architecture of Deconstruction: Derrida's Haunt*, p. 29.
2. Ibid., pp. 108–9.
3. Ibid., p. 108.
4. Ibid., p. 29.
5. Matthew Lewis, *The Monk*, p. 17. Subsequent page numbers are cited parenthetically in the text.
6. Charlotte Dacre, *Zofloya, or the Moor*, p. 82. Subsequent page numbers are cited parenthetically in the text.
7. Wigley, *Architecture of Deconstruction*, p. 104 and p. 107.
8. Ibid., p. 106.
9. Ibid., p. 118.
10. Ibid., p. 98.
11. Ibid., p. 106.
12. Ibid., p. 118.
13. Audrey Niffenegger, *Her Fearful Symmetry*, p. 207. Subsequent page numbers are cited parenthetically in the text.
14. Sigmund Freud, 'The Uncanny', p. 356.
15. Ibid., p. 356.
16. Wigley, *Architecture of Deconstruction*, p. 137.
17. Jacques Derrida, *Specters of Marx*, pp. 144–5.
18. Wigley, *Architecture of Deconstruction*, p. 109.
19. Freud, 'The Uncanny', p. 365.
20. Mary Shelley, *Frankenstein*, p. 55.
21. Ibid., p. 56.
22. Freud, 'The Uncanny', p. 356.
23. Wigley, *Architecture of Deconstruction*, pp. 29–30.
24. Ibid., p. 118.
25. Ibid., p. 120.
26. Ibid., p. 6.

References

Dacre, Charlotte, *Zofloya, or the Moor* (1806; Oxford: Oxford University Press, 2000).

Derrida, Jacques, *Specters of Marx: The State of the Debt, the Work of Mourning and the New International* (London: Routledge, 1994).

Freud, Sigmund, 'The Uncanny', in Albert Dickson (ed.), *Sigmund Freud: Art and Literature* (1919; London: Penguin, 1990), pp. 339–76.

Lewis, Matthew, *The Monk* (1796; Oxford: Oxford University Press, 1998).

Niffenegger, Audrey, *Her Fearful Symmetry* (London: Jonathan Cape, 2009).
Shelley, Mary, *Frankenstein* (1818; London: Penguin, 1994).
Wigley, Mark, *The Architecture of Deconstruction: Derrida's Haunt* (Cambridge, MA: MIT Press, 1995).

10

'As much a family as anyone could be, anywhere ever': revisioning the family in Poppy Z. Brite's *Lost Souls*

William Hughes

The Gothic family is a perplexing thing. If Gothic is, as some critics have suggested, an inherently conservative form, then the genre's representation of this most basic organizational paradigm of heterosexual culture ought rightly to be reassuring.[1] The family as presented within the Gothic seldom adequately fulfils that function, however. This appears, indeed, to be a persistent convention of the genre, as Richard Davenport-Hines suggests in his epic 1998 survey, *Gothic*:

> Often in Europe, Gothic was anti-domestic: it rejected safety and security, its protagonists ... were excluded from family life, or subverted its structures ... or had the self sufficiency to live without family encumbrances.[2]

Davenport-Hines wisely differentiates European Gothic from its later American and Asian counterparts here, though even in its customary old-world incarnation the genre arguably displays a more complex commentary upon domesticity than is implied in his generalization. Indeed, in Gothic generally, the exclusions, subversions and rejections identified by Davenport-Hines arguably fail to completely displace the domestic from its accustomed centrality in the management of social and sexual relations. In this respect, all Gothic – even that premised upon solitariness or singularity – may have an oblique claim to be a type of domestic fiction, albeit one with a radical attitude to the comforting, comfortable or contorted scenarios presented by images of marriage, family and lineal offspring. The domestic Gothic paradoxically embraces not merely those individuals who are located – or who choose to locate themselves – within a familial identity, but also defines those who reject, or who are rejected by, that socio-sanguine concept. The anti-domestic is thus, perversely, a reflex or phase of the domestic.

In Gothic, the family frequently – if not invariably – conceals secrets and shame incompatible with, or inadmissible within, the cultural narrative of conventional domestic life. In eighteenth- and nineteenth-century Gothic, the antidote to the failing family would seem to be simply the expulsion of its deficient components – the adulterous mother, the sexually predatory father, the physically or morally tainted child – and their subsequent replacement with a renewed, chastened and monogamous union between an idealized hero and heroine. Incest and wrongful inheritance, for example, are central to the plot of eighteenth-century novels such as Walpole's *The Castle of Otranto* (1764), Lewis's *The Monk* (1796) and Radcliffe's *The Italian* (1797), just as much as they inform Gothic-inflected Victorian texts such as Brontë's *Wuthering Heights* (1847) and, in the form of illegitimacy – another family secret – Collins's *The Woman in White* (1860). The retreat of Walpole's Manfred to a monastery, the deaths of Ambrosio, Schedoni and Sir Percival Glyde in *The Monk*, *The Italian* and *The Woman in White* respectively, and the demise of almost all of the blood-related protagonists in *Wuthering Heights*, indicate the consistency of this motif of domestic catharsis across the best part of a century. Even in Stoker's *Dracula* (1897), published almost 140 years after *The Castle of Otranto*, the predatory Count, who has infiltrated the family as much as its surrounding culture, is both expelled from England and then physically eradicated. *Dracula*, indeed, concludes with a most reassuring tableau, enacted some seven years later, centred upon that enduring image of domestic bliss, a married couple with their child.[3]

A future no doubt beloved of cultural and moral conservatism is thus assured because this recuperative union is both reactive and heterosexual, its boundaries and responsibilities being clearly defined at the point at which the anti-domestic is dissipated or its danger definitively contained. A joyous celebration of nuptials, such as is proposed at the end of *The Italian*, provides therefore a refreshing illusion of closure. The sexual threat posed to the heroine of Radcliffe's novel by her rapacious uncle-father-priest is as effectively dissipated as the earlier dynastic scheming of the hero's socially ambitious mother. With both parental antagonists dead, all is forgotten in a heartfelt chorus of '*O! giorno felice!*', repeated ad nauseam by the assembled domestics of the ménage at both the nuptial service and the subsequent fête.[4]

What is often overlooked in the reading of such conventional scenarios of resolution, though, is that the familial destinies of those involved are rarely depicted beyond, variously, their joyous nuptials, or the resumption of a domestic existence which the novel has depicted as having been temporarily interrupted – but ultimately not destroyed – by the intrusion of Gothicized disorder. The reassurance afforded by such corrective gestures is thus undemonstrated, shallow and premature. It is only the implicit trust that the reader is rhetorically guided to place in the stability of the domestic that ensures that such scenes may function as contextually satisfactory conclusions which demand no corrective coda and generate no uneasy questions.

This much, arguably, is true of eighteenth- and nineteenth-century Gothic, where tableaux of resolution, in the form of weddings, family groups or new beginnings, frequently conclude the more conservative exemplars of the genre. Postmodern Gothic, however, appears markedly less constrained by the persistent imperative that ensures, elsewhere in fiction and in Western culture more generally, the apparently unquestioned – or unquestionable – reproduction of the conventional paradigms of familial and heterosexual domesticity. Indeed, it is possible to discern within the contemporary Gothic a characteristic suggestion that the domestic, as it is conventionally understood, ought now to be regarded as an anachronism. This contention is paralleled, frequently, by the projection, in Gothic, of radical alternatives to the fractured and debilitated model of the mortal heterosexual family.

Such alternatives are as manifold as they are ingenious. They include – indeed, they may be defined by – associations not based upon genitally determined reproduction or lineage-defined dynasties. Revisions and revisionings of the family as diverse and innovative as post-apocalypse survivalist alliances, urban Goth subcultures, shape-shifting werewolf encampments, secretive vampire clans and exclusive homosexual communities enforce the possibility that such alternatives may be both viable and, indeed, unquestioningly *appropriate*, under the revised conditions which characterize twentieth- and twenty-first century communal life. Mutable sexual and species identities aside, such groupings may also arguably be said to respond to a human culture whose materialism and moralities have evacuated the meaning and the relevance of reproductive heterosexuality. Deprived of the support and sanction it once drew from religion, law, medicine and the social consensus more generally, the heterosexual and monogamous family of two parents plus associated offspring fails to function as a satisfactory Absolute in postmodernity. Yet, despite this diminution of its contemporary importance, the alternative communities which have replaced the earlier model of domesticity continue, perversely, to proclaim the apparent need for the excluded, the self-excluding and the downright Queer to live in a quasi-familial state corresponding to the domestic or the conjugal.

Nowhere is this more evident than in the fictionalization of the vampire at the twentieth-century *fin de siècle*. If the nineteenth-century vampire – as typified by the three canonical revenants, Polidori's Lord Ruthven, Le Fanu's Carmilla and Stoker's Count Dracula – is prototypically a solitary hunter, absorbed in his or her own afterlife and prioritizing the needs of the self alone, its contemporary equivalent is considerably more likely to be scripted as a communal being.[5] The intellectual isolation of the newly created or newly aware vampire is central to this substantial change in the deathstyle of the fictional Un-Dead which may be tentatively dated to the last quarter of the twentieth century. The vampire, in this period, has undergone a perceptible quantum shift from mere blind instinct into knowingness and introspection. Victorian vampires are uncomplicatedly what they appear to be. They have neither qualms nor questions about their nature, diet or ethical compass, and seem instinctively to know what perils to avoid just as they appreciate what delicacies to select. No one teaches Stoker's Lucy Westenra to fear the crucifix nor to respect the Host, as the Count, who inducts her into vampirism, is at best an absent parent and at worst an uncaring and selfish one.[6] Vampires, traditionally, are made, but not taught; they are a dispersed species rather than a tightly knit family, driven by selfish instinct, motivated primarily by singular self-preservation.

The postmodern impulse towards the depiction of communal (and ultimately domestic) vampire lifestyles is a natural reflex of the twentieth-century shift away from the revenant gifted with instinctual and certain knowledge, and towards one characterized by epistemological unease. The stress placed in postmodern vampire fiction upon the creation of the new revenant, or else upon the vampire's sudden discovery of its true nature, effectively shifts the status of the Un-Dead away from that of a fully functioning and independent adult and towards the vulnerability of a child in need of parenting or mentorship.

Such mentorship is seldom forthcoming. Lestat's apparently mocking refusal to answer Louis's questions regarding the traditional association of his kind with spiritual damnation in Anne Rice's *Interview with the Vampire* (1976) is well known, though it may itself stem from the elder revenant's own ignorance regarding what was once a theological and literary certainty.[7] Similar ignorance, however, punctuates subsequent Un-Dead fictions – both when a mentor is present to respond to interrogation by the newly initiated vampire, and when that individual is forced to comprehend his new situation in isolation.[8] If ignorance and fear impel the new vampire towards those who will (hopefully) bestow orientation and training, then the comfort of strength found in numbers keeps the revenant thereafter in analogous company. Rudimentary in *Interview with the Vampire*, this reconfiguration of the revenant as a social being, with a domestic life and often a familial hierarchy also, develops progressively across the closing quarter of the twentieth century and the first decade of the twenty-first. At the start of the second decade of the current century, it might be noted, the fractured vampire families of Rice's *The Vampire Chronicles* have been eclipsed by the supportive and thoroughly domestic vampire clans of Stephenie Meyers's teenage America.

Located at a *very* approximate mid-point between the tentative vampire family of *Interview with the Vampire* and the more sustaining Cullen Clan of Stephenie Meyer's *Twilight* (2005), Poppy Z. Brite's *Lost Souls* (1992) represents a landmark text in the fictional vampire's transition between the solitary and domestic states. While visualizing two types of the failed mortal family, *Lost Souls* embodies also two contrasting versions of vampiric domesticity. These latter respectively echo Rice and anticipate Meyer, as less and more successful models of sustainable community appropriate to the demands of modern, everyday Un-death.

Lost Souls arguably advances a new model of vampirism that abandons once and for all the historical association of the un-dead with an essentially positive humanity which is simultaneously superseded and debased through the fatal bite of the predator. Brite's vampires are created through sexual coitus rather than as a consequence of bodily death.[9] Their bodies are thus physiological hybrids of the human and the vampire. The novel's narrator renders this unequivocal following a wannabe Nosferatu's pointless request that Christian – the oldest revenant in Brite's novel – bite, and thus convert, him into an immortal Un-Dead. The narrator reflectively confides of Christian:

> He could not turn the boy into one of his kind any more than the boy could have bitten him and turned him human. They were of separate races, races that were close enough to mate but still as far away from each other as dusk and dawn. (90)

This innovative, but still fluid-based, relationship between the fledgling vampire and his progenitor prioritizes the literal genetic value of semen over the metaphorical or occult associations of blood. In consequence, the distinctive nature of the vampire is progressively compromised. If the rhetoric voiced by the narrator is that of racial distinctiveness, its implications are more broadly those of a species under threat from a counterpart whose features have evolved in response to quite another environment and dietary regime.

The decline of the integrity of the vampire species is signified physiologically in *Lost Souls* by the deterioration of those customary bodily features which, while functioning to serve the revenant's specific dietary needs, also maintain a continuity of association with the traditional un-dead of literature. Introducing the three vampires who make up the central un-dead family unit of *Lost Souls*, the narrator envisages the trio in the cliché language associated with the stylistic and behavioural excesses of contemporary urban youth. The language of the description shades subtly from the anarchic joy of the present to a wistful contemplation of glories now departed:

> The vampires got into town sometime before midnight. They parked their black van in an illegal space, then got hold of a bottle of Chartreuse and reeled down Bourbon Street swigging it by turns, their arms around one another's shoulders, their hair in one another's faces. All three had outlined their features in dark blots of makeup, and the larger two had teased their hair into great tangled clumps. Their pockets were stuffed with candy they ate noisily, washing it down with sweet green mouthfuls of Chartreuse. Their names were Molochai, Twig, and Zillah, and they wished they had fangs but

had to make do with teeth they filed sharp, and they could walk in sunlight as their great-grandfathers could not. But they preferred to do their roaming at night ... (5)

The association of the vampire with the clichés of shiftless, work-shy youth has a further significance, however. For all their evident youthful rebelliousness, the trio appear to have functioned as a sort of unit since at least the 1920s (37), though Zillah was born as early as 1895 (193). Though inhabiting an adult (but not visibly elderly) body, therefore, Zillah – as one mortal, though prescient, observer perceives it – is 'a being with no morals and no passions except those that could be gratified at a moment's notice, *a mad child allowed to rage out of control*' (188, my italics). The lack of self-control implied by this latter is hardly surprising. No one has trained Zillah into communal living. Implicitly born of absent fathers (9) into human matrices, and killing their mothers through the bloody process of birth (245–6), Brite's orphaned vampires elide easily into the problematic domestic spaces associated in prejudicial popular media with absent- or single-parenthood, deficient socialization and irresponsible adoption. The vampire is, evidently and consistently, a product of such unpromising social circumstances – and yet the alternatives offered by the mortal paradigm, a paradigm into which the vampire continues to stray due to promiscuous and irresponsible inter-species breeding, seem to offer little that is better.

Consider here the two mortal families – one organic, the other adoptive – associated with the central male protagonist who is alternately a troubled teenager called Jason, and a fledgling vampire named Nothing. The first of these, the single-parent family of his unmarried mother Jessy Creech, perversely inverts – while still undoubtedly exploiting – the Gothic convention of the incestuous father. In this postmodern revision of a persistent Gothic theme it is not the father who menaces his innocent child but the daughter who knowingly predates upon her parent's sexual vulnerability. Jessy's sexuality, moreover, is no simple matter of lust but is intimate to her desire to become un-dead through the act of consuming human blood – though her aspiration is, though she does not know it, utterly impossible in the context of the ironic vampire mythography which structures *Lost Souls*.

The Creech family is riddled with Gothic and vampiric signifiers, for all its evident mortality. The daughter of a suicidal mother

(57–8), Jessy is raised by a vocally Christian father (55) whose celibate widowerhood renders him both vulnerable to sexual temptation and obsessively interested in the sexuality of others.[10] Wallace Creech, to be sure, displays an unhealthy interest in his teenage daughter that goes beyond his current speculations regarding 'her lovers ... the lovers he didn't know' (77). Indeed, as the narrator intimates, his catching sight of her naked body – which she herself displays to him in the cause of draining his paternal blood – arouses both his current desires *and* repressed memories of her childhood form:

> She'd just come out of the shower, and her skin was as pink and white and dewy as spring. Her hair fell wet and straight along her cheeks. As he stared at her, she let the green towel fall from her breasts. Wallace had not seen his daughter's body since she was a young child, plump and androgynous, with pink buttons for nipples and a tiny clean fold of a sex. But now her breasts were round and smooth, with a girlish heaviness to them, and Wallace wondered how it would be to cup their weight in his hands, how it would taste if he took one of those creamy strawberry peaks in his mouth and sucked. (78)

Certainly, she is 'girlish' rather than womanly within his middle-aged gaze, and there is no suggestion here that Wallace is conflating Jessy's body with that of his dead wife, Lydia. Marital sexuality, though, is the ironic key to the whole scene.

The whole encounter, in fact, is a performative re-enactment of the thwarted seduction of Arthur Holmwood by his fiancée Lucy Westenra in Stoker's *Dracula* – a novel which Jessy has read and underlined 'in pencil and lipstick and what looked like blood' (77). For all his prurience, Creech's puritan priggishness has earlier prompted him to put down Stoker's 1897 work after reading a few paragraphs as 'he was too disgusted to continue. He hadn't known the novel was pornographic' (77). Jessy though, it might be assumed, is herself enjoying some form of transgressive, performative pleasure when she adapts Lucy Westenra's fictional words to her own present purpose, and seductively states 'I need your blood, Daddy. I'm hungry. Your Jessy's hungry. Come to me' (79). Jessy's stress on the last sentence, a phrase which Lucy vocalizes twice in *Dracula* when addressing, as 'husband', a man who is *not* her husband, is especially noteworthy.[11] Both seductive figures knowingly use the enticements of sexuality to achieve their supernatural ends, demanding sperm when, in fact, what they desire is blood. It is Jessy, though, that is the greater transgressor, for her enticements do ultimately lead to a taboo sexual encounter.

Though it is unequivocally Jessy who seduces Wallace, his inability to resist temptation is expressed in strikingly ambiguous terms in the narrator's account of the incestuous father's immediate reflection upon the encounter. Initially, his actions are associated with his supposedly over-indulgent parenting, and focused upon a deficiency of self-control and the inability to say 'no' to the only other living member of his family. The narrator recreates Creech's interior monologue of regret and attempted self-justification:

> Surely if she had not cajoled so, if she were not his daughter, his only joy, if he had not always tried to give her everything she asked for ... surely if he had lain with some other woman in the ten years since Lydia was gone ... (79, original ellipses)

Suddenly, though, self-justification is eclipsed by an apparently delicious memory, the narrator's sensual language evoking again that, at the time of the encounter, this was a pleasurable rather than a taboo experience for Creech:

> ... surely then, if the ache in his groin had not come bursting forth, he would have not let her lay him out and undo his trousers and straddle him, slipping around him as smooth and tight as sea anemones. Surely he would not have groaned and squeezed her heavy soft breasts between his fingers and thrust up and up into his daughter's wet-velvet heaven until she bent over him and he felt a metallic sting as of a razor blade beneath his jaw. (79, original ellipsis)

It is subsequently suggested by the narrator that Creech 'had begun to feel as if the thing that had happened were his fault, as if he had seduced her. As if he had forced himself into her' (79). Of course, it is not an act of rape, but the implication is that, for Wallace Creech, such a violation would be emotionally easier than admitting that his own daughter, herself, has carnally desired him – and that for a purpose which had little to do with conventional human sexuality.

Whatever the interpretation that prevails, the Christian family in its Gothicized incarnation is here typified by the lingering guilt of those who survive it. Recalling the event twenty years later, 'Wallace shut his eyes tight and shook his head. "Begone, Jessy", he muttered. "Torment me no more"' (77). Creech, it might be added, seeks to further expunge his sense of guilt by destroying a species he perceives as having been instrumental in destroying 'his memories of a child who danced and laughed, of a child who loved him, who was not a dark creature of sex and blood' (80). By his own violent actions 'he would eradicate his damnable sin. He would redeem himself' (80): it matters not that one of those he would kill would necessarily be his own grandson (285–6). From such an obsessive and possessive viewpoint, offspring are little more than possessions, functioning primarily to reassure or affirm parental values – and parental self-image.

Following the graphically detailed death of Jessy in childbirth (9–10), and in the absence of his vampiric biological father, Zillah, the unnamed child is taken by Christian from cosmopolitan New Orleans to a more prosaic northern milieu, the very heart of a bland vista of 'suburbs, stretching forever or until the end of Maryland, whichever came first' (62). Left, as cliché dictates, as 'A baby in a basket, abandoned on two strangers' doorstep some night' (72), a note pinned to his blanket proclaiming '*His name is Nothing. Care for him and he will bring you luck*' (72, original italics), Jason is the required component which will transform a childless couple into a family. As the coda to the handwritten note on his basket betrays, his adoption is not altruistic but egotistical and selfish. The family of Jason, despite its New-Age credentials, is arguably as illiberal and as alienating as Creech's dour single-parent theocracy.

Jason, indeed, is depicted as little more than a necessary accessory to two bourgeois adults who habitually choose to participate in such communal and voguish gatherings as 'a consciousness-raising group, a holistic health class, [or] an expensive dinner with other people like themselves' (75). His adoptive mother's care for him, in particular, is overbearing and patronizing, however well-meaning its intentions purport to be:

> 'My support circle meditated with our rose crystals tonight,' Mother said. 'I thought of you. I don't want to keep you from fulfilling yourself. I certainly don't want to decrease your potential ... You can get your ear pierced, after all, if you still want to. Your father or I will go with you'. (28)

Jason, of course, has already pierced his own ears – twice – 'with a thumbtack and several swigs of vodka at school' (28). His mother's attempt to appropriate his minor act of body modification is, in essence, an attempt to domesticate his rebellion, to effectively steal its personal meaning from him and to transform it into a family activity if not as wholesome as any other, then at least sanctified by parental approval. Jason, though, strives to keep such things within his own grasp, setting them aside as much as he demarcates his bedroom – which is, needless to say, decorated with 'Flowers from the graveyard' (26), a stolen bone, thrift-shop horror story collections and a clay skeleton bought at the *día de los muertos* festival in México – from the adult spaces of the house. Hence:

> He was strange to his parents, and they were incomprehensible to him. He rejected their world. There was not a thing in it that touched him, not a thing he could claim as his own. Sometimes he wondered whether there was a place for him outside the elaborate juju of his room, whether there was anyone in the world who would belong to him, whether he could ever belong to anyone. (70)

The key term here is 'belong', with its connotations of ownership and possession as much as community and integration. 'Who would want him?' the narrator continues: 'Not his parents, for sure. He had never belonged to them' (70). The family has been perverted into an institution of ownership, conformity and pride, a mode of defining the communal self as wholesome, orthodox and fit for purpose.

Ultimately, because of his outsider status, Jason must always be a disappointment to his adoptive parents, as if his lack of an organic connection to their genes implies also an inability to embody the components of the wholesome, modern lifestyle they aspire to, gleaned as it is from the promptings of television and glossy magazines. Thus, as the narrator suggests:

> Maybe the knowledge that he was not of their blood assuaged their guilt when they saw their son looking at them and knew that he had caught the distance in their faces. Maybe then they were able to justify their longing for a normal son who would keep his hair brushed out of his eyes, who would be elected student council president instead of sitting in his strange bedroom reading strange books, who would bring home little fresh-faced girlfriends in clean skirts and pink blouses. Maybe they looked at him and thought, *We did not make this creature out of our seed. He is not our mistake.* And they were right. (70, original italics)

Finding the note that confirms his status as an interloper – a situation of which the reader has been aware since the novel's prologue (10–11) – is an epiphanic moment for a child who has hitherto believed 'that he had been left at the orphanage as a newborn, that his parentage was unknown' (70). It explains – and justifies – his difference from his adoptive parents, and anticipates – though he does not yet know how – his impossible memories of a New Orleans he has never known, 'where the buildings were all gay with scrolled ironwork and the river flowed darkly past and soft laughter went on all night, every night' (73).

In Jason's mundane Maryland home there are ostensibly no Gothic secrets, 'no old love letters scented and tied with pastel ribbons, no scandals, no bloodstained lace handkerchiefs' (72). In the mind of an impressionable child, searching in his mother's drawer for the adoption papers he assumes will definitively inform him 'who his real parents were' and 'where he had come from and whether someday he might find his way back'(72), the familiar homestead assumes, however, a Gothic ambience of scarce-suppressed and impending violence. As the narrator confides:

> The shadows in the house lengthened. He became frantic, knowing with the terrible conviction of a twelve-year-old that these strangers named Rodger and Marilyn would murder him if they caught him going through their things; they would have an excuse at last. (72)

The fearful transgression which inspires such extreme images, though, is not that of searching among private possessions but rather Jason's desire to know, or to possess, a family other than that which has hitherto fostered him.

His discovery of the note – which he temporarily appropriates into his own possession (72–3) – allows him to dispossess himself effectively and ultimately from all that has been imposed upon him by two strangers who had, for whatever motivation, 'tried to make him into one of their kind' (72). Hence, his discovery of – literally – nothing leads to a self-possession taken in that very name:

> ... he ceased to be Jason. He became Nothing, for that was what the note named him. He still answered to Jason, but the name was like an echo of a half-forgotten life. *I am Nothing*, his mind whispered. I am Nothing. He liked the name. It did not make him feel worthless; on the contrary, he began to think of himself as a blank slate upon which anything could be written. (73)

Disconnected from a family that was never his, and adrift far from the colour and spectacle of his birthplace, Nothing does, however, enter into a type of community, albeit one that is ghostly and metaphorical rather than literal and present. Alone in the darkness of the only physical space that is uniquely his, Nothing ambiguously evokes the cultural spectre of widespread youthful dissociation in a nation which traditionally stresses the importance of stable family life:

> *I've got to get out of this place*, he thought just before dawn, and the ghosts of all the decades of middle-class American children afraid of complacency and stagnation and comfortable death drifted before his face, whispering their agreement. (29, original italics)[12]

Those disparate spectres, connected to him only by the common suffering of subjected youth, return to him, ultimately giving him courage as he meditates upon his midnight departure from the parental home:

> Somewhere in the music, perhaps outside the window in the cold night, somewhere above the melody and under the moon, those lonely little ghosts started whispering to him again: *You've got to get out of here. You've got to find your place, your family, before you rot and die.*
>
> 'All right, 'he said, after listening for a while. 'All right.' All at once he knew he had to leave. It was inevitable, and he wondered what he had been waiting for. (74, original italics)[13]

His abdication from his adoptive family is as much a retreat from that institution as a whole as it is from its specific incarnation in his life.

The successor to the Maryland family in which Nothing was arbitrarily placed by Christian some fifteen years earlier is vampiric rather than human. Unknowingly and ironically, Nothing has found his origins, for this family comprises the trio of vampires who were present in Christian's bar in New Orleans on the night of his conception. Significantly, Nothing chooses to participate in the trio's collectivity, and willingly embraces the proffered initiation ritual of drinking blood-laced liquor: as he says, 'I don't think drinking blood is so weird' (141). His response is, though he does not know it, decisive and determining of his fate:

> Nothing took the bottle, uncapped it, lifted it to his mouth, and sipped. There was some kind of liquor – vodka or gin, something

oily and stinging – but mingled with that was another taste, dark and sweet and a little decayed. Familiar. He brought the bottle down, blinked, then lifted it again and drank deep. (141)

The movement from sip to draught is significant. If Nothing does not yet understand his vampire nature, his new compatriots seem to suspect it, for: 'The air in the van was thick, tense; something seemed to be passing between them, something Nothing could not read' (142).[14] Later, of course, he will be attuned to this type of vampiric telepathy, which may be as much about reading body language as it is about any unprecedented or uncanny power.

In a final ritualized act of incorporation, Nothing and the three vampires drink the blood of Laine, one his Maryland school friends, 'his friend in another life' (160). A choice is again offered to Nothing, as the narrator makes clear:

Zillah smiled a dark smile and said 'Come and be one of us', and Nothing knew that he was being told to make his choice. Come and be one of us – or suffer the consequences of your refusal; die, or be alone, and never drink from the bottle of life again. *For the blood was the life* –. (160, original italics)

This moment is anticipated, however, by Nothing's own assessment that 'The blood in the wine bottle, which he had thought an exotic, delicious affectation ... was not an affectation. It was their life' (158). His willing complicity is further stressed by the narrator, thus: 'They were vampires. The cynical thought that they might be just a bunch of blood drinking psychopaths never crossed Nothing's mind' (158). Such thoughts are sufficient to eclipse the morality of the 'real world' (158), the standards of which Nothing has singularly failed to meet. Drinking blood is not an affectation akin to the fashionable bisexuality of his childhood friends (32), to recreational drug-use (158) or to the crystal-meditation of his adoptive mother.[15] Rather it is a genuine and unfeigned act, a compulsion or a basic *need* as well as a tantalizing pleasure. Though Nothing cries in the act of consuming the flesh and fluids of his former friend, he realizes that 'The taste of blood meant the end of aloneness' (160). He does not achieve communion with the ingested body but rather with those who have made it available to him.

Zillah's family is a viable homosexual community, though it is also ironically a *biological* entity.[16] Nothing is the son of Zillah by Jessy, though this remains unacknowledged until the concluding third of the novel, when Christian confides it to the assembled quartet (223). Prior to Nothing's induction into the pre-existing trio of male vampires, the group – all biologically unrelated[17] – has enjoyed a credible unity. Zillah, Molochai and Twig are even depicted by the narrator in a significant tableau, standing 'together, naked and embracing, the three of them as much a family as anyone could be, anywhere, ever' (83). Clearly, the definition of the family has deflected from its customary parameters here. It is based neither on literal consanguinity, nor on the polarity of complementary sexes, nor upon the valorization of comparative age. Its unifying factor is species-based, though this is expressed through recreational rather than reproductive sexuality and joyous polygamy rather than monotonous monogamy, as well as in the consumption of blood. It functions perfectly well as an alternative to the human family until the point at which Zillah is publicly identified as the father of Nothing – with whom he has been sexually involved for some time. Though there have been moments of tension within the family before the arrival of Nothing, possessiveness seems never to have been a lasting issue. This changes with the adoption of Nothing.

The crucial scenario which fatally fractures this apparently stable alternative family unit is scripted in the hours following Nothing's momentary preference of human to vampire company. In saving the life of the rock musicians Steve and Ghost, Nothing is implicated in the maiming of Zillah. There is a tense stand-off as Nothing attempts to extract an unconscious and bleeding Zillah from Ghost's house before the elder vampire revives and most likely kills the two musicians. At this juncture, Molochai and Twig turn upon Nothing, their motive a queer combination of hot-blooded revenge and affronted family honour: 'Now Nothing was sure Twig wanted to rip his throat open. Molochai would do it if Twig did. They would kill him and then tear into Steve and Ghost' (185). The recovered Zillah, however, punishes Nothing psychologically by seducing a girl in his place (213). Despite this perversely heterosexual challenge to his newly attained place within the homosexual vampire family, Nothing realizes the paradoxical strength that this event implies with regard to his position both within Zillah's affections and the vampiric foursome:

> But Nothing didn't care. Zillah could have this girl if he wanted her. Or any girl, any*one*. Because now Nothing knew something he

hadn't known before: Zillah wasn't just angry because Nothing had gone against him, or even because Nothing had hurt him. Zillah was jealous too, jealous of Steve and Ghost, of Nothing's love for them and their music. *The new knowledge coursed through him, making him feel weirdly powerful.* (213, original italics)

Consciousness of this emotional power over Zillah colours Nothing's parting words to the girl – who is Steve's estranged girlfriend, Ann – as the elder vampire draws him back into his arms: the younger vampire simply says 'Go find somebody else – I belong here, not you' (221).

On an earlier occasion in a Washington DC hotel suite, some time prior to the induction of Nothing into the family, Zillah is depicted momentarily with Molochai in an act of oral sexuality. This apparently exclusive coupling produces a rare moment of favouritism which temporarily fractures the trio, as the narrator notes:

> Molochai stared up at Zillah for a few moments. Then he hugged Zillah tighter, and it was as if two jagged edges fitted together inside him. He turned and saw Twig standing jealously alone, watching them. They each put out an arm to Twig, and he came to them. (83)

The scenario in which Zillah beckons a supposedly humbled Nothing back to his arms is the antithesis of this earlier gesture of inclusion and equality. Zillah addresses Nothing as much as he does Ann in this encounter:

> '... you mustn't love me. I have a lover already, if he has learned his lesson.' He held out his arms to Nothing. After the barest hesitation Nothing went to him, huddled into the curve of Zillah's arm, laid his head on Zillah's shoulder. (220)

Zillah here expresses a partnering preference which enhances his earlier physical leadership, and the exclusivity of this is exacerbated when his paternity of Nothing is revealed to the four vampires by Christian, shortly after this brief heterosexual interlude.

From this point in *Lost Souls* there is an evident division, the narrator depicting the immediate aftermath of both the sexual dalliance and the revelation of paternity through the tableau of 'Zillah, with his sleeping child in his arms; Molochai and Twig, clutching each other, still whispering' (224). The incestuous nature of the now-exclusive homosexual relationship that has divided the quartet generates two discreet reactions. For Zillah it is alluring. As he says, 'Well. That changes things, doesn't it? That makes things even better. Lovely' (224). Initiating a sexual act with his son, Zillah encourages Nothing to participate in a myth of personal possession as much as one of incestuous fantasy:

> Nothing heard himself say 'Daddy.'
> Zillah kissed his eyelids, his forehead, his lips. 'Yes, that's lovely. Call me that.'...
> 'My baby', said Zillah, and bit him gently. (233–4)

Zillah expresses a pleasurable *frisson* of human transgression on contemplating his own incestuous homosexual paedophilia. Nothing, in evident contrast to this, is apparently unperturbed by the revelation. Indeed:

> He had looked at himself in the bathroom mirror, still able to meet his own eyes, and had told himself: *For a week now you have been fucking your own father. His tongue has been in your mouth more times than you could count. You've sucked him off ... you've swallowed stuff that could have been your brothers and sisters!* (232, original italics)

Though the conventional language of revulsion is ostensibly present here, it is made clear to the reader that, in these revelations, Nothing 'could not disgust himself. He could not make himself ashamed' (232).

Clearly, Zillah's readjustment of the existing family dynamic effectively aligns this species-based alternative to the familiar paradigm of the non-vampire world. As Nothing understands, 'when Christian spoke those words outside the club – those terrifying, magical words, *You're Zillah's son* – the bond had become flesh' (233, original italics). Yet that bond is not marital but lineal, even if it is also perversely sexual, and it triggers for Zillah a new and ambiguous feeling which compromises the whole alternative nature of the family he has gathered around him. This much is suggested by the narrator's privileged view of father and son, asleep together:

> Zillah lay draped around Nothing. To someone who lifted the tin roof off the trailer and looked upon the two small figures tangled in the sheets, Zillah's position would have appeared both protective and possessive. He lay with his cheek against Nothing's smooth hair, and he thought, *Mine. More than anything was before, more than*

anything will ever be again, this is mine. My seed, my blood, my soul. (234, original italics)

In spite of Zillah's proprietorial attitude, Nothing himself remains promiscuous within their circle. His, indeed, would seem to be a more radical attitude to the relationship, for even when contemplating himself how Zillah would not let him go, he anticipates how in the future

> He would ride the highways with Molochai, Twig, Zillah, and now Christian, forever. They would drink and make wild love and never grow old. And he would never have to be alone. (233)

Nothing's sexual radicalism thus remains intact where his father's falters, the younger vampire's ongoing encounters with the others being rendered as pointedly as those he enjoys with Zillah.[18]

Later, in New Orleans, they are still 'his family' (289), but Nothing is tiring of the inconsistency of an institution that has become unsatisfactorily patriarchal in its power dynamic. As he complains, bitterly, to Zillah:

> You don't treat me like your son – you treat me like I'm half sex-slave and half lap dog. When I'm good you pat me on the head, and when I fuck up you yell at me and hurt me. But you never explain anything to me. What kind of a father are you, anyway? (288)[19]

The vampire family has thus become something akin to the human ones depicted in *Lost Souls* – all ownership, repression and violence – and, if anything, has deteriorated even beyond that model. A lack of explanation, an alternating pattern of approval and punishment, seem to suggest a strategy on Zillah's part to keep his son dependent and eager to please, to prevent him from ever feeling utterly secure in the affections of another.

On the death of Zillah, it might be added, the quartet reverts to a trio, with Nothing its strategic leader, but in no way its father figure.[20] In essence, the ascendancy that Nothing enjoys over his two older compatriots is based on physical strength and mental power, and dates back to the earlier violent encounter where Molochai and Twig came close to killing Nothing in revenge for injuring of Zillah. On that occasion, the two stare each other out:

> Twig's eyes blazed feral light.
> Nothing's eyes blazed right back at him.
> And Twig's eyes dropped. (186)

The violence here is connected with acknowledged relative power rather than unchallenged proprietorial ownership.

The Epilogue to *Lost Souls*, entitled 'Fifty Years Later', depicts Nothing as the leader of a snuff-rock trio, a live band who play to mortal nightclub audiences among the macabre paraphernalia of 'bone saws' and 'ampules of blood the audience thinks is fake' (387). In twenty-first century New Orleans, 'the endless party' of Mardi Gras continues as it has always done, and nightclubs 'have changed very little' (357). In such clubs, youthful figures, with bodies elaborately pierced and scarified, join in a community that is based upon pleasure and perception rather than genetic or possessive modes of ownership. The conventional family associated with the late twentieth century in the novel is utterly absent here, for it has been left behind, its limitations dismissed as irrelevant. 'Nothing leads his family out of the club in darkness' (359), the narrator intimates, but the term 'family' can surely only be deployed here for the benefit of a reader still locked in the mores of the twentieth century, and thus unable to fully grasp the potential that has been unlocked by this final demonstration of radical sexual and social organization.

Perhaps the most poignant reminder of the departure of the paternal family of old is one small incidental remark passed by Twig, who is considerably older than Nothing, when he seeks to wrest an ancient doubloon from the younger vampire's possession. Twig says – without irony, apparently – 'Let me see that, kiddo' (359). Catching sight of that doubloon has hitherto been an important element in the kinship ritual of the vampire species. A token of recognition between those who are – and who *know* they are – vampires, the coin was, at the novel's opening:

> scarred, tarnished, smudged with Molochai's sticky fingerprints. But the picture was still clear: the head of a beautiful man with enormous sensuous lips. Lips that would be as red as blood were they not carved in cold, heavy silver. Lips pricked by long sharp fangs. Below the man's face, in ornate letters, the word *BACCHUS* curved. (7)[21]

Sixty-five years later, that same doubloon has become debased, for 'Over the years Molochai's sticky fingerprints have worn away some of the carving: the man's lips no longer appear so full, and his sharp teeth are barely visible' (359). The overt parallel to the perceptibly retreating canine teeth (5) characteristic of those vampires born of blood diluted with that of a mortal mother is perhaps too obvious here. This parallel arguably obscures the specific and historical association of the doubloon with kinship, and with the ritualized signs of recognition which delineate vampires from non-vampires.[22] The quiet subtext of the proffering of this significant doubloon *within* a family grouping, rather than its deployment *outside*, to introduce one vampire to a stranger of the same species, intimates that such a type of outreach seems scarcely relevant in a world where vampires roam seemingly unperceived, and happily ingest their diet from 'a hypodermic needle full of blood' (358) rather than the trembling body of some victim. Tossed and spun in the air during the trio's cinematic exit from the New Orleans nightclub, the *Bacchus* doubloon has become in the twenty-first century, if not exactly a Mardi-Gras trinket, then something valuable only because of the anachronistic rituals it evokes in the minds of its possessors. The greater 'family' which constitutes the vampire species, seemingly, is now irrelevant, and no suggestion is made that the trio seek, or have ever sought, others of their own kind. Its replacement with an ostensible family of three, though, equally fails to integrate the vampires within conventional human models of domestic living which themselves may well be anachronistic within a world in which only nightclubs 'have changed very little' (357). In this family there is no father: all are eternal children – playful, irresponsible and destructive in equal measure – and the vampire's separation from humanity through a form of novel kinship is utterly complete, even where it is enacted in the very midst of human civilization.

Notes

1 David Durant, 'Ann Radcliffe and the Conservative Gothic'; Richard Davenport-Hines, *Gothic*, p. 4.
2 Davenport-Hines, *Gothic*, p. 267.
3 Bram Stoker, *Dracula*, ed. Hughes and Mason, pp. 420–1.
4 Ann Radcliffe, *The Italian*, pp. 411, 412–15.
5 The apotheosis of this, of course, is Richard Matheson's *I am Legend* (1954), where the human is configured as the solitary and abnormal predator, with the vampires the community beleaguered by his presence.
6 Stoker, *Dracula*, pp. 256, 281.
7 Anne Rice, *Interview with the Vampire*, p. 42.

8 Anne Rice, *The Vampire Lestat*, p. 109.
9 Poppy Z. Brite, *Lost Souls*, pp. 8–10, 217, 224. All references are taken from this edition. Subsequent page numbers are cited parenthetically in the text.
10 Lydia Creech's suicide is characteristically bloody in its excessive detail, Wallace finding her 'in her cooling red bathwater with her forearms slashed open from wrist to elbow' (78). Suicides, according to folklore, are prime candidates to become vampires after burial. See Paul Barber, *Vampires, Burial, and Death*, p. 30; Matthew Bunson, *Vampire: The Encyclopædia*, p. 249.
11 Stoker, *Dracula*, p. 256.
12 Cf. Brite, *Lost Souls*, pp. 31, 74.
13 Ibid., p. 31.
14 Ibid., p. 158.
15 As Jason confides earlier in *Lost Souls*, 'He realised that among these kids he called his friends he felt much more alone than he had in his room last night': Brite, *Lost Souls*, p. 32.
16 William Hughes, '"The taste of blood meant the end of aloneness"', pp. 142–57.
17 'Zillah had met them at an elegant garden party in the roaring twenties', giving them his own blood to drink as a sign of communion: see Brite, *Lost Souls*, p. 37.
18 See for example Brite, *Lost Souls*, pp. 227–8, 230, 233–4.
19 The parallel to Louis's complaint regarding Lestat in *Interview with the Vampire* cannot be ignored here.
20 The quartet was briefly a quintet following the temporary incorporation of the New Orleans vampire, Christian.
21 The doubloon is not offered to Nothing in the van, for example, as he does not yet comprehend his true nature, even though his future associates may well suspect it.
22 When the doubloon is offered to Christian by Molochai, the former responds, ritualistically, 'How – how do you come?', receiving the reassuring reply 'In peace' (7). This seemingly formal exchange is followed by a mutual ingestion of blood from the wrist, shed not with the teeth but through the deployment of the edge of a broken bottle.

References

Barber, Paul, *Vampires, Burial, and Death: Folklore and Reality* (New Haven, CT: Yale University Press, 1988).
Brite, Poppy Z., *Lost Souls* (London: Penguin, 1992).
Bunson, Matthew, *Vampire: The Encyclopædia* (London: Thames & Hudson, 1993).

Davenport-Hines, Richard, *Gothic: One Hundred Years of Excess, Horror, Evil and Ruin* (London: Fourth Estate, 1998).

Durant, David, 'Ann Radcliffe and the conservative Gothic', *Studies in English Literature, 1500–1900*, 22:3 (1982), 519–30.

Hughes, William, '"The taste of blood meant the end of aloneness": vampires and gay Men in Poppy Z. Brite's *Lost Souls*', in William Hughes and Andrew Smith (eds), *Queering the Gothic* (Manchester: Manchester University Press, 2009), pp. 142–57.

Radcliffe, Ann, *The Italian, or the Confessional of the Black Penitents*, ed. Frederick Garber (1797; Oxford: Oxford University Press, 1981).

Rice, Anne, *Interview with the Vampire* (London: Futura, 1977).

——, *The Vampire Lestat* (London: Futura, 1990).

Stoker, Bram, *Dracula*, ed. William Hughes and Diane Mason (1897; Bath: Artswork Books, 2007).

11

Gothic half-bloods: maternal kinship in Rowling's Harry Potter series[1]

Ranita Chatterjee

In discussing her Harry Potter heptalogy J.K. Rowling makes a suggestively Gothic claim for her texts: 'My books are largely about death. They open with the death of Harry's parents. There is Voldemort's obsession with conquering death and his quest for immortality at any price.'[2] Rowling, of course, refers here to the night of Voldemort's murder of Harry's parents that informs the entire series. While the subject of death itself is not Gothic, a narrative about the porous boundaries between life and death may very well be. We will recall that the central relationship/kinship that frames and animates all seven books between the boy hero Harry Potter and his nemesis Tom Riddle – infamously known as Lord Voldemort or the Dark Lord – involves their mutual death, resurrection and physically intertwined existence. Voldemort kills Harry twice. In the pre-history to the series, the first time Harry survives Voldemort's killing spell – known as the Unforgivable Avada Kedavra Curse – baby Harry goes on to live, unbeknownst to him, with a fragment of the much older, evil wizard Voldemort's soul inside of him, while Voldemort is reduced to a near-death, animal-like existence because he has lost this part of his soul. In the middle of the heptalogy, Voldemort is able to resurrect himself from a perverted foetus-like shape to a partly mature human male form by violently taking the blood of the fourteen-year-old Harry. At the end of the entire series when Voldemort kills Harry for a second time, the now seventeen-year-old Harry again survives because the Avada Kedavra Curse only kills the fragment of Voldemort's soul that has been inside Harry. Throughout the series, Voldemort attempts to murder Harry numerous times, but Harry is always able to escape death. Their literal sharing of blood and souls suggests that neither character is wholly independent. Both are a product of the violent fusion of a young boy's blood and an old man's soul. It is thus not surprising that the Harry Potter novels are generally categorized as superior examples of crossover fiction – fiction that appeals to adults, adolescents and children and that interrogates the boundaries between these three age categories. That crossover literature also explores 'other "edges" of being, such as being born and dying',[3] two prevalent themes in the Harry Potter novels, also suggests that Rowling's entire series may be considered Gothic.

I will explore how Voldemort's premeditated assassination of James and Lily Potter becomes the defining cataclysmic event that produces the Gothic kinship that structures the lives of both Harry and Voldemort. Of particular significance for my argument is the fact that their kinship ties revolve around Voldemort's lost matrilineal ancestry and Harry's dead mother's blood. As we shall see, in Voldemort's quest for immortality through a careful and repeated literal fragmentation of his soul, Voldemort attempts to trace a direct line from his dead witch mother back to the ancient pure-blood (that is, with no human intermixing) Peverell family whose last descendant was his mother. And it is Harry's human-born witch mother Lily's attempt to defend her baby on the night of Voldemort's assassination of her and her husband that transforms her actual blood into a magical shield that protects baby Harry from Voldemort's wrath. Indeed, because of her sacrifice, Voldemort seeks out Harry not only to ingest his blood, thereby overcoming Harry's protective magical barrier, but also to resurrect himself from his degraded physical state with the power of Lily's blood. Thus, I shall suggest that Rowling's Harry Potter series reconfigures the act of sacrifice as not only feminine and maternal, but also problematically generative insofar as Lily's blood both protects the hero and empowers the villain.[4]

Literal and figurative blood ties play a key role in the Harry Potter world: individuals are classified as pure-blood (only wizarding pedigree), half-blood (a mix of wizarding and human ancestry), or Muggle (only human lineage). As I will discuss, Voldemort's half-blood status makes him desire a pure-blood wizarding world. Voldemort's hatred of his human father's blood status also manifests as his hatred of the half-blood Harry Potter. In his meteoric rise to power during the so-called First Wizarding War, the newly fashioned Lord Voldemort and his Death Eater followers (militant pure-blood Dark Arts practitioners) determine the fate of Harry Potter. Based on his Death Eater's partial hearing of Professor Sybill Trelawney's prophecy that a son with the 'POWER TO VANQUISH THE DARK LORD'[5] will be born near the end of July to parents who have defied him three times, Voldemort chooses to kill baby Harry in the hopes that this act will eradicate future threats to his ascendancy in the Wizarding world. But, as readers learn in book five *Harry Potter and the Order of the Phoenix*, this prophecy could have equally applied to Harry's school friend Neville Longbottom. Because of their positions as Aurors, or elite special operatives trained in magical combat and working for the Ministry of Magic's Department of Magical Law Enforcement, Neville's parents Alice and Frank confront Voldemort three times. They are eventually captured and tortured to the point of insanity with the Cruciatus curse by Voldemort's lieutenant and most loyal Death Eater Bellatrix Lestrange. As with Harry Potter, Voldemort's actions make Neville a near-orphan. Unlike Harry who is raised by his abusive maternal Muggle relatives with no knowledge of his half-blood wizarding/Muggle heritage, Neville is raised by his pure-blood witch grandmother Augusta Longbottom and given a proper magical education. In choosing not the pure-blood but the half-blood baby boy, Voldemort selects one like himself. Voldemort is the son of the Muggle Tom Riddle and the witch Merope Gaunt. As the headmaster of the British wizarding boarding school, Hogwarts School of Witchcraft and Wizardry, and Harry's mentor Albus Dumbledore tells the teenage Harry, Voldemort 'saw himself in you before he had ever seen you' (*OP*, 842). In choosing Harry, Voldemort tries to abject (in Julia Kristeva's sense of the word as eliminate that which disturbs identity) his half-blood lineage in order to fortify his desire for pure-blood status. That Voldemort commits this horrendous crime against a baby because of a prophecy about the waning of his power further seals the connections between the two generations of male characters in a Gothic direction – by which I mean concerned with omens, warnings and familial legacies.

The second part of Trelawney's divination that Voldemort's Death Eater does not hear and, therefore, cannot warn his master against is significant for my discussion of this Gothic kinship between hero and villain. Trelawney states that Voldemort will 'MARK' this son who is fated to destroy him 'AS HIS EQUAL, BUT HE WILL HAVE POWER THE DARK LORD KNOWS NOT ... AND EITHER MUST DIE AT THE HAND OF THE OTHER FOR NEITHER CAN LIVE WHILE THE OTHER SURVIVES' (*OP*, 841). Through his choice of Harry and not Neville, Voldemort thus constitutes one of the boys as his equal other in a dialectical battle that neither, by definition, may win. Voldemort 'mark[s] him as his equal' with the infamous lightning bolt scar (*OP* 842). In so doing, Voldemort ensures Harry's future by transferring some of his dark powers to baby Harry. Voldemort's act of murdering the Muggle-born witch Lily Potter unknowingly causes another fragment of his already broken soul to attach itself to baby Harry. And it is the scar on his forehead, the external signifier of the internal presence of a part of Voldemort's soul, that gives Harry the ability 'to detect Voldemort's presence, even when he is disguised, and to know what he is feeling when his emotions are roused' (*OP*, 827). As Dumbledore explains at the end of *Harry Potter and the Order of the Phoenix*, Voldemort's actions have enabled Harry to escape the Dark Lord's wrath 'not once, but four times so far – something that neither your parents, nor Neville's parents ever achieved' (*OP*, 842). For Harry, the narrative of his parents' courage in confronting Voldemort functions as a primal scene and inscribes him in wizarding lore as 'The Boy who Lived' and later 'The Chosen One' destined to vanquish the Dark Lord.

The catastrophic night of his parents' murder also marks Harry in another way. Emerging from a deep-rooted filial love, Lily's valiant attempt to protect her baby son from the Dark Lord's Avada Kedavra spell or killing curse marks Harry (who is repeatedly told that he has his mother's eyes) with what we might call a maternal blood sacrifice. Dumbledore tells Harry of 'an ancient magic' (*OP*, 835) that transformed his mother's love and consequent sacrifice into 'a lingering protection ... [that Voldemort] never expected, a protection that flows in your veins to this day ... in your mother's blood' (*OP*, 836). Lily's loving sacrifice literally infuses Harry's blood with a powerful magical immunity against Voldemort's violence. After his resurrection in book four *Harry Potter and the Goblet of Fire*, Voldemort recounts for his Death Eaters how on the fateful night of his murder of the Potters his killing 'curse [directed at baby Harry] was deflected by the woman's [Lily's] foolish sacrifice, and it rebounded upon' himself shattering his body and soul and reducing him to 'less than spirit, less than the meanest ghost ... [sic] but still ... alive').[6] Because Voldemort blames baby Harry for his degraded existence, he regards Harry as his mortal enemy whose blood he requires for his return to physical wholeness: 'I wanted Harry Potter's blood. I wanted the blood of the one who had stripped me of power thirteen years ago ... [sic] for the lingering protection his mother once gave him would then reside in my veins too' (*GF*, 656–7). As Voldemort explains to his Death Eaters after he is resurrected, Harry's 'mother left upon him the traces of her sacrifice' (*GF*, 652–3). Thus, Harry and Voldemort both share the magical properties of Lily's blood and house a portion of the Dark Lord's soul.

Rachel Falconer points out that the literal and figurative 'blood-bond makes itself evident in the growing telepathic connection between Voldemort's mind and Harry's'.[7] However, it is also their mutual soul relationship that enables Harry's clairvoyant link to the reborn and physically whole Voldemort. When Harry regularly loses consciousness from the searing pain stemming from his lightning-bolt scar and sometimes when he dreams, Harry sees through Voldemort's eyes and experiences Voldemort's emotions. Voldemort, too, can enter Harry's dreams and 'assault ... [his] mind' (*OP*, 828). We might say that in these unconscious spaces, whether in dreams or in fainting spells, either each character becomes the other or each ceases to exist as a distinct identity. I suggest that their bond occupies a Gothic heterotopic space, to use Fred Botting's reading of Michel Foucault's term for non-hegemonic counter-sites that are neither here nor there. Although Harry's and Voldemort's internal soul and blood ties are thoroughly part of the power dynamics of the wizarding world, their undesired Gothic affiliation undoes the notion of both discrete subjectivity and individual agency. If, in David Punter's words, 'the subject-matter of the Gothic, both historically and in its contemporary manifestations, is precisely to do with these moments of destabilization, moments when the power of what the psychoanalyst Jacques Lacan refers to as *méconnaissance*, or misrecognition, becomes irresistible, and we find ourselves driven by forces beyond our own compass', then Rowling's Harry Potter heptalogy is Gothic throughout because of this central perverse kinship between a broken evil man and an heroic over-determined boy who share souls and blood.[8]

Infused with a dead mother's potent love in a magical economy of blood, inscribed with the infamous lightning-bolt scar by his arch nemesis, and consequently, unknowingly constituted as a half-blood container for a fragment of this older evil wizard's soul, young Harry Potter experiences a decidedly Gothic relationship with Lord Voldemort. Indeed, I argue that the seven novels of Rowling's Harry Potter series ultimately explore the dynamics of two related and suggestively Gothic economies: one of maternal blood exchanges and transfusions, and another of paternal soul dissections and replications. Here, I shall focus on what I call the Gothic maternal economy of blood in the Potter heptalogy.

As in many early British Gothic novels from Ann Radcliffe's classic *The Mysteries of Udolpho* (1794) to Charlotte Dacre's lesser known *Zofloya, or The Moor: A Romance of the Fifteenth Century* (1806), the absent or dead mother enjoys a commanding presence in the Harry Potter series. This is certainly the case for Harry's and Tom Riddle's/Voldemort's respective mothers Lily Evans Potter and Merope Gaunt Riddle. Upon their death, both women determine the destinies of their respective sons. This is also the case for Professor Severus Snape – head of Slytherin House at Hogwarts and a former Death Eater working as a double agent for Dumbledore – who models himself after his brilliant witch mother Eileen Prince. As is well known, Radcliffe's young Emily St. Aubert only begins her own Gothic adventure that ends with her marriage to Valancourt after her mother's death and her father's weeping over a mysterious miniature (that turns out to be a portrait of his sister Laurentini de Udolpho/Marchioness de Villeroi otherwise known as Sister Agnes). Similarly, though Dacre's young Victoria de Loredani experiences her own lascivious yet tyrannical Gothic adventures aided and abetted by a Satanic Moorish servant in a feminine version of Lewis's famous 1796 archetypal male Gothic novel *The Monk*, she continually blames her actions on the sins of her adulterous and absent mother Laurina de Loredani. Neither Harry nor Voldemort explicitly blames his mother. Yet both are situated along a particular path of socio-historical subject development in the existing hierarchical power relations of the wizarding world by the specific circumstances of his mother's death. Indeed, as an orphaned wizard who only discovers his magical identity with Dumbledore's assistance at Hogwarts, Tom Riddle is an earlier generational model for the orphaned Harry Potter whose entry into

Hogwarts and identity formation is also facilitated by Dumbledore. Although Dumbledore's affectionate concern for Tom Riddle, Harry Potter and, to a lesser extent, Severus Snape suggests that surrogate fatherhood plays a crucial role in enabling the destinies of these three unique wizards from two successive generations, it is significantly their absent witch mothers (whether Muggle-born or not) that construct their subject positions in the wizarding world.

In the sixth book, *Harry Potter and the Half-Blood Prince*, readers are given a tantalizing history of Tom Riddle's and Severus Snape's blood lines. Both Tom and Severus, who meet at Hogwarts, are half-blood wizards with Muggle fathers and witch mothers. We discover that Severus Snape was raised in a Muggle neighbourhood close to Harry's mother. Because of the abusive relationship between Snape's witch mother Eileen Prince and his Muggle father Tobias Snape, the awkward and antisocial young Severus relishes his life at school. At Hogwarts, young Snape is placed in Slytherin House. Salazar Slytherin is one of the four founders of Hogwarts whose friendship with the only other male founder of Hogwarts, Godric Gryffindor, is severed over the issue of their students' blood purity. For Slytherin only wanted pure-blood students at Hogwarts, whereas the other founders Gryffindor, Helga Hufflepuff and Rowena Ravenclaw were open to Muggle-born witches and wizards. Despite Severus's friendship and burgeoning love for young Lily Evans who is in Gryffindor, he joins the Death Eaters and refashions himself as the 'Half-Blood Prince' identifying with his mother's suggestively more aristocratic magical heritage. Moreover, young Snape's expertise in making potions also connects him to his mother Eileen Prince who was the best potions student in her time. In fact, Snape signs his *Advanced Potion-Making* textbook, which he inherited from his mother, with the moniker 'the Half-Blood Prince'.[9] Indeed, Snape follows in his mother's path by later becoming Hogwart's highly regarded Potions Professor.[10] Snape's identification with his mother, however, is complicated by her blood-status. Initially, young Snape's disgust with his abusive Muggle father's behaviour towards his pure-blood mother leads him to his fellow student Tom Riddle's pure-blood ideology and to joining the newly-formed Death Eaters. Only with his growing understanding of his own love for his Muggle-born witch friend and classmate Lily Evans (Harry Potter's mother) and his passion for chemical transformations (that is, potion-making) does the older

Snape switch his loyalties from Lord Voldemort to Dumbledore. Of course, neither Voldemort nor Harry Potter readers know this until the last book *Harry Potter and the Deathly Hallows*. Harry only discovers the extent of Snape's sacrifice after Snape's death. It is in Snape's extracted memory which the dying Snape gives Harry that Harry sees how much Snape's love for Lily has shaped his Professor's destiny. My point is that Snape's position in the wizarding world as one of Voldemort's devoted servants and secretly Dumbledore's assistant is powerfully shaped by his pure-blood witch mother.

In fact, Snape's enduring love for his childhood friend transforms the signifier of his soul's ecstasy, namely his Patronus, as they are called in the series. Remus Lupin, one of many Defence-Against-the-Darks-Arts Professors at Hogwarts, explains that the Patronus is a spectral presence of 'positive force', 'a projection of ... hope, happiness, the desire to survive'[11] that a wizard generally conjures as a shield against soul-sucking Dark Creatures such as Dementors who cause despair and depression. The shape of these corporeal, yet ethereal light-filled and bright white forms is an animal that is unique to each wizard. However, in the case of deep and abiding love, two wizards may share the same animal shape. This is the case for Snape whose Patronus is Lily's doe. For Snape, this form of kinship is complicated by Lily's son Harry: 'Loving Lily Potter, he is bound to protect her son, but equally he is bound to hate Harry for being the sign of Lily's love for another man'[12] and, therefore, associated with the despised blood lineage of his male rival James Potter. However, unlike the classic British eighteenth-century Gothic novel's obsession with primogeniture, the Harry Potter heptalogy repeatedly returns to the strength and imposing force of maternal blood lines and maternal presence. It is because of his allegiance to his mother's potion-making abilities and her love for him that Snape recognizes his own devotion to Lily and his subsequent protection of her son Harry to be his most important role.

Voldemort, too, rejects his Muggle father's parentage and adopts his maternal lineage in transforming from young Tom Riddle to Lord Voldemort. Unlike Snape's mother Eileen Prince who is a student at Hogwarts, when in a memory we meet Riddle's/Voldemort's mother Merope for the first time, she is described by Harry as a grimy, impoverished 'defeated-looking person' (*HBP*, 205). In this memory, Voldemort's grandfather Marvolo Gaunt calls her a 'dirty Squib' (*HBP*, 206), meaning a witch with no magical abilities. Marvolo defiantly claims that they are the 'last living descendants' of the great Salazar Slytherin, '[g]enerations of purebloods, wizards all' (*HBP*, 208). It is this pride in blood purity and his sister Merope's infatuation with the handsome Muggle son Tom of the village squire Thomas Riddle that causes Merope's brother Morphin Gaunt to attack the Muggle, and his father Marvolo Gaunt to attack the employee of the Ministry of Magic who comes to take Morphin away. These two crimes land the Gaunt men in the wizarding prison Azkaban. Merope's magical powers and obsessive love only blossom in the absence of her abusive and arrogant male relatives. With a love potion, she is able to secure her marriage to Tom Riddle and become pregnant. That she names her baby boy Tom Marvolo Riddle, even though her husband abandons her in horror (after she stops giving him the love potion according to Dumbledore's speculations) before their son is born, suggests that she did not relinquish her elusive desire for love from both her father and her husband. Because Merope dies shortly after giving birth and her husband Tom Riddle Sr. has no connections with her, little Tom is raised in an orphanage. Tom Riddle's disgust with his Muggle father's abandonment coupled with his painful realization that his witch mother did not even use magic to save her life results in his hatred for love, family and especially Muggles. Young Tom Riddle thus revives his pride in being the heir to Salazar Slytherin, and not the third Tom Riddle, through his metamorphosis into Lord Voldemort. Through his adoption of this grandiose title, Tom emphasizes his pure-blood Slytherin ancestry. In *Harry Potter and the Chamber of Secrets*, a young Tom Riddle tells a younger Harry that he was not going to 'use my filthy Muggle father's name forever ... I, in whose veins runs the blood of Salazar Slytherin himself, through my mother's side ... I, keep the name of a foul, common Muggle, who abandoned me even before I was born, just because he found out his wife was a witch'.[13] Both Snape and Voldemort, then, try to erase their non-wizard lineage as they aspire for blood purity. Moreover, as in a Freudian family romance where the son imagines his parents to be of noble birth, Snape and Voldemort through their personal signifiers ennoble themselves as a Prince and a Lord respectively. But, significantly for my discussion, they do so in the name of their maternal blood heritage.

It is important to recall that Harry is protected from Voldemort's wrath by the 'ancient magic' (*OP*, 835) of his mother's blood sacrifice. Because Lily dies defending her baby son from Voldemort's killing curse, her blood becomes Harry's shelter from the Dark Lord's aggression. As Dumbledore explains, 'Your mother's sacrifice made the bond of blood the strongest shield I could give you' and 'I put my trust, therefore, in your mother's blood. I delivered you to her sister, her only remaining relative' (*OP*, 836). As long as Harry thinks of his Muggle Aunt Petunia Dursley's home as his, no matter how abusive she, his Uncle Vernon and his cousin Dudley are, Voldemort cannot hurt Harry in this house. Even Voldemort recognizes this fact as he explains to his Death Eaters his inability to kill Harry: 'Dumbledore invoked ancient magic, to ensure the boy's protection as long as he is in his relations' care. Not even I can touch him there' (*GF*, 657). Indeed, Lily's shared blood ties with her horrid sister Petunia also transforms Petunia's blood into Harry's 'refuge' (836) in a corporeal manifestation of Freud's paradoxical uncanny as related both to the familiar homely or *heimlich* and unfamiliar unhomely *unheimlich*. As much as the narrative discourages our sympathies for the Dursleys, we must acknowledge that Petunia's blood ensures Harry's survival for the first eleven years of his life. Later, two pure-blood women also guarantee Harry's life: the surrogate mother Molly Weasley and his school enemy's mother Narcissa Malfoy. Despite her numerous sons, Molly is proud to provide the famous Harry Potter the love and affection he needs to sustain his newly discovered and developing wizarding identity. Near the end of the series in the final Battle of Hogwarts, in response to Voldemort's request that she confirm that Harry has indeed died, Narcissa lies to the Dark Lord. She knows that the only way for her to enter Hogwarts Castle and find her son Draco is as part of 'the conquering army'.[14] Narcissa's motivation for lying has nothing to do with Harry, but everything to do with her love for her own son Draco. Significantly, then, these two pure-blood maternal proxies rule Harry's fate.

Ironically, Lily's maternal blood also determines Voldemort's fate. As I have discussed, at the end of book four *Harry Potter and the Goblet of Fire*, Lily's blood is the last crucial element that is partially and violently taken from Harry for Voldemort's resurrection to full bodily form. Notably, Voldemort's vampiric absorption of Lily's blood symbolically makes him Harry's brother in a series that repeatedly focuses on matrilineal blood lines. In the last novel,

Harry Potter and the Deathly Hallows, Harry willingly sacrifices his self for the greater good of the Wizarding and Muggle worlds. After his spilling of this powerfully magical maternal blood, a sacrifice that repeats Lily's original act, Harry finds himself apparently having a conversation with the late Dumbledore in the crucial chapter entitled 'King's Cross'. In this liminal space from which Harry will be resurrected to rejoin his fellow wizards in the final battle against Voldemort, Dumbledore explains that it is precisely because the Dark Lord took Lily's blood and thus her protective shield inside himself that 'he tethered ... [Harry] to life while he [too] lives' (*DH*, 709). Suman Gupta suggests that 'the theme of blood or lineage' is 'analogous to race in our world'.[15] Although this interpretation aptly applies to the politics of blood in the series insofar as Lord Voldemort and his followers do advocate for and actively participate in an eugenics project to eliminate all but pure-blood wizards, Gupta's reading cannot account for the economy of blood between hero and villain. For Ximena C. Gallardo and C. Jason Smith, '[w]hile Voldemort's immediate foe is Harry, and vice versa, it is Lily Potter's eternal love that thwarts Voldemort throughout the series'.[16] As I have suggested, this is precisely because of Harry's and Voldemort's fraternal sharing of Lily's maternal blood sacrifice. While her sacrifice for Harry provides him with a defensive safeguard against Voldemort's violence and, in effect, constitutes Harry as the only one to ever survive the Dark Lord's killing curse, Lily's sacrifice also ensures Voldemort's rebirth because her act magically transforms her blood into the required potent ingredient for his resurrection. Thus, their bonds of kinship, however despised, not only follow an economy of blood exchanges, but also produce an alternative Gothic economy based not on paternal but on maternal blood lineage.

This brings me to the importance of reading the series through a Gothic lens. Children's literature, almost from its inception, has been both didactic and entertaining. This ideology also permeates the critical scholarship on crossover literature, such as Rowling's Harry Potter series. But children's and much crossover literature, as we all know, is rarely written by children or adolescents: rather like a paranoid Freudian patient, the writers of children's and adolescent literature must imaginatively recollect and recreate the emotions, thoughts and words of their young characters. Furthermore, in Rowling's long magical series that spans many years in the lives of its fictional characters and avid readers, both groups grow and develop in a mutual mirroring of emerging identities. The cross-readers of Rowling's cross-genre heptalogy may be seen as Kristeva's subject-in-process, that is, not fully abject or fully part of adult society. In the case of Harry Potter, he is neither a benevolent teenage boy nor a psychopathic older man: he is both. In ignoring this Gothic, inherently transgressive, side of Harry Potter and of children's and adolescent literature in general, we risk denying the complexities of children's circuitous and uneasy path to adulthood and our own incomplete trajectory to that elusive goal. Ultimately, I claim that in Rowling's Harry Potter series with its explorations of transgressions and regulatory controls, non-normative desires and punitive measures, conflicted family dynamics and alternative social units, bodily inscriptions and ideological interpellations, it is the economics of the maternal blood exchanges that unite its two dominant characters in a Gothic direction. Through their kinship, 'The Boy Who Lived' and 'He Who Must Not Be Named' return crossover literature to its Gothic roots.

Notes

1 At California State University, Northridge, I thank the following students who explored some of these ideas with me in my senior undergraduate seminar in Spring 2009, 'The Harry Potter Series and Critical Theories': Norma Aceves, Chris Adajar, Adina Altschuler, Samantha Berley, Araceli Blanco, Annie Carlin, Isabel Casas, Mark Cope, Sean Curran, Sara Dean, Tannaz Faal, Melissa Filbeck, Lorie Hamalian, Micah Harding, Marielle Kriesel, Nicole Miller, Sean Pessin, Sherif Rezkalla, and Kelly Rowley. I am grateful for numerous conversations on the Harry Potter series that I had with Masha Grigoryan while advising her Senior Honors thesis 'A Trinity of Choices: A Theoretical Analysis of the Harry Potter Series' (Spring 2011), and that I had with Erin Delaney for whom I was a second reader for her Master's thesis '*Harry Potter*: Out of the Cupboard under the Stairs' (Fall 2007). I also thank the College of Humanities Faculty Fellowship and Grant Program at California State University, Northridge for a much needed course release to complete this chapter (Spring 2012). Finally, I am indebted to two female family members: my sister Ronjaunee Chatterjee for introducing me to the Harry Potter novels and discussing them and this chapter with me, and my nine-year-old daughter Syontoni Hattori-Chatterjee for sharing her child's perspective on the series.
2 Geordie Greig, 'There would be so much to tell her …'.

3 See Rachel Falconer, *The Crossover Novel*.
4 There has already been a decade's worth of wide-ranging scholarship from a variety of disciplinary and critical perspectives, with obviously more attention paid to the earlier novels than the last one published in 2007, that explores the Gothic turn in specific books (such as Falconer's discussion in *The Crossover Novel* of the first chapter and outline of *Harry Potter and the Goblet of Fire*), specific scenes (such as June Cummins's analysis of Hermione's bathroom experiences in *Harry Potter and the Philosopher's Stone*), specific themes (such as Cummins's overall discussion of female development in the series) and specific elements (such as Anne Hiebert Alton's identification of the ubiquity both of Gothic architecture – dungeons, subterranean passages, secret entrances – and supernatural characters – werewolves, zombies or Inferi and Voldemort himself). See also Lena Steveker's article: through her discussion of the parallels between Stevenson's *The Strange Case of Dr Jekyll and Mr Hyde* and Rowling's novels, Steveker argues that though 'Rowling's Harry Potter series inscribes itself into the late-Victorian Gothic tradition of problematising the destabilisation of the unitary Self' (p. 75), the heptalogy 'also re-affirm[s] conceptions of identity which are clearly indebted to liberal humanism' (p. 80). I am more concerned with how the *narrative of Harry Potter*, not just particular books or sequences, invokes the Gothic through the literal and figurative blood and soul ties that connect Harry Potter and Lord Voldemort along matrilineal lines.
5 J.K. Rowling, *Harry Potter and the Order of the Phoenix*, p. 841. Subsequent page numbers are cited parenthetically in the text as *OP*.
6 *Harry Potter and the Goblet of Fire*, p. 653. Subsequent page numbers are cited parenthetically in the text as *GF*.
7 Falconer, *The Crossover Novel*, p. 67.
8 David Punter, 'Anti-canon theory', p. 520.
9 J.K. Rowling, *Harry Potter and the Half-Blood Prince*, p. 193. Subsequent page numbers are cited parenthetically in the text as *HBP*.
10 Nearly a generation later in his own potions class, Harry Potter accidentally gets to use Eileen Prince's/Snape's textbook. With the aid of young Snape's various marginal annotations that not only modify the procedural steps but also improve the effectiveness of the resulting potion, Harry for once becomes a model student supplanting his friend Hermione Granger from this coveted position.
11 J.K. Rowling, *Harry Potter and the Prisoner of Azkaban*, p. 237. Subsequent page numbers are cited parenthetically in the text as *PA*.
12 Rachel Falconer, *The Crossover Novel*, p. 67.
13 J.K. Rowling, *Harry Potter and the Chamber of Secrets*, p. 314. Subsequent page numbers are cited parenthetically in the text as *CS*.

14 J.K. Rowling, *Harry Potter and the Deathly Hallows*, p. 726. Subsequent page numbers are cited parenthetically in the text as *DH*.
15 Suman Gupta, *Re-reading Harry Potter*, p. 101.
16 Ximena C. Gallardo and C. Jason Smith, 'Happily Ever After', p. 98.

References

Alton, Anne Hiebert, 'Generic fusion and the mosaic of *Harry Potter*', in Elizabeth E. Heilman (ed.), *Harry Potter's World: Multidisciplinary Critical Perspectives* (New York and London: 2003), pp. 141–62.

Botting, Fred. 'In Gothic Darkly: heterotopia, history, culture', in David Punter (ed.), *A Companion to the Gothic* (Oxford: Blackwell, 2000), pp. 3–14.

Cummins, June, 'Hermione in the Bathroom: The Gothic, menarche, and female development in the *Harry Potter* Series', in Anna Jackson, Karen Coats, and Roderick McGillis (eds), *The Gothic in Children's Literature: Haunting the Borders* (New York and London: Routledge, 2008), pp. 177–93.

Falconer, Rachel, *The Crossover Novel: Contemporary Children's Fiction and Its Adult Readership* (New York and London: Routledge, 2009).

——, 'Young adult fiction and the crossover phenomenon', in David Rudd (ed.), *The Routledge Companion to Children's Literature* (London and New York: Routledge, 2010), pp. 87–99.

Freud, Sigmund, 'The Uncanny', in James Strachey et al. (ed. and trans.), *The Standard Edition of the Psychological Works of Sigmund Freud*, Vol. 17 (London: Hogarth Press, 1955), pp. 235–41.

Gallardo, Ximena C. and C. Jason Smith, 'Happily ever after: Harry Potter and the quest for the domestic', in Giselle Liza Anatol (ed.), *Reading Harry Potter Again: New Critical Essays* (Santa Barbara: ABC-CLIO, LLC, 2009) pp. 91–108.

Greig, Geordie, 'There would be so much to tell her …', *The Telegraph*, 10 January 2006. www.telegraph.co.uk/news/uknews/1507438/There-would-be-so-much-to-tell-her....html (Accessed 5 August 2012).

Gupta, Suman, *Re-reading Harry Potter* (Basingstoke: Palgrave Macmillan, 2009).

Kristeva, Julia, *Powers of Horror: An Essay on Abjection*, trans. Leon S. Roudiez (1980; New York: Columbia University Press, 1982).

—— *Revolution in Poetic Language*, trans. Margaret Waller (1974; New York: Columbia University Press, 1984).

Punter, David, 'Anti-canon theory', in Patricia Waugh (ed.), *Literary Theory and Criticism: An Oxford Guide* (Oxford: Oxford University Press, 2006), pp. 519–29.

Rowling, J.K., *Harry Potter and the Sorcerer's Stone* (New York: Scholastic, 1997).
——, *Harry Potter and the Chamber of Secrets* (New York: Scholastic, 1998).
——, *Harry Potter and the Prisoner of Azkaban* (New York: Scholastic, 1999).
——, *Harry Potter and the Goblet of Fire* (New York: Scholastic, 2000).
——, *Harry Potter and the Order of the Phoenix* (New York: Scholastic, 2003).
——, *Harry Potter and the Half-Blood Prince* (New York: Scholastic, 2005).
——, *Harry Potter and the Deathly Hallows* (New York: Arthur A. Levine Books, 2007).
Steveker, Lena, '"Your soul is whole, and completely your own, Harry": the heroic self in J.K. Rowling's *Harry Potter* Series', in *Heroism in the Harry Potter Series* [e-book] (Ashgate Publishing: 2011), pp. 69–83. (Accessed 2 March 2012.)

12

'They fuck you up' – revaluations of the family in contemporary British horror film: Steven Sheil's *Mum & Dad*

Johannes Schlegel

Introduction: Transgressive family horror

Horror film, like all Gothic narratives,[1] is predominantly concerned with representations and negotiations of the family, its values and ideologies. In an illuminating generalization, the film scholar Tony Williams even suggests that 'all horror films, in one way or the other, are family horror films. Some reveal the association more clearly than others'.[2] While this is an interesting claim that deserves to be investigated more thoroughly, it is a surprising fact that little to no pertinent academic discussion of 'family horror' exists. Given the attention that is currently paid to all things Gothic and horror in literary and cultural studies, this neglect seems all the more striking. To date, the only comprehensive, book-length study is Tony Williams's *Hearths of Darkness*, published in 1996, in which he seeks 'to argue for the validity of a family trajectory within horror itself' and to 'suggest [that] the genre's very form has an intrinsic relationship with family situations'.[3]

At the core of Williams's argument lies the notorious film *The Texas Chainsaw Massacre* (1974), written and directed by Tobe Hooper, which is basically acclaimed for two things: first, for kick-starting the genre of the backwoods slasher film almost single-handedly, and second, for its depiction of one of the bleakest images of the family. The film – which was initially banned in several countries but is now considered a cult classic – tells the story of the siblings Sally (Marylin Burns) and Franklin Hardesty (Paul A. Partain), who, accompanied by three friends, travel to an unspecified place in

Texas in order to visit their grandfather's grave, which is reported to have been desecrated and robbed. Afterwards, they are, due to a gasoline shortage, forced to take a detour and spend the night at an old Hardesty family homestead. They are killed off one by one by a deranged, cannibalistic family living in one of the nearby houses – all except Sally, who manages to escape after a night full of torment. In one of the film's key sequences, she awakens from unconsciousness and realizes that she is bound to a chair made of bones and other human remains and, as the cannibals' captive, is thus forced to participate in a grotesque family dinner scene. At the head of the table resides the mummified, yet still alive Grandpa Sawyer (John Dugan), with three of his descendants assembled at his side. Significantly, neither of them carries a proper name;[4] the script refers to them as the Hitchhiker (Edwin Neal), the Cook (Jim Siedow), and Leatherface (Gunnar Hansen), a mentally retarded giant constantly wearing a mask made of tanned human skin. They decide that Grandpa should bludgeon Sally to death with a hammer – just as he used to butcher cattle in a nearby slaughterhouse. However, he is physically too weak to deliver a fatal blow and Sally is able to escape. According to Williams, it is scenes like this that 'invert normal civilized values' that inform his reading of the film as 'one of the most nihilistic visions of the family, revealing a hearth of darkness that generates violence and destruction.'[5]

While this vision's radicalness is unique indeed – and maybe only equalled by both Wes Craven's *The Hills Have Eyes* from 1977 and Alexandre Aja's remake of the same title from 2006[6] – it ultimately comes into question whether the Sawyers can actually serve as representatives and epitomes of family per se and, therefore, whether '*normal* idealized family images' are indeed contradicted.[7] It seems as if Williams avoids reflecting further on the normal as category – which he seems to presuppose unconditionally – and thus fails to give consideration to the fact that normalcy is not something that is ontologically given but, first and foremost, performatively generated – that is, a discursive entity which is historic and which evolves historically: 'the idea of a norm is less a condition of human nature than it is a feature of a certain kind of society'.[8] Precisely because the normal as category can only be conceived by means of a difference – the normal versus the abnormal, the normal versus the deviant, the normal versus the transgressive, for example – it proves to be a dynamic relation requiring constant negotiations and re-affirmations. It can be argued that the exclusion of the deviating 'other', therefore, is constitutive rather than challenging the norm. The Sawyers, ultimately, cannot be perceived as other than deviant.

In spite of all the careful analogies between the Sawyers and the Hardestys in Hooper's text, a boundary consisting precisely of the state of familial identity, and therefore impermeable, remains between both families – connecting and separating them at the same time – ultimately rendering the dynamic-transgressive possible in the first place. The dual opposition, not least being manifested in the violent killings, thus cannot be eradicated entirely and the more antagonistic the families prove to be, the more the normal is constituted.

One cannot fail to notice that the cannibals, as familial entity, are rotten to the core. What becomes obvious in the above-mentioned dinner scene, for instance, is the absence of biologically female family members, since the sole female role is a queered one and is performed by a disguised and cross-dressed Leatherface. This absence proves to be total: while Sally stumbles through the house, looking for a way out, she discovers the mummified bodies of the Grandmother and her dachshund. Unlike Grandpa, however, she is clearly dead – and thus this can be read as an intertextual allusion to Alfred Hitchcock's *Psycho* (1960), in which the corporeal remains of Norman Bates's (Anthony Perkins) mother function as iconography of a perverted familial order and the neurosis inevitably following from it. Additionally, while it is stated repeatedly that Hitchhiker and Leatherface are brothers, the relation between the Cook and the other family members is highly ambiguous. On the one hand, it is suggested that he could be either their father or their brother or, on the other hand, both at the same time, since incest appears to be a more or less apparent undercurrent in the whole *The Texas Chainsaw Massacre* franchise. The mere existence of this ambiguity, however, as well as the fact that their family is so vile and perverted that to call them 'dysfunctional' seems a shallow euphemism, subverts the critical *topos* that the Sawyers are an 'embodiment of the family as such'.[9] Rather, precisely because the family is depicted as deviant and transgressive, Tobe Hooper's film does not undermine traditional family values but *ex negativo* confirms them: the Sawyers are the way they are because their familial structure is a deviant one failing to provide a safe haven in times of political and economic crisis. In this sense, horror film in general and *The Texas Chainsaw Massacre* in particular prove to be outright conservative.[10]

As narrative pattern, this dialectics of transgression and (re-)affirmation of the normative family informs almost all films of the family horror genre, especially those representatives that ostensibly seem to revalue familial values. Striking cases in point are, among others, Charles Kaufman's *Mother's Day* (1980), Joseph Ruben's *The Stepfather* (1987), or both Rob Zombie's *The House of 1000 Corpses* (2003) – a postmodern *tour de force* that is heavily indebted to *The Texas Chainsaw Massacre* – and its prequel *The Devil's Rejects* (2005).

It is against this backdrop that I will discuss Steven Sheil's *Mum & Dad* (2008) in greater detail in the following sections. I will argue that this film, as medium of a discursive transformation of familial semantics, reflects and negotiates a paradoxical notion of order and cultural discontent in a way that can no longer be described adequately with the Gothic *topoi* of transgression and the monstrous. Given that the film was released in 2008 and that it takes up recent trends in horror film, the problems to which it responds prove to be all the more pressing.

Mum & Dad: A Heathrow Airport Chainsaw Massacre

Steven Sheil's debut *Mum & Dad* was the first film that was funded by the *Film London Microwave* scheme, which challenges film-makers to shoot a feature film for no more than £100,000.[11] Although the film can never shake off its B-movie look and feel entirely, it makes a virtue of this limitation and condenses its story into a gruesome, ruthless piece of cinema which belongs to a fairly new genre of horror film for which *New York Magazine*'s chief film critic David Edelstein coined the term 'torture porn':

> As a horror maven who long ago made peace, for better and worse, with the genre's inherent sadism, I'm baffled by how far this new stuff goes – and by why America seems so nuts these days about torture … Certainly television has become the place for forensic fetishism. But torture movies cut deeper than mere gory spectacle. Unlike the old seventies and eighties hack-'em-ups (or their jokey remakes, like *Scream*), in which masked maniacs punished nubile teens for promiscuity (the spurt of blood was equivalent to the money shot in

porn), the victims here are neither interchangeable nor expendable. They range from decent people with recognisable human emotions to, well, Jesus.[12]

This cinematic trend, however, is neither an exclusively American phenomenon nor exclusive to the horror film. Regarding contemporary French *auteur* cinema, for instance, James Quant states that 'Bava as much as Bataille, Salo no less than Sade seem the determinants of a cinema suddenly determined to break every taboo, to wade in rivers of viscera and spumes of sperm, to fill each frame with flesh, nubile or gnarled, and subject it to all manner of penetration, mutilation, and defilement'.[13] It is striking, however, that most torture porn of any provenance seems to be based on familial themes and motifs. To give but three examples, all of which stirred up considerable controversy: in the French film *Frontier(s)* (2007), directed by Xavier Gens, an old Nazi family living in the French borderlands secretly strives to create and establish some kind of Aryan super-race consisting of their descendants; Alexandre Aja's *High Tension* (2003) tells the story of Marie (Cécile de France), a young woman who, due to her repressed homosexual desire for her best friend Alex (Maïwenn Le Besco), becomes schizophrenic and brutally kills her own family; in Alexandre Bustillo's *Inside* (2007), a nameless woman (Béatrice Dalle), who has lost her unborn child during a car accident, takes revenge on the person she holds responsible for this catastrophe – Sarah (Alysson Paradis), an expectant mother – by cutting the foetus out of her body.

Mum & Dad transfers this international trend to an English setting and takes it to its extremes. Its reductive plot centres on the young Polish office cleaner Lena (Olga Fedori), who has just started working at Heathrow Airport. She is befriended by her young colleagues Birdie (Ainsley Howard) and Elbie (Toby Alexander), who claim to be adopted siblings. At the end of their shift, Birdie causes Lena to miss the last bus back into the city and persuades her to spend the night at their parents' house, which is in walking distance from the airport. After arriving, Lena is suddenly knocked down from behind. When she regains consciousness, she finds herself chained to a bed in a run-down room, her vocal cords disabled. She is introduced to the eponymous Mum (Dido Miles) and Dad (Perry Benson), informing her that from now on she is supposed to live with them as their new daughter. Ultimately, after being repeatedly exposed to increasing mental and physical abuse, Lena kills Mum, Dad, and Birdie and thus is able to escape.

As if the film's thematic line of attack remained too subtle and unclear, one of its trailers as well as an early pitch of a poster explicitly refers to Philip Larkin's poem 'This be the Verse' and, by quoting its famous first line – 'They fuck you up' –, thus stimulates a certain way of 'reading' the film.[14] It is not so much dysfunctional parenting that is seen as problematic but rather functional, which is, however, nonetheless inherently and inevitably damaging. In full, the first stanza of Larkin's poem, which was published in 1974 as part of the collection *High Windows*, reads: 'They fuck you up, your mum and dad. / They may not mean to, but they do. / They fill you with the faults they had / And add some extra, just for you.' Accordingly, both Mum and Dad serve as archetypes of familial discourse, lacking any trait of an individual identity. In the mentioned sequence, in which Lena faces them for the first time, Mum merely utters 'I'm Mum. He's Dad'. Not only are their proper names not mentioned once throughout the whole film, but also the closing credits only refer to them in their familial role. Furthermore, the absence of first names and its function is emphasized by the fact that Lena, in a creepy rite of passage, is designated a new identity. Having explained to her that she had always wished for another daughter, Mum gives her the name 'Angel', since she regards her as a 'precious gift from heaven', the child she had wished for: 'I said to Dad the other day that I wanted another girl. And look, here you are.'

Consequentially, Lena is, from now on, 'Mum's little angel', which the latter not only demonstrates by constantly calling her by the name Angel, but also by cutting virtual wings into her skin. Lena's new identity is thus literally engraved onto and into her body. The 'power of the name', which is constitutive for this performative primal scene, is analysed by Judith Butler as follows:

> One is, as it were, brought into social location and time through being named. And one is dependent upon another for one's name, for the designation that is supposed to confer singularity ... First, a name is offered, given, imposed by someone or by some set of someones, and it is attributed to someone else. It requires an intersubjective context, but also *a mode of address*, for the name emerges as the *addressing of a coinage to another, and in that address, a rendering of that coinage proper*. The scene of naming appears then first as a unilateral action: there are those who address their speech to others.[15]

The sequence described so far, however, differs significantly from the description of the speech act given by Butler in that it rejects the Derridean notion of an always already iterative performative,[16] which is central to Butler's claims: 'and yet, the one who names, who works within language to find a name for another, is presumed to be already named'.[17] Precisely the fact, however, that Dad is *not* properly named ensures that the sequence has indeed to be understood as a primal scene of familial power relations, which therefore establishes the founding law of the father, or, to use a phrase coined by Jacques Lacan, 'le nom du père'.[18]

The trauma of initiation is further acted out as the sequence continues. The injured Lena is brought before Dad declaring the rules of the house, which, from now on, is the whole world to her:

> When you are in my house, you're to abide by my rules. Do you understand? In this household, family is everything. You can forget what's outside that window; it doesn't exist. From now on, this is your world. Your Mum and your Dad, your brother and your sister – that's it. You do your chores, keep your mouth shut, and your mother happy or you'll have me to answer to … In return, you get a roof over your head, you get your meals, you get all your clothes.

Since during his speech several cuts to close-ups of the family members' faces occur, indicating their compliance and affirmation, the concept of the nuclear family as relying on mutual affection is turned upside down, if not rejected, thus bringing to light a hidden conception of the modern family as a disciplining unit. In light of this inversion, one might be inclined to take *Mum & Dad* as a mere satire and deconstruction of middle-class values, which become manifest and are represented in scenes such as the previously quoted one, and which is instantiated by transferring said values to a working-class, if not underclass context. Steven Sheil's film, however, is far more ambitious than to simply settle for this. Rather, it aims at a radical revaluation of familial values, which results in a notion of the family as an entity that is intrinsically perverted, yet the ineluctable condition of being and of subjectivity. Having said this, Lena's torment turns into the coming-of-age story of a conflict between the individual and both the all-embracing and traumatic symbolic order of the real, in which any 'outside' is, albeit necessarily existent, inaccessible and thus, to some extent, imaginary. It is thus crucial to understand that, in the following, the notion of the outside has to be understood metaphorically and refers to the realm of the family.

On several occasions, *Mum & Dad* points out that the mechanism establishing and sustaining this familial order relies on the connection of sex and violence. On the morning after being incorporated to the family, Lena is brought into the kitchen to have breakfast with them. While reluctantly eating, her gaze falls upon the TV standing next to the dinner table on which hardcore porn is shown as bizarre family entertainment. Since the explicit sound remains audible throughout the whole sequence, the pornographic content is juxtaposed to Dad, who enters the kitchen carrying body parts wrapped in plastic, dripping with blood. On the one hand, this sequence does not only offer a variation of the violent-sex-motif that had already been introduced – an earlier sequence showed Dad masturbating with a piece of human liver into which he ejaculated – but also reveals that pornography itself functions as medium which renders said symbolic order and its constitutive masculine violence visible.

The sequence therefore, on the other hand, also points to the film's own mediality and thus self-referentially reflects on its own indebtedness to the voyeuristic exhibition of maimed and mutilated bodies – that is, its indebtedness to the torture porn genre. By means of this self-referentiality it becomes obvious that the film itself inevitably cannot avoid but to also distribute, proliferate and thus participate in the symbolic order. The all-embracing superstructure, which Lena – for whom nothing exists 'outside that window' any longer – has to face, holds true for the film itself and, even moreso, its surrounding cultural context: there is no possibility to reach or to imagine the outside of familial discourse. All that lies beyond the realm of a family is – yet another family. In this sense, Dad is absolutely correct in stating: 'family is everything'.

What is critically negotiated, then, is nothing less than Occidental culture and its Christian roots. This is brought to the fore by the final sequence – the family celebrates a premature Christmas – which is the film's most impressive scene and, at the same time, the only one that is truly innovative in terms of horror film. Noticeably, it is the sole sequence with diegetic music, but the tacky song being audible stands in eerie contradiction to the *mise-en-scène*, which is effectively rendered by means of montage. Initially, a close-up is shown of a hand whose palm is transfixed by a nail, thus resembling the holy wounds of Christ – an analogy that is pursued further consequently. It is followed by a shot of a head of a young man wearing a crown not of thorns, but of tinsel. Another close-up follows, this time of a bleeding stump, which in turn is rapidly followed by a counter-shot to the laughing, dancing Mum and Dad, wearing festive crowns. Another cut and close-up reveals that a candle was inserted into the young man's chest. Finally, after another close-up has shown his crotch and penis, a medium long shot reveals the family's living room, decorated as for Christmas. The frame consists of a triptych: while the left side is taken by the dancing parents and the centre by the grotesque Christ-like figure, the right side is reserved to a young disabled woman in a wheelchair: Angela, the brain-damaged, hardly viable and sole biological child to Mum and Dad.

The symbolism is rather obvious: instead of being the site of salvific history any longer, the family becomes both the manifestation of a phallocentric Christian ideology and its hegemonic and dominant code which – regardless of whether its tenets are universally or individually accepted or not – continues to shape the 'phantasmal deep structures' of Occidental cultures,[19] becoming the origin of trauma and violence, of violent as well as traumatic sex inevitably following from it. According to this, the monstrous is no longer the abject, excluded or formerly repressed,[20] that now returns and threatens and haunts the family – that is to say: the law – rather, it amalgamates with the family and the familial law itself. From this notion stems a paradox that ultimately puts an end to the monstrous as expedient category of the Gothic. In a chapter in his recent book *Limits of Horror*, tellingly entitled 'Daddy's dead', Fred Botting states that 'Monstrosity becomes a general condition rather than an exception. When monsters become, rather than mark out the limits of, humanity, it is difficult to see why the name 'monster' needs apply at all. Monsters are the norm.'[21] *Mum & Dad* is a case in point proving this rationale.

At this point, it becomes obvious what separates *Mum & Dad* from *The Texas Chainsaw Massacre*, even though it is cited more or less explicitly on several occasions and Sheil himself once referred to his film as 'The Heathrow Airport Chainsaw Massacre'. If the ending of *The Texas Chainsaw Massacre* was ambiguous – in the nick of time, Sally escapes Leatherface on the back of a passing pickup truck – then *Mum & Dad* is plain hopeless.[22] While Larkin was rather playfully able to identify a point of exit ('get out as early as you can / And don't have any kids yourself'), this is denied to a vision as forceful and consistent as *Mum & Dad*. After Lena has killed her 'parents', she is shown on her own, standing on a desolate field, screaming. To overcome the parents ultimately results in a bleak vision of Heideggerian Being-in-the-world as thrownness (*Geworfenheit*). This point is further demonstrated by the fact that, while Lena stabs Mum and Dad, in a cross-cut sequence Elbie strangles his 'sister' Angela, for whose care he was responsible, before leaving the house: to be free, you have to completely sever all ties, which results in absolute solitude.

By means of its generic radicalism and reduction, therefore, *Mum & Dad* transcends not only one of the most enduring story lines of Gothic fiction – that is to say, that of the family and its ideology under threat, be it from within or from without – but also the inherent dialectics of transgression which, as narrative pattern, as I have initially argued, informs almost all family horror in the wake of Hooper's *Texas Chainsaw Massacre*. In order to be able to understand just how radical *Mum & Dad* actually is, the following and last section focuses on the genealogy of this triadic connection between the Gothic, the family and transgression.

Gothic families, the problem of evil, and the dialectics of transgression

As literary foundation stone, not only does Horace Walpole's *The Castle of Otranto* reveal that the primal scene of Gothic fiction is a tainted marriage, but also it historically marks the birth of the genre from the spirit of two coinciding discourses: on the one hand the failure of theodicy as *grand récit*, and the consolidation of new family formations on the other hand. Gothic fiction is conceived at the intersection of these discourses.

Due to sceptical challenges, but also an inherent atrophy of the persuasiveness of prevalent explanations stemming from natural theology, the long eighteenth century witnessed an incipient and increasing dislocation of evil from traditional religious patterns of explanations.[23] In the wake of this secularizing process, however, evil loses its ontological status. While in theodicean systems, culminating in the works of William King and Gottfried Wilhelm Leibniz, evil has been unambiguously identified as something either natural, moral or metaphysical,[24] it now begins to turn into an immanent yet opaque quality. Henceforth, in the legacy of the doctrines of privation, evil is predominantly conceived of as the absence of good (*privatio boni*) and thus as a non-being. Terry Eagleton, among others, still grapples with the ensuing problems when, in his recent book *On Evil*, he states 'that evil is not fundamentally mysterious, even though it transcends everyday social conditioning. Evil as I see it is indeed metaphysical, in the sense that it takes up an attitude toward being as such, not just toward this or that bit of it. Fundamentally, it wants to annihilate the lot of it'.[25] Evil is deprived of any ontological status and, consequentially, hardly an operable or conceivable term any longer. Instead, it crystallizes into a discursive cipher and floating signifier, which, since it discharges varying phenomena of meaning, can be ascribed to an almost infinite number of occurrences.

As opposed to negative ontological approaches towards evil, structural-pragmatic ones still allow for conceiving evil positively as violation of a morally binding norm. Most prominently, Georges Bataille insisted on both the intrinsic relation between literature and transgression, and their liberating effect:

> The desire for Good limits the instinct which induces us to seek a value, whereas liberty towards Evil gives access to the excessive forms of value … The very principle of Good establishes the 'farthest point' from the social body, beyond which constituted society cannot advance, while the association with the principle of Evil establishes the 'farthest point' which individuals or minorities can temporarily reach. Nobody can go any 'farther'.[26]

The basic discursive formation, at least as far as Gothic fiction is concerned, that provides for such binding norms is that of the nuclear family, as it develops from the Early Modern period onwards.[27] In order to understand, however, why it is precisely this discursive formation that lends itself to the Gothic, which is henceforth obsessed not only with the nuclear family but also with its transgression, something has to be taken into account that Michel Foucault describes as the functionalization of this emerging family type. According to Foucault, the nuclear family as institution came into being as means of control, of surveillance and thus as regulation of infantile sexuality:

> What is now being constituted is a sort of restricted, close-knit, substantial, compact, corporeal, and affective family core: the cell family

in the place of the relational family; the cell family with its corporeal, affective, and sexual space entirely saturated by direct parent-child relationships. In other words, I am not inclined to say that the child's sexuality that is tracked down and prohibited is in some way the consequence of the formation of the nuclear family, let us say of the conjugal or parental family of the nineteenth century. Rather I would say that this sexuality is one of the constitutive elements of this family ... By highlighting the body of the child in sexual danger, parents were urgently enjoined to reduce the large polymorphous and dangerous space and to do no more than forge with their children, their progeny, a sort of single body bound together through a concern about infantile sexuality, about infantile autoeroticism and masturbation.[28]

According to Foucault, the reduction of the family to its cell unit henceforth serves to constitute what is normal by excluding the monstrous, the abnormal as, for instance, the masturbating child and thereby induced physical ailments. In a characteristic train of thought Foucault argues that neither the normal nor the abnormal is pre-existent to its respective other. Rather, both forms are generated equally and simultaneously in a single act of disjunction.

How influential the connection between transgressions of the institutionalized family's law and Gothic fiction proves to be has been described in a number of studies: in her book *The Contested Castle* (1989), Kate Ferguson Ellis distinguishes between insider- and outsider narratives and describes how each of these specifically challenges and eventually subverts domestic ideology; Valdine Clemens's *The Return of the Repressed* (1999) contextualizes Walpole's novel to the *British Marriage Act* of 1754; while Margot Gayle Backus analyses negotiations of Anglo-Irish colonial order in her monograph *The Gothic Family Romance* (1999).

These studies, by and large, tend to read the Gothic mode as subversive, as they do not take into consideration said dialectics which, however, prove to be constitutive. In their readings of Bataille's texts, both Derrida and Foucault point this out:

The limit and transgression depend on each other for whatever density of being they possess: a limit could not exist if it were absolutely uncrossable and, reciprocally, transgression would be pointless if it merely crossed a line composed of illusions and shadows. But can the limit have a life of its own outside of the act that gloriously passes through it and negates it? ... Transgression, then, is not related to the limit as black to white, the prohibited to the lawful, the outside to the inside, or as the open area of a building to its enclosed spaces. Rather, their relationship takes the form of a spiral which no simple infraction can exhaust.[29]

In refusing an 'outside' – metaphorically, but also, to some extent, literally – recent family horror in general and *Mum & Dad* in particular seem to circumvent the said narrative pattern of transgression and re-affirmation. By depicting a site where the normal and the abnormal, where the deviant and the standard coincide, the family and its code are revalued in a way that transcends mere subversion and inversion. In doing so, *Mum & Dad* does maybe not so much substitute the narrative pattern of *The Texas Chainsaw Massacre* and its numerous successors with a genuinely new model. Rather, it radicalizes it in a way that, ultimately, indeed allows observing the family as such in the first place – and thus delivers on a promise that Hooper's film was never able to keep.

Reconsidering the first sequence in which Lena faces her new 'parents', the extent to which the exclusion of anything external to the core family is pursued becomes obvious. As demonstrated by the *mise-en-scène* in general and the effective, exact positioning of the main characters in particular as well as the over-shoulder shot rendering Lena's point of view, it is foregrounded that the only way into and out of this world leads through the parents. Similar to a new-born child, therefore, Lena utterly depends on the care of her parents and siblings. Additionally, she is unable to speak for quite some time. After regaining her voice, that is to say after having 'learned' to speak, the first word that Lena utters and that comes along with a display of affection, albeit simulated, is 'Mum'. Finally, the violent rejection of the 'outside' is not only manifested in the killing of each and every outsider, of everyone that thus functions as an Other to the family and enters the familial realm of the house – the various women that are tortured and murdered by Dad, his friend and colleague, whose attention, on the occasion of his buying a used car from Dad, Lena is able to attract – but also at the beginning of the film by a rather short and inconspicuous dialogue that unfolds between Lena and Birdie as follows:

> Birdie: You got family round here?
> Lena: No. I mean I have family in London, but I live on my own here in Hounslow.

Birdie: A bit of a shithole, in't?
Lena: Na... Yeah, it is a bit of a shithole. [They laugh]
[...]
Birdie: So how come you don't live with your Mum and Dad?
Lena: We don't get on. My dad, he is ... ahm ... we just want different things.
Birdie: Like what?
Lena: Well, he wanted me to stay at home and work for the family business, and I wanted to go to College, but he wouldn't listen ...

According to this dialogue, the following torment is a repetition of Lena's original familial situation and thus is exaggerated into a primal scene of family as such. It is not so much that she suffers one familial situation after the other that eventually goes from bad to worse. Rather, it is precisely the iteration that functions as a magnifying glass rendering, due to the extreme enlargement, the revaluation of the family in the first place.

Steven Sheil's film therefore illuminates a recent turn in Gothic fiction that David Punter famously describes as a 'ceremonial' one transcending the mere transgressive: 'A ceremonial ... is the Other of transgression.'[30] In this light, the 'perverse' seems not to be transgressing and thus inevitably constituting the norm. Rather, it is in itself stabilized, which is the prevalent function of the ceremonial. According to Punter, the Gothic 'attempts the impossible task of stabilising the world through ceremonial and ritual, and in doing so necessarily involves itself in a structure of perversion which can alone give force to that stability, which can shore up our shifting perception of the "natural"'.[31] Due to its ritualistic power, the ceremonial is capable of stabilizing the perverse, and thus of altering its very nature: the perverse, not as category, but as specific historic instantiation, vanishes. This is the nature of *Mum & Dad*'s revaluation of the family. The perverse becomes the norm and the norm in itself, thus, becomes perverse. In Steven Sheil's demanding film, the family, stripped of all ideological restraints, rears its ugly head.

Ultimately, since due to its ceremonial design there is no inherent boundary that can be transgressed within the film, at least as far as the family is concerned, one might be inclined to argue that the moral boundary lies outside of the cinematic artefact – that is, within the beholder or, on a larger scale, the audience. Such an argument might be fuelled by instances of the film's self-referentiality, which I discussed earlier. The meta-level, such a position could thus claim, would stir viewers into action, make them aware of their own position as voyeur. The outside in this film, the outside of this film therefore, would be the viewer looking through the windows of this home, so to speak. To some extent, there is something to be said for that.

And yet: Once viewers start to reflect not only on their relation to the film, but on their status itself, it becomes shockingly obvious that their outside of the film – that is to say their outside of *Mum & Dad*'s family – is the inside of their very own familial position. This emphatically proves that family is everything. What *Mum & Dad* would sensitize for, then, is the fact that each and every spectator is in turn and inevitably 'fucked up' by Mum & Dad. They may not mean to, but they do.

Notes

1 Concerning this distinction, Misha Kavka argues that 'in those instances where the paranoia once evoked by shadows or ghostly figures becomes the perfectly rational fear of a lunatic killer on the loose ..., we have moved from the Gothic into the realm of horror, into the dubious comfort of screaming at what we actually see ... The horror genre, in contrast to the Gothic, demands that we see ...': see Misha Kavka, 'The Gothic on Screen', in Jerrold E. Hogle (ed.), *The Cambridge Companion to Gothic Fiction*, p. 227.
2 Tony Williams, 'Trying to Survive on the Darker Side: 1980s Family Horror', p. 168.
3 Tony Williams, *Hearths of Darkness*, p. 17.
4 Not until the sequel (*The Texas Chainsaw Massacre II*, 1986) are their names revealed.
5 Williams, *Hearths of Darkness*, p. 192f.
6 For a detailed analysis and comparison of these films see Lorena Russell, 'Ideological Formations of the Nuclear Family in *The Hills Have Eyes*'.
7 Williams, *Hearths of Darkness*, p. 13. Emphasis added.
8 Lennard J. Davis, *Enforcing Normalcy*, p. 24.
9 Again, see Williams. For a similar, contradictory argument cf. Bernice M. Murphy, *The Suburban Gothic in American Popular Culture*, pp. 136–65.
10 As early as in 1981, Rosemary Jackson pointed out the 'difficulty of reading Gothic as politically subversive'. See Rosemary Jackson, *Fantasy*, p. 58. Unfortunately, her claim has had little resonance in Gothic studies. On this, cf. also the critical review of approaches

offered by Chris Baldick and Robert Mighall, 'Gothic criticism', in David Punter (ed.), *A Companion to the Gothic*.
11 For more information on this scheme, see http://microwave.filmlondon.org.uk/.
12 David Edelstein, 'Now playing at your local multiplex'. Besides *Mum & Dad*, horror films that can be subsumed under this category are *Saw* (dir. James Wan, 2004) and its five sequels (2005–09), *Wolf Creek* (dir. Greg McLean, 2005), *Hostel* (dir. Eli Roth, 2005), and *Martyrs* (dir. Pascal Laugier, 2008).
13 James Quandt, 'Flesh & Blood. Sex and Violence in Recent French Cinema'.
14 The poster can be seen on http://microwave.filmlondon.org.uk/get_inspired/mum_and_dad/press_pr/poster_evolution/.
15 Judith Butler, *Excitable Speech*, p. 29. Emphasis in original.
16 Cf. for instance Derrida's article 'Signature Event Context' in Jacques Derrida, *Limited Inc.*, pp. 1–23.
17 Butler, *Excitable Speech*, p. 29.
18 Cf. Jacques Lacan, *The Seminar of Jacques Lacan: Book III*.
19 On this reading of the Holy Family and its code cf. also Albrecht Koschorke, *Die heilige Familie und ihre Folgen*, p. 16. Koschorke employs the term 'phantasmatische Tiefenstruktur'. My translation.
20 On this, see for instance the classic David Punter, *Gothic Pathologies*.
21 Fred Botting, *Limits of Horror*, p. 47.
22 To some extent, the fact that Sally's escape relies on masculine help (the driver) and/or a technical device which she cannot control (the pickup truck, which, in a sense, resembles the Hardesty's family van from the beginning) subverts Carol Clover's epochal reading of the establishment of 'the final girl' in the slasher film. See Carol J. Clover, 'Her Body, Himself: Gender in the Slasher Film'. See also Carol J. Clover, *Men, Women, and Chain Saws*.
23 Cf. Luca Fonnesu, 'The Problem of Theodicy', in Knud Haakonssen (ed.), *The Cambridge History of Eighteenth-Century Philosophy*. For the literary repercussions of this process see Peter-André Alt, 'Wiederholung, Paradoxie, Transgression'.
24 See William King, *An Essay on the Origin of Evil* (5th edn, London, 1781). Gottfried W. Leibniz, *Theodicy: Essays on the Goodness of God, the Freedom of Man and the Origin of Evil*. King's *Essay* was first published in Latin in 1702, the first edition of the translation into English by Edmund Law in 1732. To the said fifth edition, Law added notes and fragments from King's legacy, but also some of his own. From my point of view, no critical edition of the *Essay* exists to date.
25 Terry Eagleton, *On Evil*, p. 16.
26 Georges Bataille, *Literature and Evil*, p. 74.

27 The classic, seminal studies on this development are Philippe Ariès, *Centuries of Childhood* and Lawrence Stone, *The Family, Sex and Marriage in England: 1500–1800*. For a critical account of these see Ralph A. Houlbrooke, *The English Family 1450–1700*.
28 Michel Foucault, *Abnormal*, p. 248.
29 See Kate F. Ellis, *The Contested Castle*; Valdine Clemens, *The Return of the Repressed*; Margot G. Backus, *The Gothic Family Romance*.
30 Michel Foucault, 'A preface to transgression', p. 34f. Cf. also the essay 'From Restricted to General Economy: A Hegelianism without Reserve' in Jacques Derrida, *Writing and Difference*, pp. 317–50.
31 David Punter, 'Ceremonial Gothic', p. 41.
32 Ibid., p. 48.

References

Alt, Peter-André, 'Wiederholung, Paradoxie, Transgression: Versuch über die literarische Imagination des Bösen und ihr Verhältnis zur ästhetischen Erfahrung (de Sade, Goethe, Poe)', *Deutsche Vierteljahrsschrift für Literaturwissenschaft und Geistesgeschichte*, 79:4 (2005), 531–67.

Ariès, Philippe, *Centuries of Childhood* (Harmondsworth: Penguin, 1962).

Backus, Margot G., *The Gothic Family Romance: Heterosexuality, Child Sacrifice, and the Anglo-Irish Colonial Order* (Durham, NC: Duke University Press, 1999).

Baldick, Chris and Robert Mighall, 'Gothic criticism', in David Punter (ed.), *A Companion to the Gothic* (Oxford: Blackwell, 2000), pp. 209–28.

Bataille, Georges, *Literature and Evil* (London: Boyars, 1997).

Botting, Fred, *Limits of Horror: Technology, Bodies, Gothic* (Manchester: Manchester University Press, 2008).

Butler, Judith, *Excitable Speech: A Politics of the Performative* (London, New York: Routledge, 1997).

Clemens, Valdine, *The Return of the Repressed: Gothic Horror from The Castle of Otranto to Alien* (Albany, NY: State University of New York Press, 1999).

Clover, Carol J., 'Her Body, Himself: Gender in the Slasher Film', *Representations*, 20 (1987), 187–228.

——, *Men, Women, and Chain Saws: Gender in the Modern Horror Film* (Princeton, NJ: Princeton University Press, 1992).

Davis, Lennard J., *Enforcing Normalcy: Disabilty, Deafness, and the Body* (London: Verso, 1995).

Derrida, Jacques, *Writing and Difference* (London: Routledge, 1978).

——, *Limited Inc.* (Evanston, IL: Northwestern University Press, 1988).

Eagleton, Terry, *On Evil* (New Haven, CT, London: Yale University Press, 2010).

Edelstein, David, 'Now playing at your local multiplex: torture porn. Why has America gone nuts for blood, guts, and sadism?', http://nymag.com/movies/features/15622/ (accessed 10 November 2011).

Ellis, Kate F., *The Contested Castle: Gothic Novels and the Subversion of Domestic Ideology* (Urbana, IL: University of Illinois Press, 1989).

Fonnesu, Luca, 'The Problem of Theodicy', in Knud Haakonssen (ed.), *The Cambridge History of Eighteenth-Century Philosophy*, Vol. 2 (Cambridge: Cambridge University Press, 2006), pp. 749–78.

Foucault, Michel, 'A preface to transgression', in D.F. Bouchard (ed.), *Language, Counter-Memory, Practice: Selected Essays and Interviews* (Ithaca, NY: Cornell University Press, 1977).

——, *Abnormal: Lectures at the Collège de France, 1974–1975* (New York: Verso, 2003).

Houlbrooke, Ralph A., *The English Family 1450–1700* (London: Longman, 1984).

Jackson, Rosemary, *Fantasy: The Literature of Subversion* (London: Methuen, 1981).

Kavka, Mishka, 'The Gothic on screen', in Jerrold E. Hogle (ed.), *The Cambridge Companion to Gothic Fiction* (Cambridge: Cambridge University Press, 2002), pp. 209–28.

King, William, *An Essay on the Origin of Evil*, 5th edn (London, 1781).

Koschorke, Albrecht, *Die heilige Familie und ihre Folgen: Ein Versuch* (Frankfurt/M.: Fischer, 2000).

Lacan, Jacques, *The Seminar of Jacques Lacan: Book III (The Psychoses, 1955–1956)* (New York: W.W. Norton, 1997).

Larkin, Philip, *High Windows* (London: Faber & Faber, 1974).

Leibniz, Gottfried W., *Theodicy: Essays on the Goodness of God, the Freedom of Man and the Origin of Evil* (La Salle, IL: Open Court, 1985).

Murphy, Bernice M., *The Suburban Gothic in American Popular Culture* (Basingstoke: Palgrave Macmillan, 2009).

Punter, David, *Gothic Pathologies: The Text, the Body and the Law* (Basingstoke: Macmillan, 1998).

——, 'Ceremonial Gothic', in Glennis Byron and David Punter (eds), *Spectral Readings: Towards a Gothic Geography* (Basingstoke: Palgrave, 1999), pp. 37–53.

Quandt, James, 'Flesh & blood: sex and violence in recent French cinema', *ArtForum*, February (2004), 112–22.

Russell, Lorena, 'Ideological Formations of the Nuclear Family in *The Hills Have Eyes*', in Thomas R. Fahy (ed.), *The Philosophy of Horror* (Lexington, KY: University Press of Kentucky, 2010), pp. 102–20.

Stone, Lawrence, *The Family, Sex and Marriage in England: 1500 – 1800* (London: Weidenfeld & Nicolson, 1979).
Williams, Tony, *Hearths of Darkness: The Family in the American Horror Film* (Cranbury, NJ: Associated University Press, 1996).
——, 'Trying to survive on the darker side: 1980s family horror', in Barry K. Grant (ed.), *The Dread of Difference: Gender and the Horror Film* (Austin: University of Texas Press, 1996), pp. 164–80.

Index

Note: 'n.' following a page reference indicates the number of a note on that page.

abjection 76, 77
Addams Family, The 1
adoption 6, 8, 63–80 *passim*, 143, 180, 183–8
Aja, Alexandre, 212, 215
  High Tension 215
  The Hills Have Eyes 212
alternative family 2, 5, 8, 188
anthropological approach of kinship 3
aristocratic 12, 14–15, 17, 20, 24, 37–8, 202
  patriarchy 5, 13, 15–16, 18, 25, 27
Armstrong, Nancy 3, 13, 16, 117, 120–9, 131

Backus, Margot Gayle 3, 222
Ballard, J.G. 81
bastard 1, 24, 57
Bataille, Georges 215, 221–2
Beekman, E.M 56
Bergman, Ingmar 82–3
birth 16–20, 25, 40, 44, 70, 75–7, 158, 165, 169–71, 180, 204, 220
bisexuality 187
blood 15–16, 22, 32, 66, 72, 81, 92, 102–3, 108, 120, 148, 160, 179–87 *passim*, 191–3, 196–207 *passim*, 214, 218
  half-blood 197–8, 201–2
  lines *see* relations
  relations 3, 9, 30, 34–8, 175, 200, 203, 205–6
  relatives 45
  ties *see* relations
body 8, 31, 41, 55–7, 59–60, 66, 75–7, 109, 115–16, 120, 123, 138–9, 142–50 *passim*, 160, 166–71, 180–1, 184, 187, 193, 200, 215–16, 218, 222
Botting, Fred 66, 78n.5, 106, 113n.15, 153n.32, 200, 219, 226n.21
bourgeois 5, 8, 12, 14–18, 20, 134, 183
Boyer, Paul 33
Braidotti, Rosi 115
Breton, Marianne 18
Briefel, Aviva 91
Brite, Poppy Z. 8, 174, 178–80
  Lost Souls 8, 152n.9, 178–80, 189, 191–2
Brockden Brown, Charles 81
Brontë, Emily 67, 175
  Wuthering Heights 175

brother 17, 39, 57–8, 74, 92, 102, 143, 159–61, 163–4, 171, 204–5, 213, 217
Bruhm, Steven 107–9, 113n.18, 152n.8
Buck, Pearl S. 70, 79n.13
Buikema 60n.2
Burney, Frances 23
  Evelina 5, 23–5
Butler, Judith 4, 140, 147, 216–17

cannibalistic family 212
Carsten, Janet 3
Castricano, Jodey 48, 60n.1, 101
Chambers, Deborah 4
child 3, 15, 16, 32, 35–9, 42, 65, 68, 72, 75, 84–7, 90, 97, 125, 143, 160, 163, 175, 178, 180–1, 183, 185, 189, 215–16, 222–3
  abuse 89
  adopted 21, 63–4, 79, 143, 215
  biological 219
  evil 64, 76
  vampiric 2
childbirth 59, 183
childhood 66–7, 71, 93–4, 119, 181, 187, 203, 227
children 1, 3, 6, 16, 18–19, 32, 34–5, 37, 45, 48, 52–5, 58–9, 64–5, 68–70, 72, 81–2, 85–91, 94, 99, 101–2, 104, 118, 159–60, 165–6, 186, 193, 197, 206, 207
  evil 6, 63, 76, 77
  surrogate 106
Christian 8, 22, 69, 70, 75, 181–2, 218–19
Christie, Agatha 67
Cixous, Hélène 100
Cleary, Maryell 31
Clemens, Valdine 222
Collet-Serra 63
Collins, Wilkie 175
colonial order 3, 48–60 *passim*, 222
conception 186

conjugal 4, 32, 99, 133, 177, 222
consanguineal 4, 188
Cooper, Davina 132, 152n.3
Couperus, Louis 6, 49–50, 54–6, 60
  The Hidden Force 6, 49–51, 54
Craven, Wes 6, 7, 82–95 *passim*, 212
  The Hills Have Eyes 83–4, 212
  The Last House on the Left 82, 85, 89, 93
  A Nightmare on Elm Street 85–7, 92
  The People under the Stairs 88, 90
  Red Eye 94
  Scream 82, 92–3, 214
Cretney, Stephen 142–3
cross-dressing 6, 43, 138, 213
Cuthbertson, Catherine 18, 21
  Santo Sebastiano 18, 21

Dacre, Charlotte, 158, 161, 201
  Zofloya, or the Moor 8, 158, 160–1, 165, 171, 201
daughter 5, 14, 17–26 *passim*, 31–2, 34–5, 37–8, 40, 43–4, 55, 64–5, 69, 72, 74–5, 83, 86–9, 93–4, 98, 104, 106, 143–4, 148, 159, 163–6, 168–70, 180–2, 215–16
Davenport-Hines, Richard 174
degeneration 66
De Man, Paul 108–9, 113n.22
Derrida, Jacques 164, 167, 172n.17, 222
determinism 64–6, 68, 73
Dickens, Charles 35, 38
difference 5, 7–8, 70, 100, 107, 115–16, 122, 124–5, 133, 136, 141, 212
domestic 8, 13, 55, 68, 94, 97, 106, 108, 110, 157, 158, 161–4, 166–7, 169, 171, 174–8, 180, 193, 222
domesticity 13, 162, 164, 167, 174, 176–8

Index

Dorrestein, Renate 7, 78, 116–17, 122–4, 127
  A Heart of Stone 78, 116
  The perpetual motion machine of love 7, 116–28 *passim*
Doss, Helen 70, 72
Duncker, Patricia 7, 133–6, 140–1, 149
  The Deadly Space Between 7, 132–49 *passim*

Eagleton, Terry 221
Edelstein, David 214
Ellis, Kate Ferguson 10, 222
Exorcist, The 76, 105

Falconer, Rachel 200
father 1, 12–15, 17, 19–25, 32, 35–6, 39–41, 44, 54, 57–8, 64, 72, 74, 84, 86–7, 92–4, 103, 106–11, 134, 136–8, 143–5, 147–51, 158–9, 161, 166, 175, 180–1, 188, 190–1, 193, 202, 204, 213, 217
  adoptive 67, 151
  biological 183
  surrogate 108, 112, 202
  symbolic 97
fatherhood 7, 54, 108, 111, 202
Faulkner, William 81
Feinberg, Leslie 42
femininity 6, 50, 120, 137
feminism 115–17, 119, 122–3, 128
fertility 75
Fineman, Martha 132
foetus 105, 170–1, 197, 215
Foucault, Michel 200, 221–2, 227n.28, 227n.30
Freeman, Elizabeth 4
Freud, Sigmund 100, 134–5, 143, 146, 158, 165, 168, 170, 205

Gallardo, Ximena C. 206
Garber, Marjorie 43
Gaskell, Elizabeth 5, 6, 30–45 *passim*
  'Clopton House' 30–2, 37, 45–6

'The Grey Woman' 30, 34–5, 38, 44–5
  Lois the Witch 30, 32, 45
  'The Old Nurse's Story' 30, 34–5, 37–9, 45
gender 5, 8, 13, 38, 40, 42, 44–5, 55–6, 73, 75, 115, 122, 133–9, 142–4, 149, 150
genderqueer *see* transgender
genealogy 6, 12–13, 63, 133, 146, 220
genetic 32, 65, 68, 72–3, 77, 179, 192
Gens, Xavier 215
  Frontier(s) 215
ghost 22–3, 34–8, 48, 56, 59, 86, 98, 100, 166, 200
granddaughter 35, 37, 65, 75
grandfather 14, 18, 91, 159, 203, 212
grandmother 44, 65, 71, 74, 198, 213
grandson 13, 159–60, 171, 183
Gupta, Suman 206
Gurel, Perin 73

Halberstam, Judith 115, 147
Harwood, Sarah 4
Hawthorne, Nathaniel 81
Heijst, Annelies van 118
heir 13–14, 161–2, 164, 204
heredity 35, 65, 75
Herman, Didi 133
Herman, Ellen 68
heteronormative 30, 38, 45, 134, 136–7, 139, 142–6
heterosexual family 5, 8, 45
heterosexuality 143, 146, 177
heterotopia 149, 200
Hitchcock, Alfred,
  Psycho 81, 89, 213
Hogle, Jerrold E. 1, 2
Holt, Bertha 70, 72, 78
home 3, 6, 33, 38–9, 51, 53, 55, 66, 77, 82–4, 88, 91, 93–5, 132, 148, 157–8, 161–2, 164, 166–8, 171, 185–6, 205, 225

Index

homosexuality 43
homosexual marriage *see* same-sex union
Hooper, Tobe 82, 211, 213, 220, 223
   Texas Chainsaw Massacre 82, 211, 213–14, 219–20, 223
horror 3, 6, 7, 22, 25, 31–2, 44, 63, 66–7, 75–7, 78, 80–95 *passim*, 104, 106, 120, 146, 161, 169–70, 184, 204, 211–25 *passim*
house 1, 31, 34, 36–7, 42, 51, 56, 88–91, 161–5, 167, 171, 184–5, 188, 205, 213, 215, 217, 220, 223
Howitt, William 40
Hughes, Peter 31

identification 5, 7–9, 12–27 *passim*, 133, 135, 137, 139, 142, 144–6, 150, 202
imperialism 3, 59
incest 4, 50, 56, 74, 84, 175, 213
   interdict 137–8, 143–4, 146
individualism 121–3
infant 15–16, 18, 90, 97, 99, 104, 158, 221–2
inheritance 152, 160, 163, 165–7, 170, 175
   genetic 65, 73

Jackson, Shirley 81, 86
Jacobs, W.W. 104
   'The Monkey's Paw' 104–5
James, Henry 67
   The Turn of the Screw 67

Kaufman, Charles 214
   Mother's Day 214
King, Stephen 7, 97, 100, 102–9, 111–12
   Carrie 104, 106, 112
   The Dark Half 105–6, 112
   Firestarter 104, 106
   Lisey's Story 106

Pet Sematary 7, 97–8, 100, 103–5, 108–11
Salem's Lot 106–7
The Shining 104, 106–8
King, William 220
Klein, Christina 70–1
Kristeva, Julia 198, 207

Lacan, Jacques 200, 217
Larkin, Philip 216, 219
   'This be the verse' 216
Lathom, Francis 18
Lavater, Johann Caspar 14
Lee, Sophia 19
   The Recess 19, 20
Le Fanu, Joseph Sheridan 67, 177
Leibniz, Gottfried W. 220
lesbian 44, 118, 133, 136, 138
Lévy, Maurice 1
Lewis, Matthew 22, 158, 175, 201
   The Castle Spectre 22
   The Monk 8, 158, 165, 171, 175, 201
likeness 12, 22, 26, 98, 102–3, 105–6, 111
   see also resemblance
lineage 8, 16–17, 19, 103, 157, 159–61, 164, 171, 176, 197–8, 203–4, 206

McAleer, Patrick 105
McClintock, Anne 54, 59
McKeon, Michael 12
madwoman 49, 60, 122
Magistrale, Tony 104–5, 107
Mann, Thomas 135
March, William 6, 63, 66, 71–5, 78
   The Bad Seed 63–8, 72–8, 85, 92
marriage 4, 16, 20, 26, 33, 35, 39, 41, 44, 52, 55, 92, 133, 141–4, 159–60, 163–4, 174, 201, 204, 220
masculinity 6, 50, 85, 137
Matheson, Richard 78n.2, 81, 193n.5
matriarch 168
matrilineal 14, 197, 205

Index

Meijer, Hans 58
Meijer, Maaike 117
Mellor, Anne K. 12–13
Melville, Herman 135
Meyer, Stephenie, 178
   Twilight 178
middle-class 6, 16, 20, 58, 69, 82–4, 89–95 *passim*, 186, 217
misogyny 75, 94
Moers, Ellen 122
momism 73
monster 2, 7, 31, 75–6, 87, 112, 115–17, 122, 128, 147, 169, 219
monstrosity 7, 38, 76, 88, 115–16, 120, 147, 219
mother 5, 9, 13–26 *passim*, 32–8 *passim*, 40, 42–3, 55, 59–60, 63–4, 66, 68–9, 74–6, 85–7, 89–93, 103, 106, 108, 134, 136, 138–9, 143–4, 146, 149, 158–9, 161–71 *passim*, 176, 180, 183, 185, 193, 197–205 *passim*, 213, 215, 217
   adoptive 19, 36, 76–7, 151, 183, 187
   adulterous 175, 201
   biological 34, 36, 40, 57, 77, 92
   birth 19
   dead 15, 18, 21, 23, 197, 201
   foster 19
   indigenous 57
   substitute *see* surrogate
   surrogate 3, 163, 205
   unmarried 180
motherhood 77, 106
Muir, John 84, 85
Murphy, Bernice M. 96, 225n.9

Newman, Kim 83
Niffenegger, Audrey 8, 158, 165, 171
   Her Fearful Symmetry 8, 157–8, 160, 164, 171
Nissenbaum, Stephen 33

nuclear family 1–9 *passim*, 66, 81, 90–2, 94, 106–7, 117–18, 121–3, 125, 132, 157, 161, 217, 221–2, 225

Oates, Joyce Carol 73
Oedipal 8, 58, 107, 134–140 *passim*, 143–7
offspring 66, 76–7, 159–62, 164, 175, 177, 183
   see also progeny
orphan 25, 35, 67, 69–70, 198, 201

parents 6, 24, 35, 68, 82–3, 85–90, 92–3, 106, 119, 158–60, 166, 177, 184, 196, 198–9, 204, 215, 219–20, 222–3
   adoptive 69, 70, 77, 185
patriarch 14, 16–17, 19, 24, 54, 84, 94
patriarchal family 1, 5–6, 13, 50, 59
patriarchy 5, 14, 15, 24–7, 177
patrilineal 14, 110
Pattynama, Pamela 59
Peach, Linden 86
Perry, Ruth 4, 5
perversion 66, 171, 224
Pharr, Mary F. 105
Pisters, Patricia 4
Poe, Edgar Allan 81
   'The Fall of the House of Usher' 1
Pointon, Marcia 18
Polidori, John 177
Pollmann, Tessel 62
pregnancy 40, 76
procreation 15, 64, 68, 75, 77, 160
   see also reproduction
progeny 9, 14–15, 17, 21–2, 142, 222
   see also offspring
property 15, 17, 19, 25–6, 42, 91, 122, 166, 168
Punter, David 135, 200, 224
purity 54, 202, 204

queer 4–6, 34, 43, 134–6, 139, 144, 149, 150, 177, 188
  families 3, 5
  Gothic 108

race 55–6, 66, 70, 73, 91, 98, 206, 215
racism 71, 73, 75, 77
Radcliffe, Ann 5, 175, 201
  The Italian 5
  The Mysteries of Udolpho 201
recognition 21, 109, 112, 126, 133, 192–3
Reddy, M.T. 43, 44
Reeve, Clara, 20
  The Old English Baron 20
relatives 32, 36, 45, 49, 170, 198, 204
reproduction 2, 8, 122, 133, 136, 139, 142, 176
  assisted 132
  biological 3
  sexual 133, 141, 143
  see also procreation
resemblance 5, 7, 12, 14–15, 18–27 *passim*, 67, 102, 104–5, 111, 116, 171
  see also likeness
revenant 99, 103, 134, 177–9
Richter, David 4
Rice, Anne 2, 178
  Interview with the Vampire 178
Roman Catholicism 14, 21
Romantic 12–13
romantic love 17, 118, 124–5
Romero, George A. 90
  Night of the Living Dead 81, 90
Rosemary's Baby 76, 105
Rowling, J. K 9, 196–7, 200–1, 206–7
  Harry Potter and the Chamber of Secrets 204
  Harry Potter and the Deathly Hallows 203, 206
  Harry Potter and the Goblet of Fire 199, 205
  Harry Potter and the Half-Blood Prince 202
  Harry Potter and the Order of the Phoenix 198–9
Royle, Nicholas 101
Ruben, Joseph
  The Stepfather 214

same-sex union 8, 44, 132–3, 137, 140–5
Sedgwick, Eve Kosofsky 1, 138, 152n.9, 154n.33
sexism 73, 77
sexuality 7, 35, 52, 73, 75–6, 133–5, 137, 141, 143–4, 150, 180–2, 188–9, 221–2
Shakespeare, William 13
Sheil, Steven 9, 211, 214, 217, 219, 224
  Mum & Dad 9, 214–15, 218–20, 223–5
Sheldon, Paul 106
Shelley, Mary 2, 105, 135, 149,
  Frankenstein 105, 135, 137, 149
siblings 67, 88, 106, 127, 143, 151, 161, 164–5, 168, 211, 215, 223
single parent 45, 132, 180, 183
sister 20, 35, 91, 116–18, 120, 123, 125–8, 143, 151, 159, 160, 162, 166, 170, 201, 204–5, 217, 220
  biological 116
sisterhood 7, 116–17, 123–4, 126–8
Sleath, Eleanor, 12
  The Orphan of the Rhine 12, 20–1, 23–6
Smith, Catherine 18
Smith, C. Jason 206
Smith, Charlotte Turner 23
son 1, 12, 25, 32, 52, 54–5, 57–8, 97, 99, 103–4, 109–10, 136, 138–9, 143–4, 146, 149, 159, 162, 171, 184, 187, 190–1, 198–9, 203–5

Index

Sophocles 135
Southern gothic 63, 65–6
spectre 22–3, 37, 86, 139, 186
sperm 143, 182, 215
Spivak, Gayatri Chakravorty 60
Staat, Wim 4
Stanhope, Louisa Sidney 12
  The Confessional of Valombre 5, 12, 15–16, 24–5
  The Stepfather 214
Stephenson, Glennis 35
stepson 53–4, 57
Stevenson, Robert Louis 208n.4
  The Strange Case of Dr Jekyll and Mr Hyde 208n.4
Stoker, Bram 106, 122, 175, 177, 181
  Dracula 106, 122, 125, 175, 181
Stoler, Ann Laura 59
Stoneman, Patsy 34
Strengell, Heidi 105
Stychin, Carl 142
surrogate 106
  family 97
  father 108, 112, 202
  mother 3, 205

teenage 8, 35, 82, 85–7, 92, 178, 180–1, 198, 207
Tincknell, Estella 4
Toffoletti, Kim 115
transgender 6, 44, 46n.17
transgression 2, 9, 38, 42, 117, 137–8, 140–1, 145–6, 159–61, 185, 190, 207, 214, 220–4
triangle 136–9

twins 165–8, 170–1
Twitchell, James 1

uncanny 7, 8, 51, 53, 65, 99–104, 107, 109, 112, 132–50 *passim*, 157–8, 165, 167–71, 187, 205
unheimlich 158, 205
  see also uncanny

vampire family 2, 8, 178, 188, 191
vampires 2, 67, 106, 116, 120, 122, 125–7, 176–80, 186–93 *passim*

Wallace, Diana 35
Walpole, Horace 1, 13, 152n.13, 175, 220, 222
  The Castle of Otranto 1, 5, 13–15, 18–20, 22, 175, 220
Weber, Carl Maria von 135, 145
werewolves 176, 208
Wesseling, Lies 60n.2
Wigley, Mark 157, 161–2, 167, 171
Williams, Anne 1, 60n.2
Williams, Tony 3, 87, 211–12
womb 19, 66, 75, 124, 171
Wylie, Philip 79
Wyndham, John
  The Midwich Cuckoos 63, 76

Zarchi, Meir 82
Žižek, Slavoj 104
Zombie, Rob
  The Devil's Rejects 214
  The House of 1000 Corpses 214
zombies 208